Studies in
Jain Population and Demography

Studies in

Jain Population and Demography

Edited by

Prakash C. Jain

RAWAT PUBLICATIONS

Jaipur • New Delhi • Bangalore • Guwahati • Kolkata

ISBN 978-81-316-1018-3

Published by
Prem Rawat for **Rawat Publications**
Satyam Apartments, Sector 3, Jawahar Nagar, Jaipur 302 004 (India)
Phone: 0141 265 1748 / 7006 Fax: 0141 265 1748
E-mail: info@rawatbooks.com
Website: www.rawatbooks.com

New Delhi Office
4858/24, Ansari Road, Daryaganj, New Delhi 110 002
Phone: 011 23263290

Also at *Bangalore, Guwahati* and *Kolkata*

Typeset by Rawat Computers, Jaipur
Printed at Nice Printing Press, New Delhi

Contents

Preface

The idea of this book came to me some time in the year 2006, when I was working on an article on Jain population and demography based on 2001 census data. Although the book did not materialize then, the article was incorporated as a chapter in my book *Jains in India and Abroad* (2011). During the same year, I also began to nurse the idea of co-editing this book with Professor Vilas A. Sangave, the well-known sociologist and author of *Jain Community: A Social Survey* which opens with a chapter on Jain population. Though focussed on 1931 census, this chapter also takes into accounts the dynamics of the Jain population through the next four censuses. With great reluctance and apprehensions, I drafted a letter requesting Professor Sangave for acting as senior co-editor and give copyright permission for using the chapter in the proposed book. Unfortunately, just around the time I could muster courage to post the letter, I came across the news of his sad demise on 1 March 2011.

The manuscript remained in hibernation for a few years. Then I waited for 2011 census data to come out which happened during 2016. Following the 2011 census data on Jains, a serious debate ensued in 2017 at International School for Jain Studies, New Delhi, regarding the low growth rate of Jain population, and indeed the under-enumeration of Jain population. The last chapter in the book is the final outcome of that debate which first led to getting conducted two Jain population surveys in Delhi.

The book was also delayed due to the difficult availability of late Dr M.K. Jain's article on 1971 census data analysis on Jains (Chapter 4), which was published in 1975 in a short-lived ethnic magazine *Tirthankar* – published and edited from Indore by Dr Nemichandra Jyotishacharya, a noted Jain scholar. This small English-language monthly magazine on Jainology survived perhaps only a few issues and was nowhere to be found in major north Indian Jain or other libraries. So much so that at one stage I thought of dropping the article from this book, but then the article was too important to do that.

Finally, our search ended at the doors of editor-publisher's son Shri Vishwas Jain at Indore where a few copies of the magazine were literally locked inside a room – may be due to family dispute and/or court injunction. In this context, I am grateful to Advocate Dr Sudha Jain, a one-time colleague at ISJS, whose persistent efforts over a period of about four months in getting a copy of the article eventually paid off. Needless to say, I am more than grateful to Shri Vishwas Jain for this favour.

Delay at several stages in finalizing the manuscript turned out to me the proverbial blessings in disguise. Without this delay, the inclusion of Chapter 10 in this book would not have been possible as the two Delhi survey reports on which this chapter is based were not completed until January 2018. I am thankful to Dr Shugan C. Jain, Founder-Chairman of ISJS for not only co-authoring Chapter 10 with me, but also allowing me to use the ISJS as a platform for carrying out a number of studies on Jain population and community. His moral support has been a source of inspiration for me. At ISJS, I am also thankful to Mr Sushil Jana and Mr Shivam Saxena for getting the manuscript typed and ready for publication.

My special thanks to Dr Sulekh C. Jain, Professor Yashwant K. Malaiya and Shri Dheeraj Jain for contributing their respective articles and for their suggestions and help in putting together this volume. Thanks are also due to Shri Pranit Rawat for readily accepting the manuscript for publication and his editorial team for making the book more readable. Finally, I would like to thank my wife Dr Renu Saxena, and our daughters Dr Rashi Prakash and Ms Sanskriti Prakash for their love and support which made my academic pursuits a lot less arduous.

New Delhi **Prakash C. Jain**

Acknowledgements

The editor and publisher wish to thank the authors and the following individuals and publishers who have kindly given permission for the use of copyright material.

Princeton University Press for the excerpts 'The Jains' (pp. 183–184) from *The Population of India and Pakistan* by Kingsley Davis, 1951, Princeton University Press, Princeton, NJ.

Dr Anupam Jash, Joint Editor, *Jain Journal* for the articles (a) Jagdish P. Sharma, 'The Jains as a Minority in Indian Society and History', *Jain Journal*, 1976, Vol. 5 (April), pp. 137–148; and (b) M.K. Jain, 'A Demographic Analysis on the Jains', *Jain Journal*, 1986, Vol. 21, No. 2, pp. 33–50.

Dr Ajit Phadkule for excerpts 'Jain Population' (pp. 1–45) from *Jain Community: A Social Survey* by Vilas A. Sangave, 1980, Popular Prakashan, Bombay.

Mr Vishwas Jain for the article 'Jains in India: Where and How Many?', *Tirthankar*, 1975, Vol. 1, No. 2, pp. 8–23.

International School for Jain Studies for the chapter 'Jain Demography' (pp. 48–85) from *Jains in India and Abroad* by Prakash C. Jain, 2011, International School for Jain Studies, New Delhi.

International School for Jain Studies for excerpts 'Under-Enumeration of the Jain Population: Evidence from Two Delhi Surveys' from its two reports: (a) Jain Population in India: Hauz Khas Tehsil, 2017; and (b) Jain Population in India: New Delhi District, 2018.

Contributors

Kingsley Davis (1908–1997) was a renowned American sociologist and demographer who served at a number of universities including Princeton, Columbia and University of California at Berkeley. A prolific scholar, he is best remembered for his following major works: *Human Society* (1949), *Population of India and Pakistan* (1951), *Population Policy and Economic Development* (1961), *World Urbanization 1950–1970* (1969, 1972) and *Cities: Their Origin, Growth and Human Impact* (1973). Professor Davis served as President of the Population Association of America and the American Sociological Association and represented the United States on the United Nations Population Commission. He coined the terms 'population explosion' and 'zero population growth' and developed the theory of demographic transition.

Dheeraj Jain is Deputy Director in the Office of the Registrar General and Census Commissioner, Ministry of Home

Affairs, Government of India. Earlier he served at the Ministry of Statistics and Programme Implementation. He holds MSc and MPhil degrees in Applied Mathematics and Mathematics respectively from the Indian Institute of Technology, Roorkee. His book *Population of Jains in India: A Perspective from the Census 2011* was published in 2017.

M.K. Jain (Late) was the Deputy Registrar General in the Office of the Registrar General and Census Commissioner, Ministry of Home Affairs, Government of India during the 1990s. Besides the two articles included in this book, Dr Jain is best remembered for his work *Functional Classification of Urban Agglomerations/Towns of India*, 1991, which was published as part of Occasional Papers Series by the RG and CC Office in 1994.

Prakash C. Jain is currently the Project Director of Population and Sociological Studies at International School for Jain Studies, New Delhi. Prior to this, he was a Senior Fellow of ICSSR (2013–2015) and UGC-Emeritus Fellow (2015–2017) at the Centre for Comparative Politics and Political Theory, School of International Studies, Jawaharlal Nehru University, New Delhi. Until his superannuation in December 2011, he served the JNU as Professor of West Asian Studies. He is the author of *Racial Discrimination against Overseas Indians: A Class Analysis* (1990), *Indians in South Africa: Political Economy of Race Relations* (1999), *Population and Society in West Asia* (2001), *Non-Resident Indian Entrepreneurs in the United Arab Emirates* (2010) and *Jains in India and Abroad: A Sociological Introduction* (2011). He has also edited/co-edited books on Iran, Saudi Arabia, Indian Diaspora and the Jain community; including *Indian Diaspora in West Asia: A Reader* (2007), *Indian Trade Diaspora in the Arabian Peninsula* (2013), *Social Consciousness in Jainism* (2014) and *South Asian Migration to Gulf Countries* (2016).

Shugan C. Jain, BEng. (Delhi University), MS (Systems Engineering) (New York University), MA, PhD (Jainology, Jain Vishva Bharati Institute), has been an IT consultant, manager and CEO with MNCs for about 40 years in United States, the Netherlands, Iraq, Saudi Arabia and India. Since 2005, he has been the Founder-Chairman of International School for Jain Studies, New Delhi, where he is involved in teaching, research and publications. He has published over fifty papers and five authored/edited books. His latest publications include *Gandhi and Jainism* (2017) and *Jainism for Young Inquisitives* (2018).

Sulekh C. Jain, PhD (Mechanical Engineering), has taught at several universities in India and the United States. He has published more than fifty papers and has nine US and international patents. Following his retirement from General Electric (GE) Aircraft Engine Division in Cincinnati, Ohio, he now devotes all his energies to the promotion of Jainism and *ahimsa*-related causes and projects. He has been instrumental in the establishment of a large number of Jain centres, institutions and programmes in North America, Europe and India. For nearly 50 years, he has served the community with vision, commitment, dedication and unflagging energy. He served JAINA for eight years, first as Secretary then as President for two terms. He has been the President of two Jain centres (Cincinnati–Dayton and Houston) as well as several other organizations. He is the Founder-Chairman of the Governing Council of International School for Jain Studies, USA and Secretary of Mahavir Vision Inc., United States. His book *An Ahimsa Crisis: You Decide* was published in 2016.

Yashwant K. Malaiya is a senior faculty member at the Computer Science Department of Colorado State University, Fort Collins, USA. He has been actively associated with JAINA since its inception. Born and brought up in Damoh district of Bundelkhand, Professor

Malaiya has written several articles in both English and Hindi on Jain history, population and communities of the region.

Vilas A. Sangave (1920–2011) was an eminent sociologist and Hon. Director of Sahu Research Institute at Shivaji University, Kolhapur. Earlier, he worked at the same university as Professor and Head of the Department of Sociology until his retirement in 1980. Dr Sangave has to his credit a number of articles and books in sociology and anthropology in English and Marathi. His major books include *Jain Community: A Social Survey; Life and Legacy of Mahavir: A Social Study; History of Dakshin Bharat Jain Sabha* and *Sacred Shravanabelagola.*

Jagdish P. Sharma (1935–2010), Professor of South Asian History and the author of *Republics in Ancient India,* taught at Columbia University, University of Virginia and American University at Washington, DC, before joining the University of Hawaii in 1964 where he helped establish the South Asian Studies Programme. Professor Sharma served as Director of this programme for about 40 years. He was also a visiting professor at the Universities of Allahabad, Rajasthan and Banaras Hindu University. His academic interest was particularly focussed on Jainism and Buddhism.

Introduction

Prakash C. Jain

A number of Jain scholars have maintained that during and 300 years after the nirvana of Lord Mahāvīra (599–527 BC), the Jain population was in the vicinity of about 40 crore or 400 million.[1] These scholars further maintain that the Jain population was reduced to about 160 million during the sixth or seventh century AD, and to about 85 million by twelfth century. The Jain population further declined to about 30 million by the fifteenth century AD. Obviously, royal patronage during the ancient and medieval period played a major role in the overall growth or decline of the Jain population in India. Besides, royal patronage, persecution and/or conversion of the followers of Jainism to Hinduism and Islam had also been a factor in the decline of Jains population during certain periods of Indian history. At the same time, Jainism is not a proselytizing religion, although in principle it is open to all, irrespective of caste, creed or colour. Small experiments of proselytizing here and there in recent times have eventually failed and could not gain momentum. One can recall here the conversion of *Bhangis* (sweepers) in Udaipur by Acharya Tulsi during the early 1980s.[2]

According to one historian,

> since the beginning of the medieval period (*circa* 12th century) till the first quarter of the present (twentieth) century, the community had been continuously losing in numbers, so that which had been once a major religious group on the sub-continent was reduced to a small minority .... Most of the Brahmana, Kshatriya (Rajput), Kayastha and Sudra followers became converts to other faiths under the influence of Christian missions, Muslim Tabligh, the Arya Samaj movement or the Vaisnava, Virasaiva and other sectarian preachers.[3]

Whatever might have been the numerical strength of the followers of Jainism in the past, presently they add up to less than 5 million souls the world over. Thus, in the census of 2011, the total Jain population in India was enumerated at 4.45 million. This figure represents the largest Jain population in modern times. Incidentally, the smallest population of the Jains in India with about 11,17,000 persons was recorded in 1921 census. It is against this background that this anthology chronicles the demographic evolution of the Jain community in modern times through the 15 census enumerations beginning in 1872 – the 1872 census being partial and non-synchronic.[4]

American sociologist and demographer Kingsley Davis was perhaps the first scholar to have given some serious thought to the Indian census data pertaining to the Jain community. This was done in a brief note entitled 'The Jains' contained in his book *Population of India and Pakistan* (1951) which is reproduced here as 'Jain Population in India,1881–1941' (Chapter 1). Describing the Jains as a 'sect' (sic) who have been wealthy as well as 'remarkably successful in worldly affairs', Davis characterizes the Jain population dynamics during 1881 and 1941 to be 'numerically stationary, and to be declining as a portion of the total population'.[5]

The Jain population stagnation is partially attributed by Davis to the Jain community's 'strict observance of the taboo on widow remarriage' resulting in a 'low percentage of their women 15–39 married'.[6] The author further maintains that during the census period 1921–1931 a fifth of Jain women in this age group were widows. Additionally, Davis considers three more factors responsible for the stagnation in the Jain population: (a) low marital fertility due to better socio-economic position, (b) the tendency of some Jains to 'drift into Hinduism' by which he meant their enumeration as Hindus and (c) lack of any deliberate conversion agenda and practice in Jainism. Davis ends his note with optimistic predictions in regard to the reduction in the number of Jain widows and the growth of Jain population in the near future.

Jagdish P. Sharma's article 'Jains as a Minority in Indian Society and History' (Chapter 2) written during mid-1970s takes into account the previous 10 censuses and declares the Jains to be 'the sixth most numerous religious group', and by virtue of their numbers (about 2.6 million in 1971, that is 0.47 per cent of the total population of the country) 'a very small minority' in the Indian society. Further on, he claims that 'it is difficult to imagine their numerical strength ever being more than one per cent of India's total population at any given point in history'.[7] The rest of the article is devoted to the introduction of Jainism as a religion and philosophy, historical migration of the Jains from eastern to central, western and south India, their occupational and social status in the Indian society and so on, with quite a number of hypotheses worthy of consideration.

In Chapter 3, 'Jain Population, 1881–1971' of this book, the author Vilas A. Sangave takes a wide view of Jain population and demography from the census year 1881 to 1971 covering a period of 90 years. It explores the causes of decline in the Jain population from 1881 until 1921 and its increase in subsequent censuses. Dr Sangave explains the negative growth in terms of 'the fact that in the past many Jains used to regard themselves as

Hindus and were also regarded by others as Hindus', and therefore, they were not enumerated as Jains.[8] The 1931 census report itself had taken note of this drifting tendency of some Jains into Hinduism:

> In respects of Jains it is always doubtful whether the numbers recorded are really accurate as many record themselves as Hindus. Sometimes there is no uniformity about this practice so that the comparative figures of Jains and Hindus are always liable to a certain amount of disturbance by influences that cannot be gauged statistically'.[9]

We have already taken note of the views of Professor Kingsley Davis in this regard.

Increased religious awareness among the Jains however began to change this situation in the late 1920s and in spite of the boycott of the census enumeration by the Jains in support of Mahatma Gandhi's Non-Cooperation Movement, there appears to be appreciable increase in the Jain population in the 1931 census. Besides decadal growth rate, other population characteristics taken for consideration in the chapter are distribution of population by region/states/UTs, rural–urban background, gender and age distribution, longevity and civil conditions.

Dr Sangave cautions the readers about the nomenclature in the regional distribution of Jain population during the pre- and post-independence India in that whereas until India's independence the population distribution was shown between British and Indian states, since 1951 census it is done between states/provinces and the union territories (UTs). In this connection, it is interesting to note that during the British period about 60 per cent of the Jain population preferred to reside in the Indian states, while only 40 per cent lived in British states. The corresponding figures for the 1941 census were 64 per cent and 36 per cent respectively.[10]

The specific treatment given to the 1931 census data pertaining to the civil conditions of the Jain population is the remarkable feature of the chapter by Sangave. Accordingly, until about the middle of the twentieth century, the Jains were not only an early marrying community, but they were also a polygamous community with preponderance of widows. In Rajputana, for example, there were 247 widows per 1,000 females among the Jains. Thus, one out of four females 'was necessarily a widow'.[11]

Although child marriage and polygamy are no longer problematic to the Jain community today, widow and divorcee remarriages continue to be the major issues in most sections of the community with serious repercussions. The scriptural/social ban on widow remarriage not only affects the sex composition of the community, but also 'considerably reduces the proportion of females in the reproductive period. Obviously this situation very adversely affects the rate of increase in the Jain population'.[12] Writing more than half-a-century ago, Professor Sangave was progressive enough to come out in strong support of widow remarriage: 'if conversion is not practised the removal of ban on widow remarriage appears to be the most pressing and urgent need for the growth of Jain population'.[13]

M.K. Jain's article 'Jains in India: How Many and Where?' (Chapter 4) is the analysis of Jain demography based on the 1971 census data.[14] It details the growth and the distribution of Jain population in 69 districts along with the relationship between population growth and sex composition and urbanization of Jain population in 69 districts of India. Taking a historical perspective on Jain population, the author observed that:

> (a) the growth rate of Jain population in India caught momentum only after 1951, (b) the Jain population is mainly concentrated in Maharashtra, Gujrat, Rajasthan, Madhya Pradesh and Mysore and the growth of Jain Population during 1951–71 was considerably faster in Maharashtra and Madhya Pradesh and was significantly low in case of Gujarat and Rajasthan and (c) about 80 percent of Jain population was living in only 69 districts at the time of 1971 census, further

> the districts at the time of 1971 census, further the districts which had faster growth of Jain population during 1961–71 were also having proportionately lesser females as compared to males and also a higher proportion of urban to total Jain population at the time of 1971 census.[15]

M.K. Jain who was with the office of the Registrar General and Census Commissioner of India and eventually rose to become one of its deputies who wrote another article 'A Demographic Analysis on the Jains' in 1986 (Chapter 5), which exclusively focuses this time on the demographic characteristics of the Jain population based on the 1981 census data.[16] While considering the decline and slower growth rate in Jain population during the period 1891 and 1941, he more or less goes along with the views of Kingsley Davis who, as already mentioned, had analysed the situation in terms of the following factors: (a) higher incidence of widowhood, (b) low fertility within marital relations, (c) 'drift into Hinduism' on the part of a considerable number of Jains and (d) non-proselytizing nature of Jainism.

> The improvement in growth rate of Jain population during 1951–71 period, on the other hand, may be attributed to the heavier reduction in the mortality rate due to improved living conditions and improvement in reporting of religion in the successive censuses.[17]

Finally, the author explains the reduction in the growth rate of Jain population from 28.48 per cent to 23.17 per cent during the 1971–1981 decade by decline in the fertility rate among the Jains both in rural and urban areas. As per 1981 census data, total marital fertility rate (3.7) was lowest for the Jains as compared to other religious communities in India.

After showing variation in number of Jains through successive censuses from 1881 onward, and other usual demographic characteristics based on 1981 census data, the author goes on to discuss in detail select population characteristics of the Jain community, namely growth rate, sex ratio, level of urbanization and average household size in terms of (a) other religious communities, (b) states and UTs and (c) categories of districts with 10,000 or more Jains. In this connection, he concludes that the 'higher household size coupled with the lowest fertility level seems to indicate that the prevalence of joint family system is still in vogue on a large scale despite it being one of the most urbanized community (sic) in India'.[18] A few other major population characteristics such as literacy, work participation rate and occupational structure are not highlighted in the chapter.

Chapter 6, 'Jains in the Censuses of 1991 and 2001' by Prakash C. Jain analyses the major population characteristics of the Jain community as per the 1991 and 2001 censuses of India. The chapter highlights two remarkable features pertaining to the population dynamics of the Jain community – one each associated with the two censuses. The 1991 census data reveal the lowest ever decadal population increase since 1931, which underlines the urban middle class character of the community. This process briefly got disturbed during the decade 1991–2001 whereby as per 2001 census the decadal growth rate of the Jain population surprisingly shot up to 26.4 per cent. This has now been attributed by scholars to the sustained campaign by the Jain media as well as the leaders to appeal to the members of the Jain community to return themselves as 'Jains', and not as 'Hindus' during the census enumerations of 2001. As a result of this campaign, about 6,00,000 people had additionally 'returned' to the Jain-fold in 2001.[19] The decadal growth rate in 2011 census at 5.4 per cent only proves the fact that the low fertility rate has been the characteristic feature of the Jain community since about the 1980s.

Chapter 7, 'Jain Population and Demography, 2011' by Prakash C. Jain and Dheeraj Jain presents all the usual major population characteristics of the Jain community in India. It is remarkable to note here that for the first time in the history of census enumerations, the Jains are found in all the states and

UTs of India. Secondly, with about 95 per cent literacy, 80 per cent urbanization, lowest fertility rate (1.4) and 5.4 per cent decadal population growth rate during 2001–2011, the data clearly confirm the urban middle class character of the Jain community. Although the 2011 census data reveal an appreciable improvement in the sex ratio and child sex ratio for the Jains (954 and 889 respectively) compared to 2001 figures (940 and 870 respectively), they continue to remain the Achilles' heels of the community in most parts of the country.[20]

Chapter 8, 'Some Notes on the Jain Diaspora' by Prakash C. Jain explores the process of Jain diaspora formation in different parts of the world, its numerical strength and socio-economic status. With a very small beginning in the late nineteenth century, the Jain diaspora today is 3,00,000 strong entity. The author also highlights two important features of the Jain diaspora: (a) its non-sectarian character, particularly in North America where about half of the diasporic Jain population resides and (b) unlike in India where the Jains are mainly engaged in trade and commerce, the diasporic Jains are mostly engaged in various professions.

Written by two distinguished members of the Jain diaspora community in North America Sulekh C. Jain and Yashwant K. Malaiya, Chapter 9 titled 'Jain Population Predicament: Need to Learn from the Parsi and Jewish Situations' voices the concern about the demographic future of the Jain community in India.[21] While showing the concern, they do have in their mind two other prominent global religious minority communities, namely the Jews and the Parsis which have been displaying 'depressing' population characteristics for about past half-a-century. Whereas the global population of the Jews has been increasing very slowly and is presently about 14 million, that of the Parsis the world over and particularly in India has been numerically on the decline from 69.601 in 2001 to 57,264 in 2011 (18% decline). It is quite natural for anyone to draw parallels among these three minorities as all of them happen to be relatively well educated, affluent and dependent on trade and commerce and professional occupations.

Can the Jains learn from the Jewish or Parsis situations? 'Yes', say the authors, and suggest that the Parsi and Jewish programmes 'that attempt to help low fertility couples' can be adapted to the Jain situation. The Jains can also learn from the two communities is question how to take pride in their Jain identity and culture. Nevertheless, the issues and their answers about the Jain population predicament are not easy, warn the authors, and rightly emphasize the urgent need to have within the Jain community 'healthy debates, action plans and road maps.' This is more so for at least two important reasons: (a) Jainism as a salvation religion encourages its laity as well as ascetics to observe celibacy, sometimes even from the childhood, that has serious implications on the Jain population dynamics, (b) the modernization and development of the Jain community as a whole and its upper middle class character are bound to slow down its population growth rate leading to eventual stagnation and then to a long process of decline in due course of time.

To the best of my knowledge, articles and book excerpts contained in this book are the only ones available so far in the field of Jain demographic studies. It is interesting to note in this connection that even census data-based analysis was not undertaken by any scholar for more than half a century after the first systematic census of India in 1881. Undoubtedly, the first pioneering and comprehensive study in this regard was made during 1950s by Professor Vilas A. Sangave who initially focussed his attention on 1931 census data and then extended it up to the 1971 census. Subsequent authors, particularly M.K. Jain and Prakash C. Jain undoubtedly owe to him a lot for further analysis of other census data.

Although the long-suspected Jain population 'drift' mentioned above appeared to have been over with the 2011 census data that showed the 'normal' decadal growth rate

(5.4%) compared to the unusual growth rate in the 2001 census data (26.4%), the grievances of the Jain community leaders and opinion makers against census enumerators as well as authorities continue to remain intact for alleged under-enumeration of the Jain population. They maintain that the total Jain population in India could be any number between 1 crore (10 million) to 2 crore. The figure of 1 crore has been in circulation for at least half-a-century now. The well-known industrialist Sahu Shreyans Prasad Jain mentioned the Jain population in 1974–1975 around 1 crore.[22] This figure is often endorsed by a large number of Jains.[23] Others even go to the extent of claiming the Jain population in India around 15 million,[24] or even around 20 million.[25]

During the past two decades, a few attempts have been made to substantiate these claims. Thus, three studies of Delhi Jain population have so far come to light. In the late 1990s, a Delhi-wide Jain directory was prepared which enumerated the total Jain population at 1,85,000 as against the 2001 census-based Delhi Jain population of 1,55,122. The compilers of this directory claimed to have covered about 95 per cent of the Delhi Jain population. Thus, the Jain population of Delhi as per this study was underestimated by at least 30,000 persons, or about 20 per cent.[26]

Recently two Delhi Jain population surveys were conducted by International School for Jain Studies, New Delhi, which are not only more assertive about underestimation of Jain population but also methodologically more sophisticated.[27]. These are reported in Chapter 10, 'Under-Enumeration of Jain Population: Evidence from Two Delhi Surveys' by Shugan C. Jain and Prakash C. Jain. The two surveys done in Hauz Khas tehsil of South Delhi district and New Delhi district respectively are based on four kinds of sources of Jain population data, namely (a) Census 2011, (b) Voters list of the areas, (c) Directories of local temples/sthanaks and (d) Sample surveys of the Jain families. Whereas the Hauz Khas study reported about 95 per cent underestimation of the Jain population, the New Delhi district study suggested about 80 per cent under-enumeration. Thus, these studies have begun to confirm the long-held contention by Jain community leaders and scholars of the under-enumeration of the Jain population in census data. Needless to say, more studies in and outside Delhi are required to further confirm this phenomenon.

Notes and References

1. See Tatya Keshav Chopde, *Jain Aani Marathi Hindu* (in Marathi) (Sangli: Shree Veer Granth Mala, 1945), p. 14.
2. Syamlal, 'The Jain Movement and Socio-Religious Transformation of the "Bhangis" of Jodhpur, Rajasthan', *The Indian Journal of Social Work,* Vol. LIII (1), 1992, pp. 59–67.
3. Jain, Jyoti Prasad, *Religion and Culture of the Jains* (New Delhi: Bharatiya Jnanpith, 1983), pp. 30–31.
4. Outside the purview of census taking, attempts have been made from time to time to partially enumerate the Jain population in terms of sect, caste or territory. Amongst these attempts, mention must be made of the All-India Digambar Jain Directory, 1914; a number of Vastipatraks of Kutchhi Jain community since 1925; and a census of Chhatarpur district Jain population in the mid-1990s by Surendra Kumar Jain (1996). Mention must also be made of All-India Directories of Parwars and Golapuravs – two Digambar Jain castes of Bundelkhand region whose details are as follows: (a) Pt. Tulsiram Kavyateerth (ed.), *Digambar Jain Parwar Directory* (Amravati: Singhai Bansilal Pannalal Parwar, 1924); (b) Pt. Mohanlal Jain Kavyateerth (ed.), *Shri Akhil Bharatvarsheeya Digambar Jain Golapurav Directory* (Barayatha, Sagar: The Author, 1941).
5. Kingsley Davis, *Population of India and Pakistan* (Princeton: Princeton University Press, 1951), p. 184.
6. Ibid.
7. Jagdish P. Sharma, 'Jains as a Minority in Indian Society and History', *Jain Journal,* 1976, Vol. 5 (April), p. 139.
8. Vilas A. Sangave, *Jain Community: A Social Survey,* Second Edition (Bombay: Popular Prakashan, 1980), p. 3. First published in 1959.
9. Census of India, 1931, Vol. 9 (Bombay Cities), Part 1, p. 11, quoted in Kingsley Davis, op. cit., p. 184, n. 21.

10. Vilas A. Sangave, op. cit., p. 30, n. 7.
11. Ibid., p. 29
12. Ibid.
13. Ibid., p. 30.
14. M.K. Jain, 'Jains in India: How Many and Where?', *Tirthankar*, Vol. 1(2), 1975, 8–23.
15. Ibid., p. 8.
16. Jain, M.K., 'A Demographic Analysis on the Jains', *Jain Journal*, Vol. 21(2), 1986, pp. 33–50.
17. Ibid., p. 35.
18. Ibid., p. 47.
19. Jain, Prakash C., *Jains in India and Abroad* (New Delhi: International School for Jain Studies, 2011).
20. Ibid.
21. An earlier version of this article appeared as 'Can Jainism Survive in 21st century?', *JAINA Digest*, 2011, pp. 125–128.
22. Jain, Ravindra K., *Universe as Audience: Metaphor and Community among the Jains* (Shimla: Indian Institute of Advanced Study, 1999), p. 88.
23. Jain, Duli Chand, 'The Jain Way of Life', *Jain Journal*, Vol. XLVIII (1/4), 2013–2014, pp. 7–14.
24. Jain 'Bhagatji', Mahendra Kumar, 'Karodon ki Jansankhya vala Jain Samaj Lakhon mei Kyon?', *Jain Gazette*, Vol. 20, 14 February 2011, pp. 1–2.
25. Chavhan, Mahavir Shrimandhar, 'Janganana 2011 Aur Jain Samaj', *Jain Gazette*, 10 September 2009, p. 5.
26. Jain, Ashish (ed.), *Jain Nirdeshika, Delhi,* Two Volumes (New Delhi: Jain Welfare Society, 2000).
27. International School for Jain Studies, *Jain Population Study in India: Hauz Khas Tehsil, Delhi* (New Delhi: International School for Jain Studies, 2017) (Mimeographed); International School for Jain Studies, *Jain Population Study in India: New Delhi District* (New Delhi: International School for Jain Studies, 2018) (Mimeographed).

1

Jain Population in India, 1881–1941

Kingsley Davis

The Jain sect is far older than the Sikh, and slightly older than Hindu doctrines, but is distinguished by carrying to an extreme doctrine of radical immanence. This doctrine, the concrete expression of which is *ahimsa* (non-injury), would result in extreme asceticism, were it not for the sharp distinction among Jains between the laity and the monks. The Jains possess one of the most ancient monastic orders in India, and one of the most ascetic. The Jain laity, on the other hand, has always been remarkably successful in worldly affairs. They were already wealthy and prominent in the old regimes, and they were one of the first religious groups to take advantages of Western education, prospering exceedingly in business under British rule.[1]

Worldly success, however, is not causing the Jains to grow in numbers. On the contrary, they seem to be numerically stationary and to be declining as a portion of the total population, as the census returns show.

As a partial explanation of the stagnation, one may note that because they observe the taboo on widow remarriage more strictly than any other religious group, the Jains have a low percentage of their women aged 15–39 married. A fifth of their women in this age group were widows during the period 1911–1931. If they permitted widows to remarry to a degree that would give them the same proportion of widows as the United States had in 1930, their fertility would be increased more than 20 per cent.

Not only does widowhood cut down Jain reproduction, but the sect also has a low fertility within the marital relation. They have next to the lowest ratio of children to married women of any religious group, being outdone in this respect only by the Parsis, who have roughly the same socio-economic position as the Jains.

The low marital fertility of the Jains is doubtless connected with their social position. They are the third most urban religious group, the third most literate and the second or third most prosperous. The price they are apparently paying for their high social position is a low fertility. Since they do not acquire new converts, this low fertility helps to prevent any growth in their number.

Low fertility is probably not the factor, however. This is indicated by the case of the Parsis. The latter have, by all signs, a lower fertility than the Jains, but are slowly increasing in population. There is some evidence that the Jains are losing some members who drift into Hinduism.[2] It will be noticed, from Table 1.1, that the Jain population reached its low point in 1921, and began to climb thereafter. In this connection, it is interesting that the Jains made the greatest improvement of any group in lowering the number of widowhood. In 1921, the proportion of widows among women aged 15–39 was 20.8,

Table 1.1

Jain Population in India, 1881–1941

Census Year	*Number (000s)*	*Per cent of Population*
1881	1,222	0.49
1891	1,417	0.51
1901	1,334	0.47
1911	1,248	0.41
1921	1,177	0.39
1931	1,251	0.37
1941	1,449	0.37

Source: Various Indian census reports.

whereas in 1931 it was down to 16.9. It is also interesting to note that vigorous reform movements began within the sect around the turn of the century. It may be that the Jains will steadily increase in numbers in the near future. In any case, they will long retain their place as the sixth most numerous religious group in India, though there is a little chance of their catching up with the fast-growing Sikhs, the nearest group ahead of them.

Notes and References

1. J.N. Farquhar, *Modern Religious Movements in India* (New York: Macmillan, 1915), pp. 324–326.
2. 'In respect of Jains it is always doubtful whether the numbers recorded are really accurate as many return themselves as Hindus. Sometimes there is no uniformity about this practice so that the comparative figures of Jains and Hindus are always liable to a certain amount of disturbance by influences which cannot be gauged statistically'. *Census of India*, 1931, Vol. 9 (Bombay Cities), Part 1, p. 11.

2

Jains as a Minority in Indian Society and History

Jagdish P. Sharma

Jains are the sixth most numerous religious group today after the Hindus (82.72%), Muslims (11.21%), Christians (2.60%), Sikhs (1.89%) and Buddhists (0.70%). The Jains (0.47%) along with Buddhists, Parsis and Jews, each account for less than 1 per cent of India's total population separately.[1] In terms of numbers alone, therefore, the Jains constitute a very small minority.[2]

Scholars have long raised questions regarding the accuracy of census figures but it is generally accepted that more than any other group the Jains have been very much at fault in misrepresenting their religious affiliation (for whatever reason) to census takers. This was noticed even in 1915[3] and continued until recently.[4] Many thousands of Jains still register themselves as Hindus. Thus, it would seem that the actual number of Jains is somewhat larger than the census figures would indicate; still it would not substantially alter their status as an extremely small minority. The 1971 census reports that there were only 26,04,646 (i.e. 0.47%) Jains out of India's total population of 54,79,49,809. Even allowing for misrepresentations, their population in India would not amount to more than 3 million at the most.

If we consider the Jain population figures in the record of the last ten censuses, we notice that the Jains constituted only 0.49 per cent of the total population in 1891 (the highest ever since census figures began to be collected in 1881) and merely 0.36 per cent (the lowest ever) in 1931 (Table 2.1). Throughout the entire past century, Jains officially accounted for less than one half per cent of the total population. Their growth rate has greatly varied from the lowest decrease of –6.4 per cent in 1901–1911, to the highest rate of growth of 28.48 per cent during the last decade, and their population has more than doubled between 1881 and 1971 (12,21,896 to 26,04,646). Yet their overall strength in the total population has, in fact, declined (Table 2.2).

Table 2.1

Percentage of Jains in India's Total Population, 1881–1971

Year	Percentage
1881	0.48%
1891	0.49%
1901	0.45%
1911	0.40%
1921	0.37%
1931	0.36%
1941	0.37%
1951	0.45% (Sangave, 1959: 434)
1961	0.46%
1971	0.47% (India 1974: 13)

Source: *India 1974: A Reference Annual* (1974).

Table 2.2

Percentage of Increase in the Jain Population

1881–1891	+15.9%
1891–1901	–5.8%
1901–1911	–6.4%
1911–1921	–5.6%
1921–1931	+6.2%
1931–1941	+15.8
1941–1951	+11.7% (Sangave, 1959: 433–434)
1951–1961	+25.17% (Census of India 1961, Vol. XIX, Pt. I:245)
1961–1971	+28.48% (India 1974: 13)

Jains are found all over India and are mainly concentrated in the western and central regions. The largest concentration of Jains at present is to be found in Maharashtra (7,03,664), Rajasthan (5,13,548), Gujarat (4,51,578), Madhya Pradesh (3,45,211) and Karnataka (former Mysore: 2,18,862), while there are 1,24,728 Jains in Uttar Pradesh and 50,513 in Delhi. Only in these six states do the Jains account for more than 1,00,000 each, along with a sizeable population in the capital. But the Jains are found even in the remotest corners of India, for example, three are noted in Mizoram between Bangladesh and Burma, fourteen in the Andaman and Nicobar Islands and thirty-nine are in the former North-East Frontier, now called Arunachal Pradesh. Only in the Union Territory of Lakshadweep, west of Kerala in the Indian Ocean, were no Jains recorded for the 1971 census.[5]

Jains live mostly in big cities and towns, and it can be said that 'the Jain community is essentially urban in character'.[6] Yet another significant fact about their distribution pattern that can be drawn from pre-independent India census figures is that the Jains preferred to live in princely states and agencies as opposed to the provinces of British India. In 1901, 64 per cent of the Jains lived in Indian India, while only 36 per cent settled in the

British-ruled provinces; while the figures for 1941 show 60 per cent and 40 per cent respectively.[7]

A third significant point about Jain population distribution is that they have been heavily concentrated in the Hindu-dominated areas and only sparsely spread in the regions dominated by the Muslims. In Sangave's opinion, as Jainism is closer to Hinduism than to any other religion in India this might have resulted in the Jains choosing the Hindus as their neighbours. Lastly and surprisingly, the land where Mahavira wandered and preached during his lifetime is scarcest in Jain population.[8] It seems evident, in the light of sources available, that in the post-Mahavira days (i.e. after c. 500 BC), a section of the Jain community moved to western and central India via Mathura, while another section went directly to the Karnataka region sometime during the fourth century BC.[9]

It seems that Jain influence and concentration shifted in the course of time, but it is difficult to imagine their numerical strength ever being more than 1 per cent of India's total population at any given point in history. It was noticed above that despite there being no change in their percentage in the population as a whole, according to Sangave the factors such as the deficiency of females mortality, large numbers of unmarried males and great proportion of young widowed females effectively barred from remarriage have all combined together to lower the growth of Jain population (1959: 414). To this he adds the lack of proselytizing activities of the Jains (at least since medieval times) as well as thousands of Jains leaving the faith every year.[10] But in my view, Jain ethics and discipline are too demanding, the community pressure and conservatism so great that it does not appeal to the non-Jains, while many Jains are driven to other creeds.

Jarl Charpentier says much the same thing about Jainism, though he chooses to emphasize other aspects. According to him,

> the Jain church has never had a very great number of adherents; it has never attempted – at least not on any grand scale – to preach its doctrines through missionaries outside India. Never rising to an overpowering height but at the same time never sharing the fate of its rival, Buddhism, that of complete extinction in its native land, it has led a quiet existence through the centuries and has kept its place amongst the religious systems of India till the present day.[11]

Jains in History and Society

The Jains are strictly an Indian phenomenon. They are not found elsewhere. Some Jains might well have migrated to and settled down for a while with neighbouring countries of Nepal and Sri Lanka, but they have not accounted for more than temporary residents in historical terms. Therefore, when we speak of their role in history and society, we mean their role in Indian history and society. The Jains claim to be the oldest living religious community in India. While contemporary historians would basically agree with this view, they also would assign a similar antiquity to the Hindus. It is now generally accepted that Jainism is at least two centuries older than Buddhism and some of its elements might well be traced to the Indus Valley Civilization of the third millennium BC.[12] Jain doctrine mythologies and practices reveal that, having lived a long and continuous existence within the vastly domain Hindu population, they have been immensely influenced by the latter. Yet they have managed to retain identity and continuity. Moreover, the Jains felt a particular sense of competition and rivalry with the Ajivikas and Buddhists. The rigorous commitment of the Jains to the ascetic ideal, persistent adherence to the principle of non-injury (*ahimsa*) and close-knit community organization served them in good stead and they not only outlived, but also outdid their rivals.

I believe that it is primarily because of these three characteristics that Jains have held their own and occupied an important position in Indian society, despite a minuteness of numbers. They seem to have wielded a greater political, cultural, economic, artistic and moral influence in India than expected. In fact, Jain contributions in these areas are not only much larger in terms of time (or duration) but also greater in proportion to those of the larger minorities of Sikhs and Christians. Their overall impact on Indian society and history is also much greater than those of Parsis and Jews and in this they vie for comparison with much larger Muslim minority and more widely discussed one of the Buddhist.

Jainism is a religion of great antiquity which first flourished in eastern India in the region of Banaras and Bihar. It has a recognized series of 24 Jinas or teachers, their own canons and a well-organized body of monks and lay community that has existed through the centuries.[13] Two of the last great Jinas, Parsva and Mahavira, lived and preached in the eighth and sixth centuries BC, respectively. Mahavira's family already professed Parsva's doctrine; he himself renounced his worldly ties when he was about 30 years old, after meeting his family obligations and taking due permission of his elder brother. He did not run away like Gautama Buddha at dead of night leaving his wife and child uncared for. He searched for the truth for about 12 years, meditated and practiced severe austerities through which he came to understand and fully control his feelings and passions. He became fully aware and fearless like a lion, he became the perfected one. He became the Jina, 'conqueror' of feelings and passions (equivalent to the Buddha as 'the enlightened one') and could now go and preach his path, a path the Parsva had preached about 250 years earlier and 22 Jinas before Parsva. Mahavira claims no originality for his doctrines. He reformulated the system which already existed and there were other followers of Parsva even before Mahavira became a Jina and main spokesman for the Niganthas as the Jinas were known in the sixth century BC. Mahavira, however, more heavily emphasized the ascetic rules for the monks than had Parsva. Mahavira may have noted the moral laxities found in contemporary monks whether Jain, Ajivika or Buddhist. He set an unusually high standard of ascetic morality which had led many an earlier student of Indian philosophy and religion to regard him as an originator of a new system.

Jinas enjoyed the support and patronage of contemporary kings such as Cetaka of Vaishali, Srenika (Bimbisara) and Kunika (Ajatasatru). Later on the Mauryan emperors Chandra Gupta and Asoka also had patronized them as did the 'Jain King' Kharavela of Kalinga. It is also certain that a number of prominent merchants and aristocrats and nobles have also shown their appreciation for Jainism during the pre-Christian era. It was apparently in the days of Chandra Gupta Maurya (fourth century BC) that a section of the Jain community moved south under the leadership of Bhadrabahu. The emperor Chandra Gupta Maurya himself is said to have renounced his throne under impact of this great Jain ascetic and accompanied his followers to Karnataka (Mysore). This migration is said to have been caused by a 12-year famine. While still in the south, Chandra Gupta is said to have fasted to death in the true Jain manner.

Western India though an important Jain stronghold from the days of Kumarapala and his Jain counsellor Hemachandra in the twelfth century AD, it has had a Jain community for several centuries. The last great council to settle canonical differences was held in this region (at Vallabhi) in the fifth century. There is even the tradition of Nemi (the 22nd Jina and contemporary of Krishna) having attained *kaivalya* on Mt. Girnar in Gujarat. Historically, at any rate, Jainism can be traced back to around second century BC in the western region.[14] Sufficient evidence has also come to light that shows that even earlier in the third century, Jainism had an important place in Mathura, the famous city on river Yamuna associated with the boyhood of Krishna. Thus, it is easy to conclude that Jainism has had a long history in the western states of Gujarat, Rajasthan and Maharashtra, apart from Mathura in western Uttar Pradesh (UP).[15] In later times,

Jainism found a great patron in the Mughal emperor Akbar in the north as well as numerous ruling dynasties in the south.[16]

The Jains built monumental structures and created great works of art and architecture. No language: old or new, no subject: humanistic or scientific, no philosophical system: orthodox or heterodox escaped their attention. Jainism initially appealed to the Kshatriyas and the Vaisyas in particular, but in course of time only the merchants continued to be their faithful adherents. Through trade and commerce, Jains made a rich and enviable contribution to India's economic growth and well-being and continue to do so this day. It would not be an exaggeration to state that Jains have continuously made a rich and varied contribution to India (cf. H.L. Jain, 1962). Their role in Indian society and history has always been that of a great moral force (from there uncompromising asceticism to Gandhi's non-violence), that of upholders of diversity of thought, cultivators of work and liberation ethic. Moreover, they have been significant contributors to learning and philanthropy, widespread and successful trading and moneylending. They have been quietly committed and loyal to the law and authority with a completely clean criminal record. Few minorities can match such a record!

Jain Attitude towards Other Communities and Ruling Authorities

The very cornerstone of Jain metaphysics stand on the doctrine of *syadvada,* 'maybe-ism', according to which 'there is no judgement which is absolutely true in some sense and false in another'.[17] The Jains are committed to a philosophical position encompassing manifold viewpoints (*anekantavada*), which encourages the cultivation of many schools of thought and expects people to look at any reality or concept from differing viewpoints.[18] With this commitment to the existence of diverse viewpoints and communities, Jains seem naturally to accept the existence of various minorities in India.

Still, a number of beliefs and practices of the Jains betray the basically conservative character of the Jain community.[19] This conservatism and the acute sense of the need to survive is more evident from their attitude towards government and authority in general, no matter what its character. The Jains have had a reputation of being the ideal subjects and citizens throughout their historical existence in India. They have always been a people who took law and order seriously. Whether the power was wielded by a Hindu, Buddhist, Muslim or Christian king or ruler, the Jains were always ready and willing to accept its legitimacy and authority.[20] They always came forward with whatever help, mainly financial and intellectual, they could offer.[21] This enabled them to establish a quick rapport and smooth working relationships with all manner of government and authority in India. There are many records of Hindu kings extending patronage to the Jains (e.g. Gupta kings, etc.) as there are of Buddhist kings such as Asoka, even of some Muslim rulers (such as Akbar) and the British government. This loyalty towards ruling authority as such has enabled the Jains to ply their rich trade and attain immense prosperity throughout their history. It was essentially this loyalty, prosperity and piety that had misled a British missionary to write of them as ideal converts so optimistically and temptingly:

> There is a strange mystery in Jainism; for though it acknowledges no personal God, knowing Him neither as Creator, Father, or Friend, yet it will never allow itself to be called an atheistic system. Indeed there is no more deadly insult that one could level at a Jain than to call him a *nastika* or atheist. It is as if, though their king were yet unknown to them, they were nevertheless all unconsciously awaiting his advent amongst them, and proudly called themselves *royalists*. The marks which they will ask to see in one who claims to be their king will be the proofs of Incarnation (*avatara*), of suffering (*tapa*) and of the Majesty of a Conqueror (*Jina*). *But when once, they recognize Him, they will pour out at His feet all the wealth of their trained powers of self-denial and renunciation. Then shall He, the*

> *Desire of all Nations, whose right it is to reign, take His seat on the empty throne of their hearts, and He shall reign King of Kings and Lord of Lords for ever and ever.*[22]

Jain Ethics and Occupations

The ultimate goal of the Jains is the attainment of *Kaivalya*. This is seen as

> integration, the restoration of the faculties that have been temporarily lost through being obscured … . All beings are intended to be omniscient, omnipotent, unlimited, and unfettered … . The aim of men must be to make manifest the power that is latent within them by removing whatever hindrances may be standing in the way.[23]

These hindrances involve the stoppage of influx of the bad karmic matter that stains the *Jiva* 'life-monad' (known as *samvara*), and the cleansing of already existing stains on the *Jiva* by producing good karmic matter (known as *nirjara*). Under Jainism, this goal can only be attained after renunciation and the practice of ascetic life. Thus, the system gives primacy to the monks and only a secondary position to the laity. The monks are expected to live by the five cardinal vows of non-injury, truth, not taking what is not given, chastity and non-possession.[24]

The monks were also expected to guide and advice the lay folk towards an ethical and spiritual path. Twelve minor vows were prescribed for the laity which are only a watered down version of the five great vows.[25]

Yet the main emphasis was laid on encouraging the lay folk to take up ascetic life as soon as possible. It will be noticed that the principle of non-injury or non-violence occupies a central position both in the life of an ascetic and that of the householder. This has serious implications for the activities and occupations that the Jainas could take up.

Since the Jain lay adherents were forbidden to injure any living beings, 'they might never till the soil, nor engage in butchering, fishing, brewing, or any other occupation involving the taking of life'[26] This injunction is regarded by Noss as by far the most important in its social effect. He asserts:

> It constituted a limitation that must have seemed serious to the early followers of Mahavira; but at long last it actually proved to have economic as well as religious worth, for the Jains found they could make higher profits when they turned from occupations involving direct harm to living creatures to careers in business as bankers, lawyers, merchants and proprietors of land. The other moral restrictions of their creed, which prohibited gambling, eating meat, drinking wine, adultery, hunting, thieving and debauchery, earned them social respect[27]... .

A Jain community survey taken by a sociologist Sangave also showed that though the Jains follow different kinds of occupations, 'they are mainly money-lenders, bankers, jewelers, cloth-merchants, grocers and recently industrialists ...'. And in professions 'they are mainly found in legal, medical and teaching professions as well as nowadays many Jains are holding important responsible positions' in various departments of the union and State governments.[28]

The Jains are a rich and influential minority primarily in commercial activities. J.L. Jaini writing half a century ago said that 'Colonel Tod in his *Rajasthan,* and Lord Reay and Lord Curzon after him have estimated that half the mercantile wealth of India passes through the hands of the Jaina laity. Commercial prosperity implies shrewd business capacity and also steady, reliable character and credit'.[29] Weber also noticed Jain honesty, wealth, commercial success and their belief in non-violence and found telling comparisons with Parsis, Jews and Quakers.[30]

The above discussion shows that Jain ethics and their commitment to the principles of non-violence[31] have forced them to follow certain occupations and professions which have led them to unusual success in business enterprises. It is basically their unique ethic that the Jains, though a small minority community, 'developed most of the essentials of the spirit of modern capitalism centuries ago .... Now with capitalism entering India from the west, the Jains are unusually well-equipped to play a dynamic role in the social order' of a new India.[32]

Summary and Conclusion

The Jains have always constituted a small religious minority of Indian society throughout their historical existence. The two other criteria of language and ethnic background that define a minority do not apply to them for they speak practically every language of India and cannot be isolated ethnically from other Indian people.

An analysis of Jain population distribution shows their concentration in western India including central India. The Jains show their preference for urban as opposed to rural areas. They occupy a pre-eminent position in trade and commerce and much of India's wealth passes through their hands who compose barely ½ per cent of India's population. This honesty, reliability, loyalty, integrity and religiosity has won them immense wealth and influence in India. They compare themselves with conservative Jews in the West. Their ethic is largely given credit for this success and sense of loyalty.

Jainism, though preached and propagated by warrior princes (Kshatriyas), has come to have an entirely merchant (Vaisya) following. Most scholars have taken this to mean a downward social mobility of the Jains, that is, they became nearer to the Sudras and farther away from the Brahmanas. Yet in the Indian past birth (*jati*) alone was never the sole criterion of social concern also contributed to social status apart from the criterion of birth. The Jains, the second most educated people in India after the Parsis, were good and loyal subjects to all governments, largely urban in character and given to many social concerns and philanthropic works. They were proverbially famous for their honesty, humility, wealth and piety. An historical analysis of the ideal qualities and characteristics of each of the four social classes (*varnas*) would indicate a close relationship of the Jain Vaisyas with the Brahmanas.[33]

When scholars assign a lower status of the Jains than the Kshatriyas they seem to be repeating what traditional writers had written millenniums ago. They have neglected to consider the changing reality of Indian society and have ignored the multiplicity of factors that contributed towards social mobility. If interpreted in this light, Indian records furnish sufficient evidence to show that the Vaisya Jains have achieved an upward social mobility by most closely paralleling the culture and personality of the Brahmanas. Thus, it can be argued that the Jain, despite the change in their ascended class (Kshatriya to Vaisya), have by adopting the dominant culture traits of the Brahmanas, raised their social status during the course of Indian history.

Notes and References

1. *India 1974: A Reference Annual* (Delhi, 1974).
2. Census of India 1961, Vol. XV, Uttar Pradesh, Pt. I-A (ii):115; *India* 1974, p. 12.
3. M. Stevenson, *The Heart of Jainism* (Oxford, 1915); Indian reprint (New Delhi, 1970).
4. V.A. Sangave, *Jain Community: A Social Survey* (Bombay, 1959).
5. cf. *India* 1974: 12. Table I.10.
6. Taking India as a whole we find that in 1941, 41.4 per cent of the Jain population lived in towns, and in provinces, the urban Jain population was 48.9 per cent and in states and agencies it was 36.5 per cent. The corresponding figures for all religions were 12.9 per cent, 12.7 per cent and 13.4 per cent. There is a continuous increase in the Jain urban population in almost all provinces and states. It would also seem that the Jains are 'more urban in localities, where they are less in number and more rural in areas where they are numerous'. It seems generally to be the case that minorities find their way and flourish in cities and towns and that is why 'the Jain community is essentially urban in character' (Sangave, 1959: 4–5).
7. Sangave (1959: 3–4).

8. Ibid.
9. C.J. Shah, *Jainism in Northern India* (London, 1932); K.C. Jain, *Jainism in Rajasthan* (Solapur, 1963); P.B. Desai, *Jainism in South India and Some Jain Epigraphs* (Solapur, 1957); S.B. Deo, *History of Jain Monachism* (Bombay, 1956).
10. V.A. Sangave, 1959: 414–415.
11. Jarl Charpentier, 'The History of the Jains', in *Cambridge History of India*, Vol. I, ed. by E.J. Rapson (Cambridge, 1935), pp. 150–170.
12. R. Williams, 'Before Mahavira', *Journal of Royal Asiatic Society*, 1966, pp. 2–6; H. Zimmer, *Philosophies of India* (New York, 1956).
13. cf. J.L. Jaini, *Outlines of Jainism*, 1916; M. Stevenson, *Heart of Jainism* (Oxford, 1915); Indian reprint (New Delhi, 1970).
14. K.C. Jain, *Jainism in Rajasthan* (Solapur, 1963); C.B. Sheth, *Jainism in Gujarat* (Bombay, 1953).
15. cf. C.V. Shah, *Jainism in Gujrat* (Bombay, 1932).
16. See, Sangave, op. cit., pp. 374–386; Charpentier, op. cit.; Desai op. cit.; K.C. Shastri, *Jainism in South India* (in Hindi) (Varanasi, 1967).
17. S.N. Das Gupta, *A History of Indian Philosophy*, Vol. I (Cambridge, 1957), p. 179.
18. cf. S. Gopalan, *Outlines of Jainism* (New York, 1973), pp. 145–156.
19. Sangave regards 'inflexible conservatism' the very strength of the Jain community. He writes: 'Another important reason for the survival of the Jain community is its *inflexible conservatism* in holding fast to its original institutions and doctrines for the last so many centuries ... an absolute refusal to admit changes has been considered the strongest safeguard of the Jains' (1959: 399).
20. A possible explanation of why the Jains were ready and willing to accede to new authority and its measures is given in a case reported by J.L. Jaini: 'The Indian Penal Code, originally drafted by Lord Macaulay, takes account of almost all offences known to and suppressed by our modern civilization. Mr. A.B. Lathe ... has shown by a table how the five minor rules of conduct (the five *anu-vratas of Jainism*) cover the same ground as the twenty-three chapters and 511 sections of the code' (1916: 72).
21. Cf. 'The royal patronage which Jainism had received during the ancient and medieval periods in different parts of the country has undoubtedly helped the struggle of the Jain community for its survival. ... Apart from Jain rulers, many non-Jain rulers also showed sympathetic attitude towards the Jain religion' (Sangave, 1959: 399).

22. Concluding words of Stevenson, op. cit., p. 298.
23. Zimmer, op. cit., pp. 254–255.
24. cf. Stevenson, op. cit., pp. 234–238.
25. Twelve minor vows for the lay folk prescribe that he: (1) must not destroy life, (2) must not tell a lie, (3) must not make unpermitted use of another man's property, (4) must be chaste, (5) must limit his possessions, (6) must make a perpetual and daily vow to go only in certain directions and certain distances, (7) must avoid useless talk and action, (8) must avoid thought of sinful things, (9) must limit the articles of his diet and enjoyment for the day, (10) must worship at fixed times, morning, noon and evening, (11) must fast on certain days and (12) must give charity in the way of knowledge and money every day (based on *Tattvarthadhigama Sutra II*, 142–143 in Zimmer, 1956: p. 196, n. 14).
26. B. Nevaskar, *Capitalists without Capitalism: The Jains of India and the Quakers of the West* (Westport, 1971), p. 159.
27. J.B. Noss, *Man's Religions* (New York, 1956), p. 152, in Nevaskar, Ibid, pp. 159–160; also see Hajim Nakamura, 'Jainism', *Jain Journal*, Calcutta, Vol. VIII, No, 2 (October 1973), p. 87.
28. Sangave, op. cit., p. 279.
29. J.L. Jaini, op. cit., p. 73; c.f. Max Weber, *The Religion of India*, New York, 1958, p. 200; Nakamura, op. cit., p. 87.
30. Weber finds striking similarities between the Jains and the Jews – and calls the former 'Jews of the Far East' (1958: 11). He also notices similarities in 'honesty is the best policy' among the Parsis, Quakers and Jains. Their honesty and wealth were both proverbial. He further adds 'that the Jains, at least the Svetambara Jains nearly all became traders was due to purely ritualistic reasons … . A case similar to the Jews. Only the trader could truly practice *ahimsa*. This special manner of trading, too, determined by ritual, with its particularly strong aversion against travelling and their way of making travel difficult restricted them to resident trade, again as with Jews to banking and money-lending' (ibid.: 200).
31. Apart from the vows the Jain lay folk were also encouraged to develop the following 21 qualities: serious demeanour, cleanliness, good temper, striving after popularity, fear of sinning, mercy, straightforwardness; wisdom, modesty, kindliness, moderation, gentleness, care of speech, sociability, caution, studiousness, reverence for old age and old customs, humility,

gratitude, benevolence and attention to business (cf. Nevaskar, 1971: 159).

32. Nevaskar, op. cit., p. 235.
33. I am not thinking here of M.N. Srinivas' concept of Sanaskritization, but stating an observation gathered in the study of Indian history during the past 15 years and following the social movements of classes, especially the Vaisyas, in historical perspective.

3

Jain Population, 1881–1971

Vilas A. Sangave

Total and Growth of Jaina Population

The population of Jainas in India according to the 1971 census is only 26,04,646 in the total population of India of 54,79,49,809. The distribution of population of India as per Census of India, 1971, among the major religious communities and their percentage to total population is given in the Table 3.1.[1]

Table 3.1

Major Religious Communities and Their Population in India, 1971

Major Religious Communities	*Population*	*Percentage of Total Population*
Hindus	45,32,92,086	82.72
Muslims	6,14,17,934	11.21
Christian	1,42,23,382	2.6
Sikhs	1,03,78,797	1.89
Buddhists	38,12,325	0.7
Jainas	26,04,646	0.47

From Table 3.1, it is evident that from the point of view of population, the Jaina community is the smallest among the six major religious communities of India. Since the Jaina population is only about 26 lakh, the Jainas are only 0.47 per cent in the total population of India. It means that out of every 10,000 persons in India only 47 are Jainas.

In fact, this figure of 26 lakh of Jaina population in 1971 is much larger than the corresponding figures recorded in the last 10 Census Report of India. The total Jaina population figures as per Census Report of India from 1881 to 1971 are given in Table 3.2.

Table 3.2

Total Jaina Population in Various Census Years

Census Year	*Total Jaina Population in India*
1881	12,21,896
1891	14,16,177
1901	13,34,039
1911	12,48,182
1921	11,78,596
1931	12,52,105
1941	14,49,286
1951	16,18,406
1961	20,27,248
1971	26,04,646

From Table 3.2, it could be seen that even though the Jaina population of 1971 shows a considerable increase over the Jaina population of 1881, still the increase has not been continuous throughout these years. On the contrary, we find that during the decade of 1881 to 1891, there was slight increase in Jaina population followed by a decline in Jaina population from 1891 to 1921 and that in general there has been a steady and continuous increase in Jaina population from 1931 to 1971.

These variations in terms of percentage increase or decrease during each decade over the last 90 years are given in Table 3.3.

Table 3.3

Variation in Jaina Population Since 1881

Decade	*Percentage Increase or Decrease in Jaina Population*
1881–1891	+15.9
1891–1901	–5.8
1901–1911	–6.4
1911–1921	–5.6
1921–1931	+6.2
1931–1941	+15.8
1941–1951	+11.7
1951–1961	+25.3
1961–1971	+28.5

These figures of total Jaina population do not, however, portray the real demographic situation about the Jainas since in the census records all Jainas are not enumerated as Jainas for different reasons. Even though Jainism is a distinct religion and not a sect of Hinduism, still it is a fact in the past many Jainas used to regard themselves a Hindus and were also regarded by others as Hindus. That is why specific instructions were issued to the census enumerators that 'the Jainas should be entered as Jainas and not as Hindus, even though they themselves regard themselves as such'. Hence on some occasions more and on others less Jainas were incorrectly returned as Hindus. At the same time, the converse case of Hindus being returned as Jainas in census records did not possibly occur. Thus, this fact that the Jainas regard themselves and are regarded as Hindus necessarily vitiates the census figures and obscures the increase or decrease of Jaina population from census to census. Again, as a part of the programme of non-cooperation movement launched by Mahatma Gandhi, the Jainas boycotted the census operations of

1931. Naturally this affected to a very large extent the figures about Jainas in the Census Report of 1931. Due to these reasons, incorrect enumeration has always remained as a dominant factor in the census figures of Jainas. But the situation is showing definite improvement as a result of change in the attitude of the Jainas towards themselves. The tendency among the Jainas to regard themselves as Hindus was very prominently noticeable among the Jainas from the beginning of this century and that is why there was a continuous decline in the Jaina population during the decades from 1891 to 1921. This tendency has been largely overcome by various methods adopted during the last 50 years by the Jainas with a view to reorganizing their community. This is clearly visible from the census figures of 1941 and 1951. After independence, there has been a great religious awakening among the Jainas and nowadays the Jainas definitely regard themselves as Jainas and not as Hindus. This situation is clearly reflected in the census figures of 1961 and 1971. During 1951 to 1961, the Jaina population is increased by 25.26 per cent; in the next decade of 1961 to 1971, it registered an increase of 28.48 per cent. In spite of this increase during the last few decades, the Jainas are still sceptical about the reliability of census figures pertaining to them as they believe that the census enumerators do not, for political and other reasons, correctly record the religion of the Jainas even though the census authorities have issued instructions to the census enumerators 'to record the religion as actually returned by a respondent'.[2]

Taking the census figures as they stand, it can be safely stated that the Jaina population has been steadily increasing during the last 50 years and that this increase has been quite noticeable in the last two decades of 1951 to 1961 and 1961 to 1971. The percentage increase of Jainas during 1961 to 1971 compares very favourably with the corresponding increase in the other religious communities as given in Table 3.4.[3]

Table 3.4

Increase in Population of Major Religious Communities, 1961–1971

Major Religious Communities	*Percentage Increase 1961–1971*
Hindus	23.69
Muslims	30.85
Christians	32.6
Sikhs	32.28
Buddhists	17.2
Jainas	28.48

From these figures, it is evident that the percentage increase of the Jainas during 1961–1971 was less than that of the Christians, the Sikhs and the Muslims, but it was more than that of the Buddhists and the Hindus.

Regarding the steady increase in Jainas population, it may be further noted that this increase is not at all due to the conversion of persons of other faiths to Jainism as proselytising activities are practically conspicuous by their absence among the Jainas during the last many centuries.

Table 3.5

Proportion of Jainas per 10,000 of the Total Population

Year	*Number per 10,000 of the Population Who Are Jainas*
1881	48
1891	49
1901	45
1911	40
1921	37
1931	36
1941	37
1951	45
1961	46
1971	47

It is true that the population of Jainas in 1971 (26,04,646) increased by 113.6 per cent over the Jaina population in 1881 (12,21,896), but still we find that at present the proportion of Jaina population to total population of India is less than what it was in 1881 or in 1891. The proportion of Jainas per 10,000 of the total population in India during the last 10 censuses is given in Table 3.5.[4]

From Table 3.5, it is clear that the Jaina community now stands at 0.47 per cent of the total population of India instead of 0.48 per cent in 1881 and 0.49 per cent in 1891. In other words, per 10,000 of the total population of India, the proportion of Jainas was 48 in 1881, 49 in 1891 and 47 in 1971. It means that during the last 10 censuses, the proportion of Jainas to the total population has not improved but has actually declined to some extent. In fact, this total decline was more marked at the four censuses from 1911 to 1941. Taking into consideration the more or less settled nature of the Jaina community, the rate at which the Jaina population declined during this period was quite alarming. That is why the social demographers and the census authorities of that period discussed the problem and tried to give some causes for it.

> This (gradual decrease) is probably due in part to the practice of child marriage and the prohibition of widow remarriage, and partly also to the small size of the community, which attracting as it does no adherents from outside, cannot increase at the same rate as much larger ones. Dr. Guha suggests with some force that the Jainas have a lowered fertility and an increased infant mortality rate on account of their division into small endogamous groups, some of which in Ahmedabad do not exceed 500 souls.[5]

The relative significance of these causes for the relative decline of Jainas population will be discussed at a greater length later on.[6] But it can, however, be mentioned here that since many of these causes still hold good for the Jaina community even to the present day, it is obvious that unless strenuous efforts are made by the Jainas to remove these causes, their proportion to general population will not appreciably increase.

Regional Distribution of Jaina Population

The Jaina community is spread all over India right from Kashmir to Kerala and from Gujarat to Nagaland. The total Jaina population and the percentage distribution of Jaina population according to 1971 census and the percentage of the Jaina population to the total population, according to 1961 and 1971 censuses, in the states and union territories are given in Table 3A.2.[7] From this appendix, it is evident that even though the Jainas have dispersed over the entire country, they show signs of concentration in certain states only. The percentage distribution, in the descending order, of the Jaina population in states and union territories as per 1971 census is given in Table 3.6.

From Table 3.6, it is clear that the Jainas are concentrated largely in the western region of India. The Maharashtra state has got the maximum population of the Jainas among the different states and union territories of India and this state accounts for more than one-fourth (i.e. 27.02%) of the total population of the Jainas. Maharashtra is followed by Rajasthan (19.72%), Gujarat (17.34%) and Madhya Pradesh (13.25%), and these four states account for more than three-fourths (i.e. 77.33%) of the total population of the Jainas. The states of Mysore (8.40%) and Uttar Pradesh (4.79%) stand next in importance from the point of view of concentration of the Jaina population. Thus, in these six states 90.52 per cent of the Jainas are concentrated and the rest 9.48 per cent of the Jainas are scattered over the remaining 23 states and union territories of India.

This distribution of the Jaina population brings out one fact clearly that the Jainas are concentrated in the Hindu-dominated areas and are very sparsely populated in the areas dominated by the Muslims. Jainism is more near to Hinduism than to any other prominent religion in India, and this might have resulted in the Jainas choosing the Hindus as their neighbours.

Table 3.6
Percentage Distribution of Jaina Population in India by State/UTs, 1971

States/Union Territories	*Percentage Distribution of Jaina Population*
Maharashtra	27.02
Rajasthan	19.72
Gujarat	17.34
Madhya Pradesh	13.25
Mysore	8.4
Uttar Pradesh	4.79
Delhi	1.94
Tamil Nadu	1.58
West Bengal	1.24
Haryana	1.2
Bihar	0.97
Punjab	0.82
Andhra Pradesh	0.62
Assam	0.52
Orissa	0.25
Kerala	0.13
Manipur	0.05
Jammu and Kashmir	0.04
Chandigarh	0.04
Nagaland	0.02
Himachal Pradesh	0.02
Goa, Daman and Diu	0.02
Tripura	0.01
Dadra and Nagar Haveli	0.01
Meghalaya	0.01
Pondicherry	0.01
Arunachal Pradesh	Negligible
Andaman Islands	Negligible
Laccadive Islands	–

A very remarkable feature of the distribution of the Jaina population is the practical dearth of the Jainas in the eastern region of India, comprising the states of Bihar, Orissa and West Bengal where the Jaina religion has its origin, and which had come under the direct spell of Lord Mahavira. It is really surprising to note that the Jainas are most scarce in Bihar where Lord Mahavira lived, preached and flourished. Similarly, it is strange to find that there are very few Jainas in Orissa where the caves of Udayagiri and Khandagiri bear witness to its early popularity in the early centuries of the Christian era. The same is the case with West Bengal as there are practically no Jainas among the indigenous inhabitants of West Bengal. The continued predominance of the Jaina population in the past in the eastern region of India could be seen from the Saraka of West Bengal, Chhota Nagpur and Orissa who are the Hinduized remnants of the early Jaina people to whom local legends ascribe the ruined temples, defaced images and the abandoned copper mines of that part of Bengal. Their name is a variant of Sravaka (Sanskrit – hearer), the designation of the Jaina laity.[8] But it seems that the Jaina religion was not in a position to wield a continuous hold on the population and later on with the advent of Muslim predominance in that part of the country even the lay Jainas had no course open but to migrate to other areas and especially to the western areas.

The relative absence of the Jainas in Tamil Nadu and Andhra Pradesh and their comparative insignificance in southern parts of Mysore are other noteworthy features in the distribution of the Jaina population. The Jainas reigned supreme in South India for a considerable period, and there are ample evidence to show that in every walk of life their influence was felt by all people. In many places of South India, the Jaina religion was the state religion and numerous villages and towns seem to have been occupied by Jainas only, as can be seen from the names of villages or places such as 'Samana-halli', or the village of the Sramanas, 'Sravana-Belgola' or the white pond of the Sramanas and 'Savanur', 'Savanadurga' and so on. But now only the temples and the colossal statues of Gommateshwara bear witness to its great popularity in the past. This sudden disappearance of the Jaina population from the land where they had a continuous hold for a very long time can, it seems, be attributed to the vigorous persecutionist policy followed by the non-Jainas against the Jainas.

Even though the Jaina population is concentrated mainly in the states of western region of India, it is pertinent to note that the Jainas form a very small proportion of the total population of the respective states. The states and union territories in which 0.25 per cent or more of the population is made up of the Jainas, as per 1971 census, are given in Table 3.7.

Table 3.7

Percentage of Jaina Population to Total Population in Select State/UTs, 1971

States/Union Territories	*Percentage of Jaina Population to Total Population*
Rajasthan	1.99
Gujarat	1.69
Maharashtra	1.4
Delhi	1.24
Madhya Pradesh	0.83
Mysore	0.75
Dadra and Nagar Haveli	0.41
Chandigarh	0.39
Haryana	0.31

From Table 3.7, it will be noticed that only in the states and union territories of Rajasthan, Gujarat, Maharashtra, Delhi, Madhya Pradesh and Mysore, the percentage of the Jaina population to total population is more than the corresponding percentage of 0.47 for India as a whole. Even in these states and union territories, we find[9] that the percentage of the Jaina population to total population of the respective state and union territory shows a great variation during the last two censuses of 1961 and 1971. The increase in Maharashtra was from 1.23 per cent to 1.40 per cent, in Delhi from 1.11 per cent to 1.24 per cent, in Madhya Pradesh from 0.77 per cent to 0.83 per cent, in Mysore from 0.74 per cent to 0.75 per cent and the decline in Rajasthan was 2.03 per cent to 1.99 per cent, in Gujarat from 1.99 per cent to 1.69 per cent and in Chandigarh from 0.86 per cent to 0.39 per cent.

From the statement[10] showing the distribution of the Jaina population into states and union territories of India, at the last three census of 1951, 1961 and 1971 and the percentage increase of the Jaina population during the last two decades 1951–1961 and 1961–1971, it will be noticed that the regional distribution pattern of the Jaina population does not show any change during this period and that the Jaina population reveals a steady increase in all states and union territories except in the states of Jammu and Kashmir and Punjab and in the union territory of Chandigarh. The percentage increase, during the last two decades, of the population of the Jainas from the states where they are mostly concentrated is given in Table 3.8.

Table 3.8

Percentage Increase of Jaina Population during the Decades 1951–1961 and 1961–1971 in Select States/UTs Where They Are Mostly Concentrated

State	Percentage Increase of Jaina Population During the Decade	
	1951 to 1961	1961 to 1971
Gujarat	+9.31	+10.21
Madhya Pradesh	+36.73	+39.24
Maharashtra	+43.86	+44.88
Mysore	+24.66	+25.52
Rajasthan	+13.80	+25.43
Uttar Pradesh	+24.93	+2.15

From Table 3.8, it is clear that Maharashtra state, which has got the maximum number of Jainas in India, the Jaina population registered increase of 43.86 per cent and 44.88 per cent during the two decades of 1951 to 1961 and 1961 to 1971 respectively. The state of Madhya Pradesh comes next in order in this respect and its corresponding figures are 36.73 per cent and 39.24 per cent. These figures for the states of Maharashtra and Madhya Pradesh compare most favourably with the figures of 25.26 per cent and 28.48 per cent increase in the Jaina population in India as a whole during the decades of 1951 to 1961 and 1961 to 1971 respectively.[11]

Apart from the state-wise distribution of the Jaina population, it is interesting to consider the district-wise distribution of the Jaina population in India. Since the small population of the Jainas is scattered over all parts of India, we find that there is not a single district in the country in which the Jainas form even 10 per cent of the population of that district. Only in two districts, namely, Kutch (6.72%) in Gujarat and Jalor (5.20%) in Rajasthan, the proportion of the Jaina population to the total population of the district exceeds 5 per cent. If we go down to the level of 2 per cent, we find that there are in all 29 districts in India in which at least 2 per cent of the population is made up of the Jainas. The statement showing the names of these 29 districts arranged in order of the percentage of the Jaina population of the district to the total population of the district is given in Table 3A.5. The statement also gives the rural and urban distribution of the Jaina population in each of these 29 districts. It means that only in these 29 districts in India, there is some concentration of Jainas because in India as a whole the proportion of the Jaina population to the total population is only 0.47 per cent. Thus, these 29 districts matter most from the point of view of the study of the concentration of the Jaina population in India. The state-wise break-up of these 29 districts is given in Table 3.9.

Table 3.9

Distribution of Jaina Population in Districts Where They are Heavily Concentrated, 1971

State		Number and Names of Districts
Rajasthan	12	Jalor, Pali, Sirohi, Udaipur, Bikaner, Barmer, Ajmer, Churu, Bhilwara, Chittaurgarh, Tonk and Jodhpur
Madhya Pradesh	7	Sagar, Ratlam, Damoh, Indore, Mandsaur, Guna and Ujjain
Gujarat	6	Kutch, Ahmedabad, Surendranagar, Bhavnagar, Jamnagar and Banaskantha
Maharashtra	3	Kolhapur, Greater Bombay and Sangli
Mysore	1	Belgaum

Regarding the location of these districts, it is very pertinent to note that these are situated in the western region of the country and that not only many of these districts in each state are contiguous but most of these districts from the adjoining states are also contiguous. These districts, on the basis of their contiguity in each state, can be divided into specific groups as given in Table 3.10.

Table 3.10

Distribution of Jaina Population by Districts – Contiguity in Five Major States

State	Group No.	District	Jaina Population of the District
Rajasthan	I	1. Jalor	34,751
		2. Barmer	25,218
		3. Jodhpur	24,669
		4. Pali	44,596
		5. Sirohi	19,197
		6. Udaipur	78,507
		7. Chittaurgarh	23,406
		8. Bhilwara	26,911
		9. Tonk	14,917
		10. Ajmer	37,253
		Total of Group I	3,29,425

Cont'd...

...Cont'd

State	*Group No.*	*District*	*Jaina Population of the District*
	II	1. Bikaner	22,266
		2. Churu	25,786
		Total of Group II	48,052
Madhya Pradesh	I	1. Mandsaur	23,531
		2. Ratlam	18,992
		3. Ujjain	17,380
		4. Indore	26,135
		Total of Group I	86,038
	II	1. Sagar	37,017
		2. Damoh	15,105
		3. Guna	15,904
		Total of Group II	68,026
Gujarat	I	1. Kutch	57,107
	II	1. Banaskantha	31,755
	III	1. Jamnagar	29,952
	IV	1. Bhavnagar	39,143
		2. Surendranagar	28,224
		3. Ahmedabad	1,04,047
		Total of Group IV	1,71,414
Maharashtra	I	1. Greater Bombay	2,44,721
	II	1. Kolhapur	93,264
		2. Sangli	59,457
		Total of Group II	1,52,721
Mysore	I	1. Belgaum	1,10,135

From Table 3.10, it will be seen that Group I of Rajasthan is a formidable group of 10 districts comprising 3,29,425 Jainas. The other groups having more than 1 lakh of Jainas are (a) Group I of Maharashtra (2,44,721 Jainas), (b) Group IV of Gujarat (1,71,414 Jainas), (c) Group II of Maharashtra (1,52,721 Jainas) and Group I of Mysore (1,10,135 Jainas). Further it is interesting to find that in the three adjoining states of Rajasthan, Madhya

Pradesh and Gujarat, Group I of (Southern) Rajasthan, Group I of (Western) Madhya Pradesh and Group II of (Northern) Gujarat are contiguous to each other. These three contiguous Groups from three states could be considered to form a regional pocket of the Jainas in the western pocket. Similarly in the two adjoining states of Maharashtra and Mysore, Group II of (Southern) Maharashtra and Group I of (Northern) Mysore are contiguous to each other. These two contiguous groups from two states of Maharashtra and Mysore could be considered to form a regional pocket of the Jainas in the southern area and could be conveniently termed as the southern pocket. Between these two pockets, the southern pocket is of great significance from the point of view of concentration of a considerable number of Jaina population in a limited area as it covers 2,62,856 Jaina persons from only 3 districts compared to the western pocket which covers 4,47,218 Jaina persons from 15 districts. Thus the southern pocket of Kolhapur, Sangli and Belgaum districts stands out as a unique geographical area in the context of the distribution of the Jaina population in India.

The three districts in the southern pocket are also significant from different aspects of Jaina population like the total population of the district, the proportion of rural population and the density of population. The districts having more than 50,000 Jaina population are given in Table 3.11.

Table 3.11

Districts with More Than 50,000 Jaina Population in Major States, 1971

District	*State*	*Jaina Population of District*
Greater Bombay	Maharashtra	2,44,721
Belgaum	Mysore	1,10,135
Ahmedabad	Gujarat	1,04,047
Kolhapur	Maharashtra	93,264
Udaipur	Rajasthan	78,507
Sangli	Maharashtra	59,457
Kutch	Gujarat	57,107

From Table 3.11, it is evident that the district of Greater Bombay has got the maximum number of Jaina population compared to any district in India. But since Bombay is a big metropolitan city and the financial capital of India, the large majority of Jainas in Bombay are not indigenous persons but are mainly migrants from other parts of India. The situation in Ahmedabad district is not much different from that of Greater Bombay district. Out of 1,04,047 Jaina population of Ahmedabad district, 97,641 Jainas reside in the urban areas – and mostly in Ahmedabad city – and only 6,406 Jainas reside in the rural areas of the district. Compared to these two districts, the districts of Belgaum, Kolhapur and Sangli stand out prominently from the point of view of the total Jaina population in a district.

Regarding the proportion of rural Jaina population in a district also, the three districts of Belgaum, Kolhapur and Sangli compare most favourably with other districts. The districts having more than 25,000 rural Jaina population are given in Table 3.12.

Table 3.12

Districts with More Than 25,000 Rural Jaina Population

District	*State*	*Rural Jaina Population of the District*
Belgaum	Mysore	90,702
Kolhapur	Maharashtra	72,859
Udaipur	Rajasthan	55,790
Sangli	Maharashtra	44,776
Kutch	Gujarat	44,476
Pali	Rajasthan	32,195
Jalor	Rajasthan	29,877

From Table 3.12, it is clear that the Belgaum district has got the maximum number of rural Jaina population in a district. In the total Jaina population of 1,10,135 in the Belgaum district, only 19,433 Jainas reside in the urban areas and 90,702 Jainas reside in the rural areas of the district. The same is the case of

Kolhapur district which stands next to Belgaum district in this respect. The rural to urban composition of the Jaina in Kolhapur district is 72,859 to 20,405. This unusually high proportion of rural Jaina population in a district is not found elsewhere in India.

From the point of view of the density of Jaina population in a district also, the three districts of Kolhapur, Belgaum and Sangli are practically top most in India. From the statement[12] showing the district-wise density of Jaina population arranged in the descending order as per 1971 census, it will be noticed that Greater Bombay District has got the maximum density (i.e. 405.84 per sq km) of Jaina population in India. But this district is a separate category by itself as Greater Bombay is an entirely urban district and it is obvious that in a metropolitan centre such as Bombay the density of population is bound to be unusually high. Ahmedabad district stands next of Bombay in the density of Jaina population (e.g. 11.95 per sq km) but there is a great preponderance of urban Jaina population in this district due to the important commercial and industrial city of Ahmedabad. The Jaina population of Ahmedabad city alone is 86,318 out of 11,04,047 Jaina population of Ahmedabad district. The district of Kolhapur (11.57 per sq km), Belgaum (8.21 per sq km) and Sangli (6.94 per sq km) come next in the district-wise density of Jaina population but they stand out very prominent compared to the other districts in India. The districts of Greater Bombay and Ahmedabad could not be compared with these three districts as the former districts are essentially urban in character. The district of Kolhapur, Belgaum and Sangli are not urban-dominated districts but still the density of Jaina population is very high compared to the other districts which show more concentration of Jaina population and especially to the districts of Kutch, Jalor and Pali which show more percentage of the Jaina population to the total population of the district concerned.[13] In fact there is a difference of only 0.38 in the density of the Jaina population between Ahmedabad district (11.59 per sq km) and Kolhapur district (11.57 per sq km). The combined density of the Jaina population in the three districts of Kolhapur, Belgaum and Sangli works out as 8.75 per sq km, and this is practically double the density of the Jaina population in Udaipur district which comes next to Sangli district in this respect. Thus, the intense concentration of the Jaina population in the southern pocket consisting of three districts of Kolhapur, Sangli and Belgaum is a unique feature in the distribution of the Jaina population in India.

Rural–Urban Distribution of Jaina Population

The Jainas are essentially urban dwellers. This is the only religious community in India whose total numbers in urban areas exceed their number in rural areas.[14] Out of 26,04,646 total population of Jainas in India as per 1971 census, 15,58,240 Jainas reside in urban areas and 10,46,406 Jainas reside in rural areas. It means that the percentage of urban and rural population among the Jainas is 59.83 and 40.17 respectively. These figures for all religions in India are 19.90 and 80.10 respectively.

The urban character of the Jaina population can be noticed from another point of view. The Jainas in India form only 0.47 per cent of the total population of the country. But the Jainas constitute 1.43 per cent of the urban population and only 0.24 per cent of the rural population of the country.

The Jainas are not only more urbanized persons but their preference to live in urban areas is continuously increasing in this century. The figures showing the percentage of Jainas residing in the urban areas at the last seven census reports are given in Table 3.13.

From Table 3.13, it is evident that the percentage of urban Jaina population has doubled during the last 70 years and that there is an increasing tendency among the Jainas to prefer to reside in urban areas than in rural areas.

Table 3.13

Percentage of Urban Jaina Population in Different Census Year, 1901–1971

Census Year	Percentage of Urban Jaina Population
1901	30
1911	29.6
1921	33.9
1931	34.6
1941	41.4
1951	Not Available
1961	53.9
1971	59.8

Further, the urban character of Jaina population is not uniform over different states and union territories of India. From the statements showing the distribution of urban[15] and rural[16] population of Jainas as per 1971 census, it will be clear that the Jainas are more urban in the areas where they are few in number and more urban in the areas where they are few in number and more rural in the areas where they are comparatively large in number. That is why the proportion of the Jainas living the urban areas is 99.39 per cent in Jammu and Kashmir, 99.20 per cent in Nagaland, 98.32 per cent in Pondicherry, 91.97 per cent in Punjab, 86.08 per cent in Andhra Pradesh, 82.00 per cent in West Bengal and 81.29 per cent in Goa, Daman and Diu. It is obvious that there is a very sparse population of the Jainas in these states and union territories.[17] Similarly, the proportion of the Jainas living in the rural areas is 65.91 per cent in Mysore, 53.54 per cent in Rajasthan, 37.74 per cent in Madhya Pradesh, 36.44 per cent in Maharashtra and 33.74 per cent in Gujarat as these are the states where the Jaina population is mostly concentrated.[18]

Thus, the preferences of the Jainas to live in urban areas is their characteristic feature. This is due to the fact that in any region with a pronounced majority of one religion it will be found that persons not of that religion are mainly to be seen in the towns. A Parsi or a Christian, unless by an accident brought up in a village, will not find himself at home in rural conditions. This type of phenomenon is common all over the world. Everywhere the country is homogeneous and native, the town heterogeneous and cosmopolitan. All minorities thus find their way to and flourish in towns and that is why the Jaina community is essentially urban in character.

Sex Distribution of Jaina Population

The sex composition of the Jainas reveals a clear deficiency of females. There are only 940 females per 1,000 males in the Jaina community. The sex ratio among the Jainas during the last eight censuses is given in Table 3.14.

Table 3.14

Sex Ratio among the Jainas During the Censuses, 1901–1971

Census Year	*Number of Females per 1,000 Males*
1901	929
1911	940
1921	931
1931	940
1941	930
1951	927
1961	924
1971	940

From Table 3.14, it will be seen that the population of females to males in the Jaina community has been varying and that the proportion of females continuously decline from 1931 onwards to 1961. The proportion of females to males became the lowest, 924 in 1961 and it registered a rise to 940 in 1971. In this connection, it may be mentioned that no definite tendency is conclusively revealed by these figures and that the alternate variation in figures at many censuses seems to be the result of incorrect enumeration of females among the Jainas during the census operations.

The proportion of females to males in the major religious communities in India as per 1971 census is given in Table 3.15.

Table 3.15

Sex Ratio by Religious Community

Religious Community	*Number of Females per 1,000 Males*
Christians	986
Buddhists	962
Jainas	940
Hindus	930
All	930
Muslims	922
Sikhs	859

From Table 3.15, it will be noticed that the proportion of females to males among the Jainas is less compared to that among the Christian and the Buddhists but is more compared to the Sikhs, the Muslims and the Hindus.

Further even among the Jainas there is a wide variation in their sex composition from state to state. From the statement[19] showing sex distribution among the Jaina population of different states and union territories of India as per 1971 census, it will be seen that the proportion of females to males is largely greater than the average (940) in Pondicherry (1,026), Gujarat (1,021), Rajasthan (1,010), Andaman and Nicobar Islands (1,000) and Jammu and Kashmir (993) and the proportion is much smaller than the average (940) in Tripura (349), Arunachal Pradesh (392), Nagaland (555) and Dadra and Nagar Haveli (586). This difference is mainly due to the fact that the proportion of females to males among the Jainas is generally more among the states (such as Gujarat and Rajasthan) where they are mostly concentrated and it is generally less among the states and union territories (such as Tripura and Arunachal Pradesh) where they are very sparsely populated and are settled there temporarily for business purpose.

There are various causes which contribute to the deficiency of females, namely (a) concealment of females, (b) excess of males at birth, (c) female infanticide, (d) neglect of female children, (e) higher female mortality and (f) religious conversion of males. It is very difficult to say which of these factors are responsible for creating disparity among males and females in the Jaina community. The Jaina population being literate and intelligent would not indulge in concealing the females at the time of the census. Since the exact figures of sex of children at birth are not available, we cannot say whether there is any excess of males at birth in the Jaina community. The Jainas are sufficiently advanced and as such there could not be any possibility of practising female infanticide by them. It is true that in a society where the female children are considered to be a burden, they are liable to be neglected. But this neglect perhaps arises out of the economic condition of parents and as economic condition of the Jaina community is comparatively good, there are very less chances of females being neglected. Female mortality is different at various age periods. The death rate among females is higher than that of males in the 5–10 years age group. This is due to the neglect of female children which varies to some extent with economic circumstances and, as said above, female mortality on this account must be low in the Jaina community. A study of specific death rate shows that after the age of 5, only in the 40 and over age groups, the female death rate is lower than that of male. This means that the female death rate is higher in the age period of 5–40. If the female ratio for any community is declining, it might be due to the fact that the mortality amongst women aged between 5 and 40 might be more than offsetting the female superiority in the age groups 1 to 5 years and over 60 years. There is every probability that female death rate between the age period 5 and 40 might be higher in the Jaina community as many Jaina females are married at an early age and are called upon to bear children too early and possibly too often. But, due to the lack of figures of female death rate at various age periods it is difficult to pronounce to what extent the high female mortality is responsible for the deficiency of females in the Jaina community. No religious conversion is resorted to by the Jaina community and we should not, on this account, assume the excess of males among the Jainas.

With all these factors operating to reduce the number of females, the females wastage in the Jaina community had been considerably low as compared with that in other communities. Table 3.16 shows the female ratio in the first year of life as compared to that at all ages censused in 1931, indicating the comparative wastage of female life from whatever causes.[20]

Table 3.16

Comparative Wastage of Female Life by Religious Community in India, 1931

Community	*Females per 1,000 Males (of Population Returned by Age)*		*Variation Per Cent between Columns 2 and 3*
	Aged 0–1	*All Ages*	
Sikh	947	784	–17.2
Muslim	999	904	-9.5
INDIA	1,013	941	–7.1
Hindu	1,017	953	–6.3
Christian	1,002	952	–5.0
Parsi	981	940	–4.2
Jaina	972	941	-3.2
Tribal	1,045	1,009	–3.4

Further, it is generally recognized that the ratio of females to males increases inversely with social standing among the Hindus.[21] This was well illustrated by figures in the former Bombay Presidency in 1931 where the whole Hindu population was divided up according to education and social status into advanced, intermediate, backward and depressed classes. For the advanced classes, the ratio of women to men was 878 per 1,000, for intermediate classes it was 935 per 1,000, for the aboriginal tribes it was 956 per 1,000, for other backward classes it was 953 per 1,000, while for the depressed classes it rose to 982 per 1,000 males. The Jainas (excepting Chaturtha, Panchama and Shetwal castes thereof) were put under advanced class in the former Bombay Presidency at that time. It would be interesting to note the ratio of females to males in each of the various castes in the Jaina community and to verify whether the connection that the ratio of females to males varies inversely according to social status is also true in the case of several castes of the Jaina community. The population figures of several castes in the Jaina community are not readily available, and special efforts will have to be made to ascertain the sex composition of various castes in the Jaina community.

Age Distribution of Jaina Population

According to Sundbarg, a normal population has about one-half of its total between the ages of 15 and 50, and the proportion of those above that age group to those below it indicates whether the population is increasing, decreasing or stationary.[22] The youngest of the three population groups must be double the oldest if the population is to continue to grow, just short of that point it may be stationary and if the elder continues to exceed the younger, the population must be regressive or decreasing. These Sundbarg's categories need readjustment before they can be satisfactorily applied to the Indian conditions as the epidemics and other causes affect the elder population more in this country and the average age is lower than what it is in other countries. The distribution of the Jaina population according to Sundbarg's categories, as per 1931 census, was as given in Table 3.17.

Table 3.17

Distribution of Jaina Population According to Sundbarg's Categories, 1931

Year	*Percentage of Jaina Population Aged*		
	0–15 Years	*15–50 Years*	*50 Years and Above*
1931	36.7	51.7	11.6
1921	35.5	51.6	12.9
1911	33.6	53.9	12.5

This clearly shows that the Jaina community was progressive at that time. Figures for the age distribution of the population based on religion have not been made available since 1941 census report.

Even though the Jaina community was progressive in this respect in 1931, it was the least progressive when compared with the other communities in India. The population of different communities arranged in order of progressiveness as determined from the 1931 census[23] is given in Table 3.18.

Table 3.18

Age Distribution by Religious Communities, 1931

Community	*Percentage of Population Aged*		
	0–15 Years	*15–50 Years*	*50 Years and Above*
Tribal	43.9	47.8	8.3
Muslim	42.9	49.3	8.5
Christian	41.7	49.2	9.1
Jew	37.7	53.6	8.7
Hindu	39.2	50.9	9.9
Sikh	39.5	48.2	12.3
Jaina	36.7	51.7	11.6
Parsi[24]	27.2	56.7	16.1

It would be interesting to see the age distribution of the Jaina and other communities. This is required not because there is any inherent connection between a man's religious belief and the number of years he lives. But in the social conditions of India, religion is a real cleavage of peoples. It is due to the fact that in the social organization of Indian life, each religion is associated with several customs and practices of its own which have a very important effect upon age. From the age distribution[25] of all communities in the Bombay Presidency in 1931 given in Table 3A.11, it is evident that there was very little difference in the age groupings of Hindus and Muslims, either for males or females. Jainas had fewer persons in the age groups from 0 to 20 years than had either Hindus or Muslims. On the other hand, Jainas had more persons in the ages above 40. In this respect, the Jainas resembled the Zoroastrians who exhibited in an extreme form a lopsidedness in the age distribution. Up to the age 20, the Jaina distribution was the same as that of the Christian. This tendency in the Jaina community to have less persons in the age group of 0–20 years and more in the age group above 40 years as compared with other communities was observed all over India as could be seen from the mean age of the Jainas which was higher than that of the Hindus, Muslims and other people. This is evident from the statement[26] showing mean ages by sex for all religions according to the 1931 census.[27] Moreover, the above tendency appeared to be persistent in the Jaina community as would be clear from the statement[28] showing age distribution of 10,000 persons of each sex in the Jaina community in the Bombay Presidency from 1881 to 1931.[29]

Fertility and Longevity of the Jainas

As an indication of comparative fertility, the proportion borne by children of 0–10 years age group to married females of 15–40 years age group can be examined. Such figures for different religious communities were available up to 1931 Census Report. The figures for some communities, as stated in 1931 Census Report,[30] are given in Table 3.19.

Table 3.19

Comparative Fertility Data by Religious Communities, 1931

Community	*Number of Children Aged 0–10*	*Number of Married Women Aged 15–40*	*Number of Children Aged 0–10 to Each Married Aged 15–40*
Tribal	24,43,237	12,47,270	1.96
Christian	17,60,983	9,08,570	1.94
Sikh	11,94,647	6,21,095	1.92
Muslim	2,29,72,076	1,28,70,165	1.78
Jaina	3,19,953	1,95,063	1.64
Hindu	6,61,77,624	4,03,78,332	1.64
Parsi	19,404	12,142	1.60

Even though the fertility of Jaina women was low as compared with that of Christian, Sikh and Muslim women, it did show some signs of improvement as seen from Table 3.20.[31]

Table 3.20

Improvement in Fertility Figures of Jaina Women, 1911–1931

Year	*Number of Children Aged 0–10*	*Number of Married Women Aged 15–40*	*Number of Children Aged 0–10 to Each Married Women Aged 15–40*
1931	3,19,953	1,95,063	1.64
1921	2,79,748	1,71,458	1.63
1911	2,93,714	1,96,754	1.49

Similarly the proportion of persons aged 60 and over to those aged 15 to 40 is an indication of comparative longevity. Such figures[32] for some communities according to 1931 census are given in Table 3.21 in the ascending order of comparative longevity.

The comparison of these figures of fertility and longevity suggests that fertility and longevity, though not quite in inverse ratio, approach such a position. Moreover, from the figures of longevity given in Table 3.21, it would be seen that only among the Tribal, Hindu and Jaina communities the longevity was more among females than what was among males and that the

Table 3.21

Comparative Longevity by Religious Community 1931

Community	*Sex*	*Number Aged 60 and Over*	*Number Aged 15–40*	*Percentage of Column 3 to Column 4*
Tribal	M	1,23,846	14,55,660	8.5
	F	1,39,208	15,29,419	9.1
Hindu	M	47,82,296	5,00,89,524	9.5
	F	50,44,122	4,83,54,902	10.4
Muslim	M	15,47,638	1,61,79,065	9.6
	F	12,77,130	1,50,11,484	8.5
Jaina	M	28,276	2,66,275	10.6
	F	30,340	2,46,619	12.3
Sikh	M	1,47,828	9,63,229	15.3
	F	1,06,023	7,19,448	14.7
Parsi	M	3,957	24,150	16.4
	F	3,730	23,348	16

difference was more marked among the Jainas. The longevity figures of Jaina males and females from 1911 to 1931, as per 1931 census, are given in Table 3.22.

Table 3.22

Longevity among Jainas by Gender, 1911–1931

Year	*Sex*	*Number Aged 60 and Over*	*Number Aged 15–40*	*Percentage of Column 3 to Column 4*
1931	M	28,276	2,66,275	10.6
	F	30,340	2,46,619	12.3
1921	M	31,498	2,51,201	12.5
	F	35,498	2,25,803	15.7
1911	M	29,747	2,79,635	19.6
	F	35,177	2,53,854	13.9

From Table 3.22, it could be noticed that no definite conclusions or tendencies could be drawn from them except that the marked difference between the longevity of males and females remained unaltered.

Distribution of Jaina Population by Civil Condition

Information regarding the distribution of the Jaina population according to the three well-known categories of civil condition, namely unmarried, married and widowed, was used to be supplied through the census reports up to 1931. This information was very useful in realizing the correct position in different communities about the various aspects of marriage such as the age of marriage and the proportion of the widowed. Such information has not been made available since the census report of 1941, and hence it becomes very difficult to draw definite conclusions regarding the distribution of population by civil condition applicable to the present time. But in the case of the Jaina community the information about civil condition up to 1931 serves a useful purpose in the sense that it is the only source which gives a proper picture about the nature and extent of civil condition among the Jainas till 1931. On this basis, we can have idea in the matter pertaining to the Jainas at present as there has been no appreciable change in the marital practices of the Jainas during the last 40 years. The distribution of 1,000 of each sex of various communities according to their civil condition as per 1931 census is given in Table 3.23.

Table 3.23

Distribution of 1,000 of Each Sex of Various Communities as per Their Civil Condition, 1931

Community	*Sex*	*Unmarried*	*Married*	*Widowed*
INDIA	M	476	470	54
	F	388	505	157
Hindu	M	463	480	57
	F	324	507	169
Jaina	M	503	415	82
	F	337	442	221
Sikh	M	550	370	80
	F	411	475	114
Muslim	M	500	456	44
	F	358	513	129

From Table 3.23, it would be seen that Hindus, except the Muslims, had got the highest number of females married and the lowest number of females unmarried. The Jainas had fewer unmarried females except the Hindus, fewer married females and more widowed, both male and female, than the general figures. The proportion of unmarried females was nearly the same in the Hindu and Jaina communities, but the difference was more prominent in the disparate proportion of married females and widows, on account of the high proportion of widows amongst the Jainas. This unusually high proportion of widowed, especially among the females, seemed to be the predominant feature of the Jaina community up to 1931 as could be seen from the statement given in Table 3.24.

Table 3.24

Marital Status of the Jainas Community by Gender, 1931

Unit	*Year*	*Sex*	*Unmarried*	*Married*	*Widowed*
INDIA	1931	M	503	415	82
		F	337	442	221
	1921	M	507	392	101
		F	327	420	253
	1911	M	493	418	89
		F	301	446	253
	1901	M	473	436	91
		F	299	470	231
Bombay	1931	M	472	457	71
		F	327	471	202
	1921	M	480	434	86
		F	307	456	237
	1911	M	466	452	82
		F	281	474	245
	1901	M	545	470	76
		F	272	499	229
	1891	M	459	480	61
		F	269	516	215
Rajasthan	1931	M	517	390	93
		F	321	432	247

From Table 3.24, it would be seen that the proportion of widows had continued to increase till 1921 and it suddenly fell in 1931. This did not mean that the situation had improved but it was the result of comparatively greater increase in the proportion of married persons due to the fear of the Child Marriage Restraint Act, popularly known as the Sharada Act. The child marriage seemed to be quite common among the Jainas as would be evident from the statement given in Table 3.25 showing the number of females per 1,000 aged 0–15 who were returned as married for the six decades till 1931.

Table 3.25

Major Religious Communities of India; Married Females Aged 0–15 per 1,000 Females of That Age, 1881–1931

Community	*Married Females Aged 0–15 per 1,000 Females of That Age*					
	1881	*1891*	*1901*	*1911*	*1921*	*1931*
Hindu	208	193	186	184	170	199
Muslim	153	141	131	123	111	186
Jaina	189	172	164	130	117	125
Sikh	120	143	101	88	72	80
Christian	33	37	38	37	32	43

From the statement[33] showing the distribution by main age- periods of the 10,000 unmarried, married and widowed in the five main religions and all religions together for 1931 in the Bombay Presidency, it would be seen that the Jainas had 497 females per 10,000 married under 5 years of age, Hindus had 360, Christians 294, Muslims 166 and Zoroastrians 36. In the 5–10 years age group, Hindus had 2,498 females married, Jainas 1,925, Christians 1,085, Muslims 985 and Zoroastrians 67. Between the ages 10 and 15, Hindus had 4,613 females married, Jainas 3,998, Muslims 2,637, Christians 1,756 and Zoroastrians 185. Thus, it would be clear that the Jainas had the highest number of infant girls married and that both Hindus and Jainas had very high figures for marriages of girls under the age of 15.

Again, from the same statement, it would be seen that the highest proportion of married persons was found for all religions in the 40–60 age group for males (8,094 per 10,000) and in the 15–20 age group for females (8,604 per 10,000). In the case of Jainas, the highest proportion of married persons was found in the 20–40 age group for males (7,421 per 10,000) and in the 15–20 age group for females (8,650 per 10,000).

Further, from the above statement, it would be clear that the difference in the proportion of males and females in the last age group with respect to civil conditions was considerable in the various communities. Of 10,000 males aged 60 and over, 866 Zoroastrians were unmarried, 496 Christians, 331 Jainas and 297 Muslims as against only 186 Hindus. Of widows aged 60 years and over, there were 8,954 per 10,000 amongst Jainas, 8,434 amongst Hindus, 8,037 amongst Muslims, 7,605 amongst Christians and 6,308 amongst Zoroastrians. In every community, the majority of males in the 60 and over age group were married, and the majority of the females were widows. The disproportion between the married men and widowers in the last age group was least in the case of Jainas, who had 5,497 married males as against 4,172 widowers.

Apart from the fact that the Jainas were an early marrying community, one could expect that due to the impact of Western ideas, there would not have been married persons up to the age of 10. But from the statement[34] showing the distribution of Jaina population in the Bombay Presidency by civil condition of 1,000 of each sex and main age periods from 1881 to 1931, it would be seen that there were persons married as well as widowed in the early age groups and moreover their number had not been appreciably reduced as was expected in the case of the Jaina community which was considered to be more advanced, well-placed in the economic life and having a high proportion of literate population. Further, with respect to the proportion of widows it would be seen that the Jainas continued to top the list of widows. In Rajputana where the Jaina population is mostly concentrated, there were 247 widows per 1,000 females. This means that out of four females one female was necessarily a widow. There is not much change in this regard in recent times.

Due to this unusually high proportion of widows, who are effectively debarred from marrying again, the sex composition of the community becomes very unbalanced. The ban on widow remarriage considerably reduces the proportion of females in the reproductive period. Obviously this situation very adversely affects the rate of increase in the Jaina population as compared to the rate of increase in population of other communities. Along with the sex ratio, the practice of religious conversion also serves as a contributive factor in affecting the rate of increase in population of a community. For example, the rate of increase in population of Christian community is highly influenced by the inclusion of converts in the community. In the case of Jaina, there is no possibility of increase in the population due to the factor of additions of newcomers to their religion as the practice of religious conversion is never restored by the Jainas. On the contrary there are indications of Jainas being converted to other religions. Thus, if conversion is not practised, the removal of ban on widow remarriage appears to be the most pressing and urgent need for the growth of Jaina population.

Notes and References

1. Census of India, 1971: Series 1 – India: Paper 2 of 1972 on 'Religion', p. iii.
2. Census of India, 1971: Series 1 – India: Paper 2 of 1972 on 'Religion', p. xiii.
3. Census of India, 1971: Series I – India: Paper 2 of 1972 on 'Religion', p. iii.
4. Also vide Table 3A.1 'The Statement showing the number per 10,000 of the population who are Jainas at the Census from 1881 to 1941'.
5. *Census of India*, 1931, Vol. I, Part I, p. 389.
6. Vide Chapter 7.
7. The position of regional distribution of Jaina population before independence is given in Table 3A.3. This appendix shows the distribution of Jaina population among the former British provinces and Indian states according to census from 1911 to 1941. From this appendix, it would be seen that during

pre-independence period the Jainas had preferred Indian state of British provinces as their permanent abodes. According to 1941 figures, 60 per cent of the Jainas lived in Indian states and only 40 per cent were in the British provinces. The corresponding figures for 1901 census stood at 64 per cent and 36 per cent respectively.

8. Census of India, 1901, Vol. I, Part I, p. 523.
9. Vide Table 3A.2.
10. Vide Table 3A.4.
11. Vide Table 3A.4.
12. Vide Table 3A.6.
13. Vide Table 3A.5.
14. Census of India, 1971: Series I – India: Paper 2 of 1972 on 'Religion', p. 23.
15. Vide Table 3A.7
16. Vide Table 3A.8. Also vide Table 3A.9. 'The Statement showing number per 1,000 of the Jaina population who live in towns according to census reports from 1901 to 1941'.
17. Vide Table 3A.2 and Table 3A.4.
18. Vide Table 3A.2 and Table 3A.4.
19. Vide Table 3A.10.
20. Vide Census of India, 1931, Vol. I, Part I, p. 206. Such figures are not available in the subsequent census.
21. Census of India, 1931: Vol. I, Part I, p. 198.
22. Census of India, 1931, Vol. I, Part I, p. 87.
23. Census of India, 1931, Vol. I, Part I, p. 87.
24. The Parsi population is stationary.
25. *Census Report, Bombay Presidency*, 1931, Part I, p. 88.
26. Vide Table 3A.11.
27. Census of India, 1931, Vol. I, Part I, p. 90.
28. Vide Table 3A.12.
29. *Census Report, Bombay Presidency*, 1931, Vol. I, Part I, p. 102.
30. Census of India, 1931, Vol. I, Part I, p. 89.
31. Ibid.
32. Census of India, 1931, Vol. I, Part I, p. 89.
33. Vide Table 3A.8.
34. Vide Table 3A.14.

APPENDIX

Table 3A.1

Statement Showing the Number Per 10,000 of the Population Who Are Jainas at the Census from 1881 to 1941

Province or State	*Number Per 10,000 of the Population Who Are Jainas*						
	1881	*1891*	*1901*	*1911*	*1921*	*1931*	*1941*
INDIA	48	49	45	40	37	36	37
Provinces	23	22	21	19	18	17	19
Madras	8	8	7	7	6	7	6
Bombay	132	127[1]	123[1]	108[1]	111[1]	111	127
Bengal	–	1	1	1	3	2	2
UP	18	18	18	16	15	14	19
Punjab	21[2]	21[2]	21[2]	20[2]	17	15	13
Bihar	–	1	1	1	1	1	1
CP and Berar	55	52	56	50	49	50	50
Assam	–	2	3	3	5	3	7
Ajmer-Merwara	528	497	418	405	372	348	323
Coorg	6	7	6	6	12	5	2
Delhi	–	–	–	–	96	84	124
Panth-Piploda	–	–	–	–	–	–	118
States and Agencies	140	140	136	114	104	101	96
Baroda	214	208	247	214	203	198	164
Central India	54	87	–	–	74	76	76
Deccan	–	–	–	–	–	–	302
Gwalior	–	–	–	–	122	128	131
Hyderabad	8	24	18	16	15	15	15
Kashmir and Feudatories	–	2	1	1	2	2	2
Mysore	26	27	25	30	35	45	45
Rajputana	375	338	349	316	284	268	247
Western India	–	–	–	564	535	509	434

1. Includes Sindh
2. Includes Delhi

Table 3A.2

Statement Showing Distribution of Jaina Population 1971 Census

States/ Union Territories	*Jaina Population*	*Percentage Distribution of Jaina Population*	*Percentage of Jaina Population to Total Population*	
			1961	*1971*
INDIA	26,04,646	100.00	0.46	0.47
States				
1. Andhra Pradesh	16,108	0.62	–	–
2. Assam	12,917	0.50	–	–
3. Bihar	25,185	0.97	–	–
4. Gujarat	4,51,578	17.34	–	–
5. Haryana	31,173	1.20	–	–
6. Himachal Pradesh	626	–	–	–
7. Jammu and Kashmir	1,150	–	–	–
8. Kerala	3,336	–	–	–
9. Madhya Pradesh	3,45,211	–	–	–
10. Maharashtra	7,03,664	–	–	–
11. Manipur	1,408	–	–	–
12. Meghalaya	268	–	–	–
13. Mysore	2,18,862	–	–	–
14. Nagaland	627	–	–	–
15. Orissa	6,521	–	–	–
16. Punjab	21,383	–	–	–
17. Rajasthan	5,13,548	–	–	–
18. Tamil Nadu	41,097	–		–
19. Tripura	375	–	–	–
20. Uttar Pradesh	1,24,728	–	–	–
21. West Bengal	32,203	–	–	–
Union Territories				
1. Andaman and Nicobar Islands	14	0.00	0.01	–
2. Arunachal Pradesh	39	0.00	NA	–
3. Chandigarh	1,016	0.04	0.86	0.39
4. Dadra and Nagar Haveli	303	0.01	0.21	0.41
5. Delhi	50,513	1.94	1.11	1.24
6. Goa, Daman and Diu	556	0.02	0.01	0.06
7. Laccadive, Minicoy and Amindivi Islands	–	–	–	–
8. Pondicherry	237	0.01	0.02	0.05

Table 3A.3

Statement Showing Distribution of Jaina Population among the Former British Provinces and Indian States According to Census from 1911 to 1941

Province or State	1911	1921	1931	1941
INDIA	12,48,182	11,78,596	12,52,105	14,49,286
Provinces	4,58,578	4,55,855	4,53,569	5,78,372
Madras	2,92,995	25,493	31,206	30,136
Bombay	2,10,725	2,12,867	1,98,670	2,66,231
Bengal	6,206	12,863	9,167	11,126
UP	75,427	67,887	67,954	1,02,768
Punjab	39,637	34,432	35,284	38,233
Bihar	4,282	4,213	3,626	4,602
CP and Berar	70,258	68,286	77,895	84,593
Assam	2,398	3,397	2,636	6,639
NWFP	4	3	–	1
Orissa	158	98	108	139
Sind	1,349	1,534	1,144	3,687
Ajmer-Merwara	20,302	18,422	19,497	18,827
Andaman and Nicobar Islands	–	–	–	–
Baluchistan	10	17	32	7
Coorg	97	202	83	34
Delhi	–	4,098	5,345	11,287
Panth-Piploda	–	–	–	62
States and Agencies	7,89,604	7,22,741	7,98,536	8,70,914
Assam	110	106	107	201
Baluchistan	–	–	–	–
Baroda	43,462	43,223	48,408	46,866
Bengal	576	506	502	582
Central India	87,471	44,431	50,268	57,374
Chhattisgarh	–	–	–	2,158
Cochin	–	101	210	355
Deccan (and Kolhapur)	–	–	–	58,226
Gujarat	–	–	–	5,540
Gwalior	–	38,906	45,079	52,714
Hyderabad	21,026	18,584	21,543	24,853
Kashmir and Feudatories	345	529	597	910
Mysore	17,630	20,732	29,613	32,858
NWFP	–	–	–	1

Cont'd...

...Cont'd

Province or State	*1911*	*1921*	*1931*	*1941*
Orissa	–	–	–	99
Punjab	7,138	6,889	7,448	6,844
Punjab Hill	–	–	408	449
Rajputana	3,32,397	2,79,222	3,00,748	3,41,788
Sikkim	–	7	2	7
Travancore	–	33	41	62
UP	308	224	214	210
Western India	–	–	2,03,626	2,12,796
Madras	150	–	31	21

Table 3A.4

Statement Showing Distribution and Percentage Increase of Jaina Population (1951, 1961 and 1971 Census)

States/Union Territories	1951	1961	1971	Percentage Increase	
				1951 to 1961	1961 to 1971
INDIA	16,18,406	20,27,248	26,04,646	+25.26	+28.48
States					
1. Andhra Pradesh	4,891	9,012	16,108	+84.26	+78.74
2. Assam	4,169	9,339	12,917	+124.01	+38.31
3. Bihar	8,165	17,598	25,185	+115.53	+43.11
4. Gujarat	3,74,867	4,09,754	4,51,578	+9.31	+10.21
5. Haryana	–	25,844	31,173	–	+20.62
6. Himachal Pradesh	64	463	626	+1261.76	+35.21
7. Jammu and Kashmir	–	1,427	1,150	–	–19.41
8. Kerala	1,398	2,967	3,336	+112.23	+12.44
9. Madhya Pradesh	1,81,328	2,47,927	3,45,211	+36.73	+39.24
10. Maharashtra	3,37,593	4,85,672	7,03,664	+43.86	+44.88
11. Manipur	150	778	1,408	+418.67	+80.98
12. Meghalaya	–	129	268	–	+107.52
13. Mysore	1,39,873	1,74,366	2,18,862	+24.66	+25.52
14. Nagaland	76	263	627	+246.05	+138.40
15. Orissa	1,248	2,295	6,521	+83.89	+184.14
16. Punjab	45,096	21,507	21,383	–52.31	–0.58
17. Rajasthan	3,59,772	4,09,417	5,13,548	+13.80	+25.43
18. Tamil Nadu	22,165	28,350	41,097	+27.90	+44.96
19. Tripura	36	195	375	+441.67	+92.31
20. Uttar Pradesh	97,744	1,22,108	1,24,728	+24.93	+2.15
21. West Bengal	19,607	26,940	32,203	+37.40	+19.54
Union Territories					
1. Andaman and Nicobar Islands	1	3	14	+200.00	+366.67
2. Arunachal Pradesh	–	NA	39	–	NA
3. Chandigarh	–	1,035	1,016	–	–1.84
4. Dadra and Nagar Haveli	–	120	303	–	+152.50
5. Delhi	20,174	29,595	50,513	+46.70	+70.68
6. Goa, Daman and Diu	–	68	556	–	+717.65
7. Laccadive, Minicoy and Amindivi Islands	–	–	–	–	–
8. Pondicherry	–	76	237	–	+21,481

Table 3A.5

Statement Showing the Districts Having More Than Two Percentage of Jaina Population to the Total Population of the District (1971 Census)

District	*State*	*Jaina Population of the District*			*Total Population of the District*	*Percentage of Jaina Population to Total Population of the District*
		Rural	*Urban*	*Total*		
1. Kutch	Gujarat	44,476	12,631	57,107	8,49,769	6.72
2. Jalor	Rajasthan	29,877	4,874	34,751	6,67,950	5.20
3. Pali	Rajasthan	32,195	12,401	44,596	9,70,002	4.60
4. Kolhapur	Maharashtra	72,859	20,405	93,264	20,48,049	4.55
5. Belgaum	Mysore	90,702	19,433	1,10,135	24,23,342	4.55
6. Sirohi	Rajasthan	11,201	7,996	19,197	4,23,815	4.53
7. Udaipur	Rajasthan	55,790	22,717	78,507	18,03,680	4.35
8. Greater Bombay	Maharashtra	–	2,44,721	2,44,721	59,70,575	4.10
9. Bikaner	Rajasthan	4,035	18,231	22,266	5,73,149	3.88
10. Sangli	Maharashtra	44,776	14,681	59,457	15,39,820	3.86
11. Ahmedabad	Gujarat	6,406	97,641	1,04,047	29,10,307	3.57
12. Sagar	Madhya Pradesh	18,662	18,355	37,017	10,62,291	3.49
13. Surendra-nagar	Gujarat	5,662	22,557	28,224	8,45,454	3.34
14. Barmer	Rajasthan	16,126	9,092	25,218	7,74,805	3.25
15. Ajmer	Rajasthan	13,588	23,665	37,253	11,47,729	3.25
16. Ratlam	Madhya Pradesh	4,092	14,900	18,992	6,26,534	3.03
17. Churu	Rajasthan	2,414	23,372	25,786	8,74,439	2.95
18. Bhavnagar	Gujarat	10,139	29,004	39,143	14,05,285	2.79
19. Jamnagar	Gujarat	14,599	15,353	29,952	11,11,343	2.70
20. Damoh	Madhya Pradesh	10,643	4,462	15,105	5,73,263	2.64
21. Indore	Madhya Pradesh	1,508	24,627	26,135	10,25,150	2.55
22. Bhilwara	Rajasthan	20,606	6,305	26,911	10,54,890	2.55
23. Banaskantha	Gujarat	20,802	10,953	31,755	12,65,383	2.51
24. Chittaurgarh	Rajasthan	12,623	10,783	23,406	9,44,981	2.48
25. Mandsaur	Madhya Pradesh	11,563	11,968	23,531	9,61,522	2.45
26. Tonk	Rajasthan	9,078	5,839	14,917	6,25,830	2.38
27. Jodhpur	Rajasthan	7,101	17,568	24,669	11,52,712	2.14
28. Guna	Madhya Pradesh	6,190	9,714	15,904	7,83,748	2.03
29. Ujjain	Madhya Pradesh	3,440	13,940	17,380	8,62,516	2.02

Table 3A.6

Statement Showing District-wise Density of Jaina Population (Arranged in Descending Order), 1971 Census

District	*State*	*District Area in sq km*	*Jaina Population of the District*	*Density of Jaina Population per sq km*
1. Greater Bombay	Maharashtra	603	2,44,721	405.84
2. Ahmedabad	Gujarat	8,707	1,04,047	11.95
3. Kolhapur	Maharashtra	8,059	93,264	11.57
4. Belgaum	Mysore	13,410	1,10,135	8.21
5. Sangli	Maharashtra	8,563	59,457	6.94
6. Udaipur	Rajasthan	17,267	78,507	4.55
7. Ajmer	Rajasthan	8,479	37,253	4.39
8. Ratlam	MP	4,859	18,992	3.91
9. Sirohi	Rajasthan	5,135	19,197	3.74
10. Indore	MP	3,910	26,135	3.68
11. Sagar	MP	10,246	37,017	3.61
12. Pali	Rajasthan	12,391	44,596	3.60
13. Bhavnagar	Gujarat	11,155	39,143	3.51
14. Jalor	Rajasthan	10,640	34,751	3.27
15. Ujjain	MP	6,081	17,380	2.86
16. Surendranagar	Gujarat	10,488	28,224	2.69
17. Bhilwara	Rajasthan	10,450	26,911	2.58
18. Bhanskantha	Gujarat	12,702	31,755	2.50
19. Mandsaur	MP	9,726	23,531	2.45
20. Chittaurgarh	Rajasthan	10,858	23,406	2.16
21. Jamnagar	Gujarat	14,125	29,952	2.12
22. Damoh	MP	7,301	15,105	2.07
23. Tonk	Rajasthan	7,200	14,917	2.07
24. Churu	Rajasthan	16,829	25,786	1.53
25. Guna	MP	11,017	15,904	1.44
26. Kutch	Gujarat	45,612	57,107	1.25
27. Jodhpur	Rajasthan	22,860	24,669	1.08
28. Barmer	Rajasthan	28,387	25,218	0.89
29. Bikaner	Rajasthan	27,231	22,268	0.82

Table 3A.7

Statement Showing Distribution of Urban Population of Jainas, 1971 Census

States/Union Territories	*Total Population*	*Urban Population*			*Percentage of Urban Population to Total Population*
		Males	*Females*	*Total*	
INDIA	26,04,646	8,18,878	7,39,362	15,58,240	59.83
States					
1. Andhra Pradesh	16,108	7,921	5,944	13,865	86.08
2. Assam	12,917	5,112	3,110	8,222	63.65
3. Bihar	25,185	9,432	8,160	17,592	69.85
4. Gujarat	4,51,578	1,52,145	1,47,051	2,99,196	66.26
5. Haryana	31,173	11,091	10,471	21,562	69.17
6. Himachal Pradesh	626	198	163	361	57.67
7. Jammu and Kashmir	1,150	570	573	1,143	99.39
8. Kerala	3,336	1,090	879	1,969	59.02
9. Madhya Pradesh	3,45,211	1,12,769	1,02,176	2,14,945	62.26
10. Maharashtra	7,03,664	2,39,659	2,07,609	4,47,268	63.56
11. Manipur	1,408	571	419	990	70.31
12. Meghalaya	268	74	47	121	45.15
13. Mysore	2,18,862	40,361	34,266	74,627	34.09
14. Nagaland	627	400	222	622	99.20
15. Orissa	6,521	2,053	1,781	3,834	58.79
16. Punjab	21,383	10,181	9,484	19,665	91.97
17. Rajasthan	5,13,548	1,20,924	1,17,646	2,38,570	46.46
18. Tamil Nadu	41,097	15,806	12,682	28,488	69.32
19. Tripura	375	105	55	160	42.67
20. Uttar Pradesh	1,24,728	46,161	40,935	87,096	69.83
21. West Bengal	32,203	15,171	11,237	26,408	82.00
Union Territories					
1. Andaman and Nicobar Islands	14	2	3	5	35.71
2. Arunachal Pradesh	39	19	11	30	76.92
3. Chandigarh	1,016	542	474	1,016	100.00
4. Dadra and Nagar Haveli	303	–	–	–	–
5. Delhi	50,513	26,162	23,638	49,800	98.59
6. Goa, Daman and Diu	556	244	208	452	81.29
7. Laccadive, Minicoy and Amindivi Islands	–	–	–	–	–
8. Pondicherry	237	115	118	233	98.32

Table 3A.8

Statement Showing Distribution of Rural Population of Jainas, 1971 Census

States/Union Territories	Total Population	Rural Population			Percentage of Rural Population to Total Population
		Males	Females	Total	
INDIA	26,04,646	5,23,992	5,22,414	10,46,406	40.17
States					
1. Andhra Pradesh	16,108	1,171	1,072	2,243	13.92
2. Assam	12,917	2,701	1,994	4,695	36.35
3. Bihar	25,185	4,012	3,581	7,593	30.15
4. Gujarat	4,51,578	71,331	81,051	1,52,382	33.74
5. Haryana	31,173	4,972	4,639	9,611	30.83
6. Himachal Pradesh	626	139	126	265	42.33
7. Jammu and Kashmir	1,150	7	–	–	–
8. Kerala	3,336	708	659	1,967	40.98
9. Madhya Pradesh	3,45,211	67,646	62,620	1,30,266	37.74
10. Maharashtra	7,03,664	1,31,177	1,25,219	2,56,396	36.44
11. Manipur	1,408	198	220	418	29.69
12. Meghalaya	268	88	59	147	54.85
13. Mysore	2,18,862	73,459	70,776	1,44,235	65.91
14. Nagaland	627	3	2	5	0.80
15. Orissa	6,521	1,364	1,323	2,687	41.21
16. Punjab	21,383	898	820	1,718	8.03
17. Rajasthan	5,13,548	1,34,487	1,40,491	2,74,978	53.54
18. Tamil Nadu	41,097	6,184	6,425	12,609	30.68
19. Tripura	375	173	42	215	57.33
20. Uttar Pradesh	1,24,728	19,462	18,170	37,632	30.17
21. West Bengal	32,203	3,138	2,612	5,795	18.00
Union Territories					
1. Andaman and Nicobar Islands	14	5	4	9	64.29
2. Arunachal Pradesh	39	9	–	9	23.08
3. Chandigarh	1,016	–	–	–	–
4. Dadra and Nagar Haveli	303	191	112	303	100.00
5. Delhi	50,513	362	351	713	1.41
6. Goa, Daman and Diu	556	60	44	104	18.71
7. Laccadive, Minicoy and Amindivi Islands	–	–	–	–	–
8. Pondicherry	237	2	2	4	1.68

Table 3A.9

Statement Showing Number per 1,000 of the Jaina Population Who Live in Towns According to Census Reports from 1901 to 1941

Province or State	*1941*	*1931*	*1921*	*1911*	*1901*
INDIA	414	346	339	296	300
Provinces	489	373	398	354	316
Madras	215	229	164	106	81
Bombay	471	322[1]	419[1]	369[1]	316
Bengal	794	616	650	592	545
UP	483	458	397	397	271
Punjab	770	613	530	533	543[2]
Bihar	520	496[3]	312[3]	378[3]	–
CP and Berar	405	321	297	255	CP 260 Berar 349
Assam	444	334	342	233	287
NWFP	–	–	1,000	750	–
Orissa	309	–	–	–	–
Sind	112	–	–	–	–
Ajmer-Merwara	463	333	340	283	266
Baluchistan	–	1,000	529	900	–
Coorg	706	602	203	670	–
Delhi	954	857	822	Not Given	–
States and Agencies	365	331	302	262	276
Assam	940	844	764	973	–
Baluchistan	–	–	–	–	–
Baroda	499	421	406	388	446
Bengal	875	711	609	351	–
Central India	435	363	311	240	302
Chhattisgarh	583	–	–	–	–
Cochin	1,000	995	1,000	992	1,000
Deccan (and Kolhapur)	206	–	–	–	–
Gujarat	710	–	–	–	–
Gwalior	420	377	250	–	–
Hyderabad	348	285	268	182	229
Kashmir and Feudatories	882	995	994	977	991
Mysore	1,000	1,000	1,000	927	–

Cont'd...

...Cont'd

Province or State	*1941*	*1931*	*1921*	*1911*	*1901*
NWFP	276	252	311	201	250
Orissa	1,000	–	–	–	–
Punjab	566	507	464	508	–
Punjab Hill	782	–	–	–	–
Rajputana	340	308	280	235	246
Travancore	1,000	1,000	1,000	1,000	–
UP	833	579	589	578	–
Western India	397	375	–	–	–
Bihar and Orissa States	–	3	50	132	–
Bombay State	–	228	306	283	–
CP State	–	495	464	399	–
Punjab State Agency	–	488	–	–	–

1. Includes Sindh
2. Includes NWFP
3. Includes Orissa

Table 3A.10

Statement Showing Sex Distribution of Jaina Population, 1971 Census

States/Union Territories	*Total*	*Males*	*Females*	*Number of Females Per 1,000 Males*
INDIA	26,04,646	13,42,870	12,61,776	940
States				
1. Andhra Pradesh	16,108	9,092	7,016	771
2. Assam	12,917	7,813	5,104	653
3. Bihar	25,185	13,444	11,741	873
4. Gujarat	4,51,578	2,23,476	2,28,102	1,021
5. Haryana	31,173	16,063	15,110	940
6. Himachal Pradesh	626	337	289	857
7. Jammu and Kashmir	1,150	577	573	993
8. Kerala	3,336	1,798	1,538	855
9. Madhya Pradesh	3,45,211	1,80,415	1,64,796	913
10. Maharashtra	7,03,664	3,70,836	3,32,828	897
11. Manipur	1,408	769	639	830
12. Meghalaya	268	162	106	654
13. Mysore	2,18,862	1,13,820	1,05,042	922
14. Nagaland	627	403	224	555
15. Orissa	6,521	3,417	3,104	908
16. Punjab	21,383	11,079	10,304	930
17. Rajasthan	5,13,548	2,55,411	2,58,137	1,010
18. Tamil Nadu	41,097	21,990	19,107	869
19. Tripura	375	278	97	349
20. Uttar Pradesh	1,24,728	65,623	59,105	901
21. West Bengal	32,203	18,354	13,849	754
Union Territories				
1. Andaman and Nicobar Islands	14	7	7	1,000
2. Arunachal Pradesh	39	28	11	392
3. Chandigarh	1,016	542	474	874
4. Dadra and Nagar Haveli	303	191	112	586
5. Delhi	50,513	26,524	23,989	904
6. Goa, Daman and Diu	556	304	252	829
7. Laccadive, Minicoy and Amindivi Islands	–	–	–	–
8. Pondicherry	237	117	120	1,026

Table 3A.11

Statement Showing the Mean Ages by Sex of the Different Provinces and States and for Religions According to 1931 Census

Provinces	*All Religions*		*Hindu*		*Jaina*		*Muslim*	
	M	*F*	*M*	*F*	*M*	*F*	*M*	*F*
INDIA	23.2	22.8	23.5	23.3	24.6	24.5	22.4	21.5
Ajmer-Merwara	23.8	23.5	23.7	23.6	25.8	26.1	23.9	22.8
Assam	27.7	21.6	23.9	22.2	–	–	22.0	20.1
Baluchistan	25.2	20.0	–	–	–	–	–	–
Bengal	23.3	21.7	–	–	–	–	–	–
Bihar and Orissa	23.0	23.6	23.4	24.0	–	–	22.6	23.0
Bombay	23.4	22.8	–	–	24.9	23.7	–	–
CP and Berar	23.7	23.8	24.2	24.3	25.0	25.0	24.2	23.3
Coorg	25.0	23.2	–	–	–	–	–	–
Delhi	24.4	22.2	24.4	22.4	–	–	24.4	21.8
Madras	24.4	24.3	24.5	24.4	27.3	27.3	23.1	23.0
NWFP	22.6	21.8	24.0	21.9	–	–	23.2	22.5
Punjab (including Agency)	24.3	23.1	24.7	23.4	–	–	23.8	22.7
UP	24.5	24.5	*24.1	*24.3	*–	–	23.8	23.3
Baroda	23.7	23.6	23.7	23.6	25.2	25.8	24.0	23.9
Central India Agency	23.3	23.2	23.3	23.3	26.1	25.7	24.3	23.2
Gwalior State	23.4	23.2	24.4	24.2	26.0	23.7	24.2	23.2
Hyderabad State	23.5	22.6	–	–	–	–	23.6	22.9
Jammu and Kashmir	23.6	23.1	26.9	25.2	–	–	23.5	22.5
Cochin State	23.7	24.1	23.9	24.6	24.0	21.5	23.0	22.5
Travancore State	23.0	22.8	23.3	23.3	–	–	22.2	21.6
Mysore State	25.1	24.4	24.7	23.8	25.5	24.6	23.9	21.9
Rajputana Agency	23.5	23.4	23.6	23.5	24.8	25.8	23.5	22.7
Western India State Agency	22.6	22.8	–	–	–	–	–	–

* Brahmanic Hindu only

Table 3A.12

Statement Showing Age Distribution of 10,000 of Each Sex in the Jaina Community in the Bombay Presidency from 1881 to 1931

Age	*1931*		*1921*		*1911*		*1901*		*1891*		*1881*	
	Males	*Females*	*Males*	*Females*	*Males*	*Females*	*Males*	*Females*	*Males*	*Females*	*Males*	*Females*
0–5	1,199	1,525	955	1,184	1,025	1,265	973	1,137	1,074	1,314	1,004	1,205
5–10	1,151	1,233	1,147	1,333	1,014	1,178	1,137	1,249	1,070	1,211	1,102	1,211
10–15	1,123	1,106	1,199	1,101	1,172	1,014	1,230	1,125	1,111	956	1,249	1,085
15–20	973	933	904	815	979	823	908	793	945	795	904	768
20–40	3,429	3,134	3,592	3,221	3,610	3,322	3,479	3,281	3,526	3,273	3,558	3,342
40–60	1,708	1,586	1,735	1,721	1,750	1,794	1,829	1,809	1,798	1,785	1,766	1,800
60 and Above	417	483	468	625	450	604	444	606	476	666	418	589

Table 3A.13

Statement Showing Distribution by Main Age Periods and Civil Condition of 10,000 of Each Sex and Religion in the Bombay Presidency According to 1931 Census

Age Periods	Sex	All Religions			Hindu			Muslim			Jaina			Zoroastrian			Christian		
		U	M	W	U	M	W	U	M	W	U	M	W	U	M	W	U	M	W
0–5	M	9,835	158	7	9,822	171	7	9,885	111	4	9,857	132	11	9,951	49	–	9,821	163	16
	F	9,667	323	10	8,629	360	11	9,828	166	6	9,488	497	15	9,964	36	–	9,687	294	19
5–10	M	9,324	658	18	9,249	731	20	9,587	400	13	9,625	359	16	9,913	87	–	9,311	649	40
	F	7,758	2,192	50	7,446	2,498	56	8,993	985	22	8,005	1,925	70	9,928	67	5	8,878	1,085	37
10–15	M	8,638	1,325	37	8,491	1,472	37	9,168	806	26	9,214	756	30	9,844	156	–	8,954	998	48
	F	4,212	5,687	101	5,275	4,613	112	7,308	2,637	55	5,874	3,998	128	9,810	185	5	8,190	1,756	54
15–20	M	5,487	4,392	121	5,091	4,788	121	6,758	3,114	128	6,363	3,514	123	9,387	604	9	7,538	2,382	80
	F	1,086	8,604	310	842	8,830	328	1,750	8,006	244	950	8,650	400	8,127	1,726	57	4,407	5,459	134
20–40	M	1,660	7,893	447	1,351	8,225	424	2,568	6,868	564	2061	7,421	518	5,252	4,620	128	3,476	6,304	220
	F	263	8,436	1,301	211	8,415	1,374	344	8,621	1,035	129	8,092	1,779	3,536	6,032	432	1,286	7,820	894
40–60	M	313	8,094	1,593	254	8,159	1,587	495	7,831	1,674	519	7,401	2,080	1,246	8,050	704	789	8,333	878
	F	111	4,612	5,277	101	4,495	5,404	111	5,102	4,787	57	3,696	6,247	9,66	6,142	2,892	443	5,169	4,388
60 and Above	M	214	6,415	3,371	186	6,452	3,362	297	6,246	3,457	331	5,497	4,172	8,66	5,945	3,189	496	7,024	2,480
	F	90	1,561	8,349	83	1,483	8,434	95	1,868	8,037	99	947	8,954	350	3,282	6,368	389	2,006	7,605

Note: U: Unmarried, M: Married, W: Widow, M: Male, F: Female

Table 3A.14

Statement Showing Distribution of Jaina Population in the Bombay Presidency by Civil Condition of 1,000 of Each Sex and Main Age Period 1881–1931

Age	1931		1921		1911		1901		1891		1881	
	Males	Females	Males	Females	Males	Females	Males	Females	Males	Females	Males	Females
					Unmarried							
All Ages	472	327	480	307	466	281	454	272	459	69	–	–
0–5	936	949	988	966	980	961	988	970	990	962	982	866
5–10	962	801	979	843	974	820	971	807	964	758		
10–15	921	587	925	545	900	439	871	565	845	383	820	337
15–20	636	95	724	71	667	45	609	42	596	22	563	18
20–40	206	13	225	17	213	10	185	9	203	5	199	4
40–60	52	6	63	8	64	6	60	4	60	4	64	3
60 and Above	33	10	38	6	44	5	54	5	41	1	47	1

Cont'd...

...Cont'd

Age	1931		1921		1911		1901		1891		1881	
	Males	Females	Males	Females	Males	Females	Males	Females	Males	Females	Males	Females
						Married						
All Ages	457	471	434	456	452	474	470	499	480	516	–	––
0–5	13	50	10	31	71	37	12	29	10	37	17	130
5–10	36	192	18	145	21	173	26	182	35	238		
10–15	76	400	69	427	91	530	121	403	148	601	172	634
15–20	352	865	260	877	314	897	370	903	393	940	431	947
20–40	742	809	699	768	715	763	749	804	754	839	749	813
40–60	740	369	705	372	714	370	762	423	789	450	777	417
60 and Above	550	95	579	106	538	85	530	170	612	105	611	116
						Widowed						
All Ages	71	202	86	237	82	245	76	229	61	215	–	–
0–5	1	1	2	3	9	2	–	1	–	1	1	4
5–10	2	7	3	12	5	7	3	1	1	4		
10–15	3	13	6	28	9	31	8	32	7	16	8	29
15–20	12	40	16	52	19	58	21	55	11	38	6	35
20–40	52	178	76	215	72	227	65	187	43	156	52	183
40–60	208	625	232	620	222	624	178	573	151	546	159	580
60 and Above	417	895	443	888	418	910	410	825	347	894	342	883

4

Jains in India

How Many and Where?

M.K. Jain

At the time of 1971 census, that is, just three years before the twenty-fifth centenary of the 'Nirvana' of Lord Mahavira – the last among 24 forerunners (Tirthankaras) of Jainism, there were more than 2.6 million followers of this religion in India.[1] Numerically this is the sixth largest religion in India and its followers are mainly spread over western part of India. It is an ascetic religion, and it lays much emphasis on the *ahimsa* (non-violence). Followers of this religion were already wealthy and prominent in the old regimes, and they were one of the first religious groups to take advantage of Western education prospering exceedingly in business under British rule.[2] Analysing census data on the socio-economic and other characteristics of different religious communities in India, Kingsley Davis observed that they (Jains) are the third most literate and the second or third most prosperous religious group in India.[3] The censuses after independence have stopped publishing data regarding socio-economic and demographic characteristics of the

Table 4.1

Per cent Change (Decennial) in the Jain Population During 1881–1971

Year	Per cent Change in Jain Population (Decade)	Year	Per cent Change in Jain Population (Decade)
1881	–	1931	6.28
1891	15.94	1941	15.81
1901	–5.83	1951	11.67
1911	–6.47	1961	25.17
1921	–5.26	1971	28.48

religious communities in India, and they only report about sex composition and rural–urban distribution of the population of religions in India. On the basis of availability of these meagre data on Jain population in India from the recent censuses, an effort is made in this chapter to discuss briefly: (a) the growth of Jains in India from past few decades of nineteenth century to the present one, (b) interstate variations in the growth and distribution of Jain population during 1951–1971 and (c) trends in population growth of Jains in the districts where Jains were found to be more than 10,000 in number.

From the figures in Table 4.1, it can be observed that after an increase of about 16 per cent during the initial decade of 1881–1891, the Jain population continued to decline till 1921 and thereafter the growth rate was below normal and fluctuated from 6 per cent to 16 per cent and then to 12 per cent during 1921–1931, 1931–1941 and 1941–1951 respectively. The last two decades, that is, 1951–1961 and 1961–1971 witnessed a considerably faster rate of growth of Jain population.

The factors which contributed to the decline and thereafter stagnation of Jain population during 1891–1941 as discussed by Kingsley Davis are: (a) higher incidences of widowhood coupled with a taboo on widow remarriage, (b) low fertility within the marital relations, (c) loss of members of this community due to drift into Hinduism because of misstatement of religion and (d) no population gains through conversion[4] because the religion is not of proselytizing nature like that of Christianism or Islam.

Again the fluctuation in the growth rate during 1931–1941 and 1941–1951 might be attributed to the partition of the country during the latter decade. Similarly the impact of this partition of the country may also be visualized from a sharp increase in the proportion of Jain population as shown by the figures given in Table 4.1 because prior to 1951 census, this was consistently declining during 1901–1931 and remained constant at 0.37 at the time of 1941 census while in 1951 it increased by 22 per cent. After 1951, the growth rate of Jain population was fairly high as compared to its previous growth rates and the reasons for this may be traced into the heavy reductions in mortality rates and improvement in living conditions in India. However, due to small size of Jain community, its proportion to the total population of India at the time of three consecutive censuses of 1951, 1961 and 1971 increased by point 0.01 only during each decade.

Table 4.2

Population by Religion, Per cent of Population in Each Religion and Per cent Change in Population (Decennial) During 1881–1971

Year	*Religion*					
	Hindus	*Muslims*	*Christians*	*Sikhs*	*Buddhists*	*Jains*
			I. Population (in Millions)			
1881	187.849	49.953	1.778	1.853	0.167	1.222
1891	207.560	57.068	2.164	1.905	0.243	1.417
1901	206.861	62.119	2.776	2.189	0.293	1.334
1911	217.197	67.835	3.666	3.008	0.337	1.248
1921	216.249	71.005	4.497	3.234	0.369	1.177
1931	238.624	79.305	5.963	3.325	0.439	1.251
1941	270.187	94.446	7.427	5.691	0.457	1.449
1951	303.575	35.414	8.392	6.219	0.181	1.618
1961	366.503	46.939	10.726	7.845	3.250	2.207
1971	453.292	61.418	14.224	10.379	3.812	2.605
			II. Proportion to Total Population (Percentage)			
1881	75.09	19.97	0.71	0.74	0.07	0.49
1891	74.24	20.41	0.77	0.68	0.09	9.51
1901	72.87	21.88	0.98	0.77	0.10	0.47

Cont'd...

...Cont'd

Year	Religion					
	Hindus	*Muslims*	*Christians*	*Sikhs*	*Buddhists*	*Jains*
1911	71.68	22.39	1.21	1.00	0.11	0.41
1921	70.73	23.23	1.47	1.06	0.12	0.39
1931	70.67	23.49	1.77	1.28	0.13	0.37
1941	69.46	24.28	1.91	1.46	0.12	0.37
1951	84.07	9.81	2.32	1.72	0.05	0.45
1961	83.51	10.69	2.44	1.79	0.74	0.46
1971	82.72	11.21	2.60	1.89	0.70	0.47
III. Decennial Growth/Decline in the Population (Per cent)						
1881–1891	10.49	14.24	21.66	2.76	45.41	15.94
1891–1901	–0.34	8.85	28.29	14.91	20.29	–5.83
1901–1911	5.00	9.20	32.08	37.42	15.12	–6.47
1911–1921	–0.45	4.67	22.66	7.52	9.63	–5.47
1921–1931	10.35	11.69	32.66	33.73	18.80	6.28
1931–1941	13.24	19.09	24.50	31.60	4.28	15.81
1941–1951	12.36	–274.97	12.99	9.28	–196.06	11.67
1951–1961	20.29	25.61	27.38	25.13	1,670.71	25.17
1961–1971	23.69	30.85	32.60	32.18	17.20	28.48

Sources: 1. Kingsley Davis, *Population of India and Pakistan* (New York: Russell and Russell, 1951), pp. 178–179.

2. Census of India, 1961, Religion, Paper No. 1 of 1963 (New Delhi: RGO, 1963), pp. ii–vii.

3. Census of India, 1971, Religion, Paper No. 2 of 1972 (New Delhi: RGO, 1972), pp. 2–5.

A comparison of Jain population growth and proportionate distribution of Jains with other religious population (Table 4.2) reveals that the trends of Jain population growth closely resembles to the trends of Hindu population growth during 1881–1971. In case of change in the proportion of both the population to the total population, it can be observed that the proportion of Hindus to total population had consistently declined during 1881–1941 and after an increase from 69.46 to 84.07 during 1950–1951 (which was only due to the creation of

Pakistan), this proportion again showed a decline during 1951–1971. The proportion of Jain population had also registered a decline during the period of 1891–1931 but after 1951 it is having marginal gains during each census. This similarity in the trends of population growth of Jain and Hindu communities may be attributed to only one factor, that is both the communities have a common social structure. When the trends of population growth of Jains are compared with other major religious communities (such as Muslims, Christians, Sikhs and Buddhists) of India it may be observed that Muslim, Christians and Sikhs had faster population growth till 1941 than the Jain population growth. During 1941–1951, this was discontinued due to the partition of the country but again during 1951–1971 this trend continued, while the population growth of Buddhists in India varied widely from one decade to another due to several reasons such as partition and mass conversion and reversion. The similar trend of increase can also be observed in case of the proportionate distribution of religious population to the total population. Thus, it can be easily ascertained that Jain population growth had close resemblance to the Hindu population growth during this period.

The percentage distributions of Jain population in different states at the time of 1951, 1961 and 1971 censuses (Table 4.3) point out that around 85 per cent of the total Jain population was concentrated in five states, namely, Maharashtra, Rajasthan, Gujarat, Madhya Pradesh and Mysore. And another 10 per cent was living in Uttar Pradesh, Delhi and Punjab (including Haryana and Chandigarh). When the proportion of Jains to the total population is considered, it can be found that it was very much small in all the states and even in either of these above-mentioned states it was not found to be more than 3 per cent at the time of any of these censuses.

Table 4.3

Percentage Distribution of Jain Population in Different States and Union Territories, 1951, 1961 and 1971

States/ Union Territories	*1951*		*1961*		*1971*	
	Percentage of Total Population	*Percentage of Jain Population*	*Per:entage o, Total Population*	*Percentage of Jain Population*	*Percentage of Total Population*	*Percentage of Jain Population*
INDIA	0.45	100.00	0.46	100.00	0.47	100.00
Andhra Pradesh	0.01	0.30	0.03	0.44	0.04	0.62
Assam[1]	0.05	0.26	0.08	0.47	0.12	0.51
Bihar	0.02	0.50	0.04	0.87	0.04	0.97
Gujarat	2.31	23.16	1.99	20.21	1.69	17.34
Jammu and Kashmir	–	–	0.04	0.87	0.04	0.97
Kerala	0.01	0.09	0.02	0.15	0.02	0.04
Madhya Pradesh	0.70	11.20	0.77	12.33	0.83	13.25
Madras	0.07	1.37	0.09	1.40	0.10	1.58
Maharashtra	1.06	20.86	1.23	23.96	1.40	27.02
Mysore	0.72	8.64	0.74	8.64	0.75	8.40
Orissa	0.01	0.04	0.01	0.11	0.03	0.25
Punjab[2]	0.28	2.79	0.26	2.39	0.22	2.06
Rajasthan	2.25	22.23	2.03	20.20	1.99	19.72
Uttar Pradesh	0.15	6.04	0.17	6.32	0.14	4.79
West Bengal	0.08	1.21	0.08	1.33	0.08	1.2
Delhi	1.06	1.25	1.11	1.46	1.24	1.94
Himachal Pradesh	N	N	1.11	1.46	1.24	1.94
Manipur	0.03	0.01	0.10	0.04	0.13	0.05
Tripura	0.01	N	0.02	0.01	0.02	0.01
Dadra and Nagar Haveli	–	–	0.21	N	0.41	0.01
Goa, Diu and Daman	–	–	0.01	N	0.06	0.02
Pondicherry	–	–	0.02	N	0.05	0.01

Cont'd...

...Cont'd

States/ Union Territories	*1951*		*1961*		*1971*	
	Percentage of Total Population	*Percentage of Jain Population*	*Percentage of Total Population*	*Percentage of Jain Population*	*Percentage of Total Population*	*Percentage of Jain Population*
NEFA	–	–	–	N	0.01	N
Nagaland	–	–	0.07	0.01	0.12	0.02

1. Assam in 1971, includes Meghalaya.
2. Punjab in 1971, includes Haryana and Chandigarh.
N: Negligible

Sources: 1. Census of India, 1961, Religion, Paper No. 1 of 1963 (New Delhi: RGO, 1963), pp. ii–vii.
2. Census of India, 1971 Religion, Paper No. 2 of 1972 (New Delhi: RGO, 1972), pp. 2–5.

Inter-state variation in the growth rate of Jain population as can be observed from Table 4.4 highlights that out of the five states where Jains are found to be mainly concentrated, Maharashtra and Madhya Pradesh had higher growth rate than the overall growth rate of Jain population during both the decades of 1951–1961 and 1961–1971. As contrary to this, in Gujarat it was substantially low, that is around 10 per cent during this period and in Rajasthan it was lower in the earlier decade but increased to 25 per cent during the latter decade of 1961–1971, while in the only remaining state of Mysore, it remained constant around 25 per cent during this period. In the next group of states, that is Uttar Pradesh, Delhi and Punjab (including Haryana and Chandigarh), there were wide variations in the growth rate, that is in Uttar Pradesh it was about 25 per cent in the earlier decade but reduced to very low level (about 2%) in the following decade and in Punjab it improved from 7 per cent to 11 per cent during these two decades. As contrary to these, in Delhi, which is more or less a city territory, the growth rate was quite high even in the previous decade and again it increased substantially and went to 70 per cent in the following decade of 1961–1971. In other states of India, where the

Table 4.4

Population Distribution of Jains and Percentage Growth of Jain Population in Different States and Union Territories of India, 1951, 1961 and 1971

States/Union Territories	*Population*			*Growth Rate*	
	1951	*1961*	*1971*	*1951–1961*	*1961–1971*
INDIA	16,18,406	20,27,267	26,04,646	25.17	28.48
Andhra Pradesh	4,891	9,012	16,108	84.26	78.74
Assam[1]	4,169	9,468	13,185	127.10	39.26
Bihar	8,165	17,598	25,185	115.53	43.11
Gujarat	3,74,882	4,09,754	4,51,578	9.30	10.21
Jammu and Kashmir	–	1,427	1,150	–	–19.41
Kerala	1,398	2,967	3,336	112.23	12.44
Madhya Pradesh	1,81,328	2,47,927	3,45,211	36.73	39.24
Madras	22,165	28,350	41,097	27.90	44.96
Maharashtra	3,37,578	4,85,672	7,03,664	43.87	44.88
Mysore	1,39,873	1,74,366	2,18,862	24.66	25.52
Orissa	1,248	2,295	6,521	83.89	184.14
Punjab[2]	45,096	48,386	53,572	7.30	10.72
Rajasthan	3,59,772	4,09,417	5,13,548	13.80	25.43
Uttar Pradesh	97,744	1,22,108	1,24,728	24.93	2.15
West Bengal	19,607	26,940	32,203	37.40	19.54
Union Territories					
Andaman and Nicobar Islands	1	3	14	200.00	366.67
Delhi	20,174	29,595	50,513	46.70	70.68
Himachal Pradesh	34	463	626	326.47	35.21
Laccadive, Minicoy and Amindivi Islands	–	–	–	–	–
Manipur	150	778	1,408	418.67	80.98
Tripura	36	195	375	441.67	92.31
Dadra and Nagar Haveli	–	120	303	–	152.50

Cont'd...

...Cont'd

States/Union Territories	*Population*			*Growth Rate*	
	1951	*1961*	*1971*	*1951–1961*	*1961–1971*
Goa, Diu and Daman	–	68	556	–	717.65
Pondicherry	–	76	237	–	211.84
NEFA	NA	NA	39	NA	NA
Nagaland	76	263	627	246.05	138.40

1. Assam in 1971, includes Meghalaya.
2. Punjab in 1971, includes Haryana and Chandigarh.
NA: Not available

Source: Same as for Table 4.2.

proportion of Jain population was very small, the growth rates varied from one state to another and from earlier decade to latter decade in case of a particular state, for example, Assam, Bihar, Andhra Pradesh and Orissa had more than 80 per cent population growth during 1951–1961, while except Orissa in all these states the growth rate was reduced by more than 50 per cent and even in Kerala where it was 112 per cent in the previous decade, it reduced to only 12 per cent in the next decade. In case of Orissa, it increased from 84 per cent to 184 per cent during the same period. Thus, there was no consistency in the growth rate of these states. One interesting feature which can be discerned from this table is the fact that pace of population re-distribution of Jains was considerably faster during the previous decade than the following decade. This is because the higher growth rates in some of these states during the earlier decade could only be attributed to the migration of Jains into these states from other states as is evident from the lower growth rate of Gujarat, Punjab and Rajasthan.

The growth and distribution of Jain population in 351 districts of India reveals that at the time of 1971 census nearly 80 per cent of the Jain population was living in only 69 districts as it can be observed from Table 4.5.

Table 4.5

Number of Districts and Per cent of Total Jain Population Classified into Various Size Classes, 1971

Population Size	Number of Districts	Per Cent of Total Jain Population
1,00,000 and above	3	17.62
50,000 to 99,999	5	13.00
20,000 to 49,999	27	30.08
10,000 to 19,999	34	19.26
Up to 9,999	275	20.04
NIL	7	0.00
Total	351	100.00

The first three districts which had more than 1,00,000 Jains were Greater Bombay, Belgaum and Ahmedabad and another five districts having Jain population between 50,000 and 99,999 were Kolhapur, Udaipur, Sangli, Kutch and Delhi.

When all these districts (excluding seven districts where no Jains were recorded both in 1961 and in 1971) are classified according to the different ranges of growth rates during 1961–1971, it is observed that more than half of the districts had growth rate higher than the overall growth rate of Jain population in India which was 28.48 per cent during this period. But apart from them there were as many as 60 districts in India where Jain population had declined as one could see from the figures in Table 4.6.

Table 4.6

Number of Districts Classified According to Different Ranges of Growth Rate of Jain Population during 1961–1971

Growth Rate (Per cent)	Number of Districts
100 and above	65
50.1–100	47
28.5–50	79
10–28.5	70
Up to 10	23
Negative	60
Total	344

In Table 4.6, all 344 districts which had population growth during the decade 1961–1971 are classified, but as mentioned earlier that about 80 per cent of Jain population was concentrated in 69 districts only, therefore it appears to be more reasonable to study the population growth in these districts. The classification of these districts according to the aforesaid growth rate ranges is given in Table 4.7.

Table 4.7

Districts with 10,000 and Above Jains Population in 1971 Classified by Different Ranges of Growth Rates of Jain Population during 1961–1971

Growth Rate (Per cent)	*Number of Districts*
More than 100	1
50–100	11
28.5–50	20
10–28.5	26
Up to 10	7
Negative	4
Total	69

The one district where Jain population doubled during 1961–1971 was Parbhani of Maharashtra and the last four districts which had suffered a decline in the population were Kutch, Mehsana, Pali and Meerut. Thus, this classification indicates that little less than half of the districts in this group had growth rate higher than the overall growth rate of the Jain population in India. Further it could have been more interesting to study the demographic and socio-economic characteristics such as fertility, mortality, migration and labour force participation of the Jain population in these districts. Due to non-availability of data such attempt could not be made. However, a brief analysis of the sex composition and the level of urbanization (per cent of urban to total Jain population) in association with the rate of growth of Jain population is made in the following paragraph. The figures related to population, growth rate, sex ratio (females per 1,000 males) and the level of urbanization for each of these districts are given in the Table 4.8.

Table 4.8

Districts Having Jain Population 10,000 and Above in 1971 (Arranged According to Their Population Size), Their Growth Rate during 1961–1971, Sex Ratio and Level of Urbanization in 1971

District/State	Jain Population 1971	Growth Rate Jain Population Per cent (1961–1971)	Sex Ratio (F/M × 1,000) of Jain Population	Level of Urbanization of Jain Population (Urban Pop./Total Pop. × 100)
I. Districts Having Jain Population Above 100,000				
1. Greater Bombay (Maharashtra)	2,44,721	57.13	836	100.00
2. Belgaum (Mysore)	1,10,135	21.82	951	17.64
3. Ahmedabad (Gujarat)	1,04,047	28.69	931	93.84
II. Districts with Jain Population Ranging from 50,000 to 99,999				
4. Kolhapur (Maharashtra)	93,264	28.27	917	21.88
5. Udaipur (Rajasthan)	78,507	25.02	977	28.94
6. Sangli (Maharashtra)	59,457	22.91	941	24.69
7. Kutch (Gujarat)	57,107	–10.23	1,357	22.12
8. Delhi	50,513	70.68	904	98.65
III. Districts with Jains Population between 20,000 and 49,999				
9. Poona (Maharashtra)	46,463	49.02	910	76.04
10. Pali (Raj.)	44,596	3.34	1,169	27.81
11. Bhavnagar (Gujarat)	39,143	8.12	975	74.10
12. Jaipur (Rajasthan)	37,427	50.37	896	80.34
13. Ajmer (Rajasthan)	37,253	35.27	933	63.52

Cont'd...

...Cont'd

District/State	Jain Population 1971	Growth Rate Jain Population Per cent (1961–1971)	Sex Ratio (F/M × 1,000) of Jain Population	Level of Urbanization of Jain Population (Urban Pop./Total Pop. × 100)
14. Sagar (MP)	37,017	31.07	922	49.58
15. Jalor (Rajasthan)	34,751	21.33	1,183	14.02
16. Rajkot (Gujarat)	31,868	14.49	1,006	90.11
17. Banaskantha (Gujarat)	31,755	5.52	1,035	34.49
18. Jamnagar (Gujarat)	29,952	8.10	1,010	51.26
19. Ahmednagar (Maharashtra)	28,331	21.27	922	39.36
20. Surendranagar (Gujarat)	28,224	3.36	1,010	79.92
21. Meerut (UP)	27,665	34.22	960	64.04
22. Bhilwara (Rajasthan)	26,911	25.06	948	23.43
23. Indore (MP)	26,135	39.43	901	94.23
24. Churu (Rajasthan)	25,786	27.06	1,252	90.64
25. Barmer (Rajasthan)	25,416	23.82	1,000	35.77
26. Jodhpur (Rajasthan)	24,669	14.30	925	71.21
27. Mehsana (Gujarat)	24,046	8.43	1,040	55.50
28. Mandsaur (MP)	23,531	30.74	904	50.86
29. Chittaurgarh (Rajasthan)	23,406	24.09	924	46.07
30. Dharwad (Mysore)	22,285	26.04	898	34.88
31. Bikaner (Rajasthan)	2,2265	32.76	1171	81.88

Cont'd...

...Cont'd

District/State	Jain Population 1971	Growth Rate Jain Population Per cent (1961–1971)	Sex Ratio (F/M × 1,000) of Jain Population	Level of Urbanization of Jain Population (Urban Pop./Total Pop. × 100)
32. Nasik (Maharashtra)	21,460	42.50	952	65.18
33. Agra (UP)	21,255	20.02	809	78.32
34. Sholapur (Maharashtra)	21,008	36.12	949	53.97
35. Surat (Gujarat)	20,292	47.60	887	75.20
IV. District Having Jain Population up to 10,000				
36. Jalgaon (Maharashtra)	19,571	20.88	918	50.28
37. Jabalpur (MP)	19,376	39.22	899	70.52
38. Nagpur (Maharashtra)	19,269	20.81	1,065	55.78
39. Sirohi (Rajasthan)	19,197	10.71	1,205	41.65
40. Ratlam (MP)	18,992	25.58	917	78.45
41. Calcutta (WB)	18,937	11.10	727	100.00
42. Bijapur (Mysore)	17,972	25.72	917	39.17
43. Thana (Maharashtra)	17,627	99.38	814	93.83
44. Aurangabad (Maharashtra)	17,489	45.75	950	43.73
45. Vadodara (Gujarat)	17,394	19.28	964	73.64
46. Ujjain (MP)	17,380	52.28	935	80.21
47. Kheda (Gujarat)	17,330	4.98	1,053	64.59
48. Madras (TN)	17,164	89.76	780	100.00
49. Jhansi (UP)	16,005	30.81	899	50.23
50. Guna (MP)	15,904	45.32	893	61.08
51. Bangalore (Mysore)	15,422	67.92	779	96.99

Cont'd...

...Cont'd

District/State	Jain Population 1971	Growth Rate Jain Population Per cent (1961–1971)	Sex Ratio (F/M × 1,000) of Jain Population	Level of Urbanization of Jain Population (Urban Pop./Total Pop. × 100)
52. Akola (Maharashtra)	15,153	43.35	993	55.52
53. Damoh (MP)	15,105	64.02	926	29.54
54. Tonk (Rajasthan)	14,917	48.63	909	39.14
55. Dhulia (MP)	13,036	23.62	890	51.18
56. Durg (MP)	12,792	78.71	916	65.49
57. Muzaffarnagar (UP)	12,151	28.42	886	62.41
58. Sabarkantha (Gujarat)	12,143	15.30	1,063	46.69
59. Bhind (MP)	12,003	28.37	901	24.29
60. Parbhani (Maharashtra)	11,983	107.46	1,308	33.79
61. S. Kanara (Mysore)	11,947	8.00	953	15.53
62. Nagpur (Maharashtra)	11,851	57.56	897	81.07
63. Valsad (Gujarat)	11,193	26.20	947	60.05
64. Vidisha (MP)	10,836	47.77	910	67.90
65. Sehore (MP)	10,733	78.97	905	82.97
66. Banswara (Rajasthan)	10,441	43.66	949	22.09
67. Buldhana (Maharashtra)	10,305	46.40	934	48.17
68. Kota (Rajasthan)	10,169	37.27	856	71.06
69. N. Arcot (Madras)	10,051	8.58	986	25.39

Source: Census of India, 1971, Religion, Paper No. 2 of 1972 (New Delhi: RGO, 1972), pp. 34–79.

Table 4.9

Sex Ratio and Level of Urbanization of Jain Population of Those Districts Where Their Population Was Found to Be Above 10,000 in 1971 as Classified According to the Different Ranges of Growth Rates During 1961–1971

Growth Rate (Per cent)	Number of Districts	Sex Ratio (F/M × 100)	Per cent Urban Total Population	Name of Districts
More than 100	1	1,308	33.79	Parbhani
50 to 100	11	855	91.86	Ujjain, Sehore, Damoh, Durg, Greater Bombay, Thana, Nagpur, Bangalore, Madras, Jaipur and Delhi
28.5 to 50	20	932	69.11	Ahmedabad, Surat, Guna, Vidisha, Mandsaur, Indore, Sagar, Jabalpur, Nasik, Poona, Sholapur, Aurangabad, Buldhana, Akola Bikaner, Ajmer, Tonk, Banswara, Kota and Jhansi
10 to 28.5	26	960	41.38	Rajkot, Sabarkantha, Vadodara, Valsad, Bhind, Ratlam Dhulia, Jalgaon, Ahmednagar, Sangli, Kolhapur, Belgaum, Bijapur, Dharwad, Churu, Nagpur, Sirohi, Jodhpur, Barmer, Jalor, Bhilwara, Udaipur, Chittaurgarh, Muzaffarnagar, Agra and Calcutta
Up to 10	7	1,001	55.50	Jamnagar, Surendranagar, Bhavnagar, Kheda, Banaskantha, South Kanara and North Arcot
Negative	4	1170	36.56	Kutch, Mehsana, Pali and Meerut

Source: Census of India, 1971, Religion, Paper No. 2 of 1972 (New Delhi: RGO, 1972), pp. 34–79.

From Table 4.9, it can be observed that except at the highest level, that is, for the districts which had more than 100 per cent population growth, in all other categories, the sex ratio declines with the increase of growth rate. This phenomenon may be regarded as an indication of the fact that with the higher growth rate, the sex composition of the Jain population tends to become more imbalanced as a result of male-dominated migration into those districts. The same is true for the districts where the Jain population had declined but in their case the imbalance was in opposite way, that is, the females were exceeding the males because of migration of males to other areas. From this table, it may also be observed that with the exceptions of first and last but one category, in the remaining categories the level of urbanization increases with the increase in the growth rates. This observation broadly indicates that those districts which had higher level of urbanization were also having higher growth rate in the preceding decade.

The foregoing discussion about growth and distribution of Jains in India may be summarized and concluded with the following remarks:

1. The population of Jains in the beginning of the present century was declining due to the rigid social structure of the community, while after this period it started increasing and during the last two decades the growth was considerably faster as compared to the previous decades. Further, a comparison of Jain population growth closely resembles the growth of Hindu population in India, and this may be due to the fact that there is no difference between the culture and norms of the communities. Jain social structure is almost similar to the Hindus' social structure.

2. The Jain population was mostly concentrated in the five states, namely, Gujarat, Madhya Pradesh, Maharashtra, Mysore and Rajasthan during the last three censuses of 1951, 1961 and 1971. Further, the growth of Jains in those states varied quite significantly, for example, in Maharashtra and Madhya Pradesh it was higher than the overall growth rate of Jain population, while in Gujarat and

Rajasthan it was on the lower side and in Mysore it was close to the overall growth rate of Jains during 1951–1961 and 1961–1971.

3. At the district level, about 80 per cent of total Jain population was living in only 69 districts out of 351 districts in India. An analysis of population growth and its interrelationship with the sex composition and level of urbanization in these districts suggests that the sex composition of the districts which had growth rate between 50 and 100 per cent during 1961–1971 was quite imbalanced, that is, the sex ratio (the proportion of females to males) was quite low and in case of those districts which had growth rate up to 10 per cent, the sex composition was almost balanced but then in those districts which had a decline in Jain population the sex composition was more favourable to females. Further, the classification of these districts according to the level of urbanization and the growth rate ranges reveals that the districts which had higher growth rate were also having higher level of urbanization.

Thus, the present discussion, which is very much limited in scope because of its dependency on census data, successfully highlights the area of concentration up to district level and also points out to the interrelationship between population growth, sex composition and the level of urbanization in the districts where about 80 per cent of the Jain population was living at the time of 1971 census. In this connection, it may however be mentioned that if a demographic survey of at least 35 districts (where about 60 per cent of total Jain population was living in the year 1971) is conducted may provide better understanding of the process of population growth and re-distribution of Jain community in India.

Notes and References

1. Census of India, 1971, Religion, Paper 2 of 1972 (New Delhi: RGO, 1972), p. 23.
2. Farquhar, J.N., *Modern Religious Movement in India* (New York: Macmillan, 1915), pp. 324–326. Grisword, H. De Witt, *Insights into the Modern Hinduism* (New York: Henry Holt, 1934), pp. 114, 147 and 150; in K. Davis, *Population of India and Pakistan* (New York: Russell and Russell, 1951), p, 183.
3. Ibid., p. 184.
4. Kingsley Davis, op. cit., p. 184.

5

A Demographic Analysis on the Jains

M.K. Jain

Numerically Jains form a very small segment of the Indian population. Approximately, 3.19 million followers of this religion account for 0.48 per cent of the total population as at 1981 and thus ranked sixth religious group after Hindus (82.63), Muslims (11.63), Christians (2.43), Sikhs (1.96) and Buddhists (0.71).[1] It has been amply demonstrated in one of the earlier studies that

> the Jains have always constituted a small religious minority of Indian society throughout their historical existence. The two other criteria of languages and ethnic background that define a minority do not apply to them for they speak practically every language of India and cannot be isolated ethnically from other Indian people.[2]

If we look at figures on the population growth of Jains in India we notice that after an initial growth during 1881–1891, the number of Jains declined continuously till 1921 and registered very slow growth thereafter during next 30 years period. In the post-independence period, the number of Jains roughly doubled, that is, from 1.62 million to 3.19 million during 1951–1981. Thus, the decadal percentage growth among Jains has greatly varied from the lowest, that is, a decline of 6.47 (1901–1911) to the highest growth of 28.48 (1961–1971). Similarly, the strength of the Jains in total population also fluctuated in the pre-independence period and improved marginally in the latter censuses.

Table 5.1

Variations in the Number of Jains Since 1891

Census Year	*Number of Jains (in 000s)*	*Percentage of Total Population*	*Decadal Per cent Change in Number of Jains*
1881	1,222	0.49	–
1891	1,417	0.51	15.94
1901	1,334	0.47	–5.83
1911	1,248	0.41	–6.47
1921	1,177	0.39	–5.26
1931	1,251	0.37	6.28
1941	1,440	0.37	15.81
1951	1,618	0.45	11.67
1961	2,027	0.46	25.17
1971	2,605	0.47	28.48
1981*	3,193	0.48	23.17

*Excluding Assam where census was not held in 1981 owing to disturbed conditions.

Sources: 1. Kingsley Davis, *Population of India and Pakistan* (New York: Russell and Russell, 1951), pp. 178–179.

2. Census of India, 1961, Paper No.1 of 1963, Religion (New Delhi: RGO, 1963), pp. ii–vii.
3. Census of India, 1971, Paper No. 2 of 1972, Religion (New Delhi: RGO, 1972), pp. 2–5.
4. Census of India, 1981, Paper No. 4 of 1984, Household Population by Religion of Head of Household (New Delhi: RGO, 1984), p. 26 (figures amended as per Errata issued subsequently by this office).

The decline in the number of Jains in the earlier decades of the present century and a slower growth during 1921–1941, according to Davis, was due to several factors such as (a) higher incidence of widowhood occupied with a taboo on widow remarriage, (b) low fertility within the marital relations, (c) loss of members of this community due to drift into Hinduism because of misstatement of religion and (d) no population growth through conversion because the religion is not of proselytizing nature such as the Christianity or Islam.[3] The improvement in growth rates of Jain population during 1951–1971 period, on the other hand, may be attributed to the heavier reduction in mortality rates due to improved living conditions and improvement in reporting of religion at the successive census. Whereas the reduction in the growth rate in the last decade may partly be due to a decline in the fertility among Jains. For instance, it has been noted that the total marital fertility rates (TMFR)[4] of Jainas have gone down from 5.1 to 4.2 in rural areas and from 4.3 to 3.5 in urban areas during 1971–1981. Moreover, at the national level, TMFR for Jains as per 1981 census is the lowest (3.7) as compared to Muslims (4.9), Sikhs and Buddhists (having an identical rate 4.5) followed by Hindus and Christians (which had an identical rate of 4.2).[5]

Figures on the dispersal of Jains as presented in the Table 5.2 show that all the states and union territories (except Lakshadweep) are having Jains and their number varied from 9,39,392 in Maharashtra to merely 11 each in Andaman and Nicobar Islands and Mizoram. Besides, Maharashtra, Rajasthan, Gujarat and Madhya Pradesh also had sizeable Jain population, and these four states accounted for more than three-fourth of the total Jains. Two other states, namely, Karnataka and Uttar Pradesh (having more than 1 lakh population each), accounted for 9 and 4 per cent of total Jains respectively. Thus, nine-tenth of the total Jains are enumerated in these six states only. Of the remaining Jains, about 4 per cent are enumerated in Delhi, Haryana and Punjab and 3 per cent in Tamil Nadu and West Bengal. The proportion of Jains in total population is the highest

Table 5.2

*Number and Percentage of Jains in the States and Union Territories, 1981**

S. No.	States/Union Territories	Population	Percentage of Jains w.r.t	
			All India	Total Population
	INDIA	31,92,572	100.00	0.48
1.	Andhra Pradesh	18,642	0.58	0.03
2.	Bihar	27,613	0.86	0.04
3.	Gujarat	4,67,768	14.65	1.37
4.	Haryana	35,482	1.11	0.27
5.	Himachal Pradesh	1,046	0.03	0.02
6.	Jammu and Kashmir	1,576	0.05	0.03
7.	Karnataka	2,84,508	8.91	0.77
8.	Kerala	3,605	0.11	0.02
9.	Madhya Pradesh	4,44,960	13.94	0.85
10.	Maharashtra	9,39,392	29.42	1.50
11.	Manipur	975	0.03	0.07
12.	Meghalaya	542	0.02	0.04
13.	Nagaland	1,153	0.04	0.15
14.	Orissa	6,642	0.21	0.03
15.	Punjab	27,049	0.85	0.16
16.	Rajasthan	6,24,317	19.56	1.82
17.	Sikkim	108	N	0.03
18.	Tamil Nadu	49,564	1.55	0.10
19.	Tripura	297	0.01	0.02
20.	Uttar Pradesh	1,41,549	4.43	0.13
21.	West Bengal	38,663	1.21	0.07
22.	Andaman and Nicobar Islands	11	N	N
23.	Arunachal Pradesh	42	N	0.01
24.	Chandigarh	1,889	0.06	0.42
25.	Dadra and Nagar Haveli	372	0.01	0.36
26.	Delhi	73,917	2.32	1.19
27.	Goa, Daman and Diu	602	0.02	0.06
28.	Mizoram	11	N	N
29.	Pondicherry	277	0.01	0.05

N: Negligible

* Excluding Assam where census was not held and Lakshadweep where no Jains were enumerated in 1981.

Source: Same as for Table 5.1 (Serial No. 4).

in Rajasthan (1.82) followed by Maharashtra (1.50), Gujarat (1.37) and Delhi (1.19). Apart from these, in two other states that is Karnataka and Madhya Pradesh only, this percentage is above the national average, whereas in the remaining states and union territories, this is quite insignificant.

Keeping in view the fact that nine-tenth of the Jains are concentrated in the six states listed earlier, the patterns of population redistribution of Jains since 1951 among these states have been only discussed here. It is seen from Table 5.3 that the number of Jains in Maharashtra, Madhya Pradesh and Karnataka has more than doubled during the last 30 years period. This growth has remained highest in Maharashtra (178%). In Gujarat, on the other hand, it remained very much slow (25%) followed by Uttar Pradesh (45%). The decadal per cent change in the population of Jains, among the states, is noted to be considerably faster in Maharashtra during the earlier two decades of 1951–1961 and 1961–1971 which however, declined in the last decade (1971–1981). A similar trend is also noted in Madhya Pradesh. As opposed to this, in Karnataka it was comparatively faster in the last decade than the earlier two decades. In Gujarat, growth of Jains as stated earlier remained quite slow during all the three decades as it varied from 9 per cent in 1951–1961 to 10 in 1961–1971 and even less than 4 in 1971–1981. In the remaining state of Uttar Pradesh, it declined from about 25 per cent to just 2 and increased thereafter to approximately 13 during these three decades.

As a result of this uneven pace of population growth of Jains, the percentage share of Jains of these states in the total population of Jains in India increased from approximately 21 to 29 in Maharashtra and from 11 to about 14 in Madhya Pradesh. Whereas in the remaining four states it declined continuously during this period except for Karnataka where after a gradual decline during 1951–1971, it increased at the 1981 census. This decline again is more conspicuous in Gujarat where it declined from 23 in 1951 to 20 in 1961, 17 in 1971 and approximately 15 in 1981. Thus, it may be discerned from the above analysis that as a result of varying pace of population growth resulting largely from the inter-state migration, the population of Jains is gradually being redistributed among these states. For instance, Gujarat which ranked first with regard to the percentage of Jains in 1951 has lost its position to Maharashtra and Rajasthan in 1981.

Table 5.3

Variations in the Number and Percentage of Jains and Decadal Per cent Population Change in Six Major States, Since 1951

S. No.	States	1951	1961	1971	1981
		I. Number of Jains			
1.	Gujarat	3,74,882	4,09,754	4,51,578	4,67,768
2.	Karnataka	1,39,873	1,74,366	2,18,862	2,84,508
3.	Madhya Pradesh	1,81,328	2,47,927	3,45,211	4,44,960
4.	Maharashtra	3,37,578	4,85,672	7,03,664	9,39,392
5.	Rajasthan	3,59,772	4,09,417	5,13,548	6,24,317
6.	Uttar Pradesh	97,744	1,22,108	1,24,728	1,41,549
		II. Percentage of Total Number of Jains of India			
1.	Gujarat	23.16	20.21	17.34	14.65
2.	Karnataka	8.64	8.60	8.40	8.91
3.	Madhya Pradesh	11.20	12.23	13.25	13.94
4.	Maharashtra	20.86	23.96	27.02	29.42
5.	Rajasthan	22.23	20.20	19.72	19.56
6.	Uttar Pradesh	6.04	6.02	4.79	4.43
		III. Per cent Population Change During			
		1951–1981	*1951–1961*	*1961–1971*	*1971–1981*
1.	Gujarat	24.78	9.30	10.21	3.59
2.	Karnataka	103.40	24.66	25.52	29.99
3.	Madhya Pradesh	145.39	36.73	39.24	28.90
4.	Maharashtra	178.27	43.87	44.88	33.50
5.	Rajasthan	73.53	13.80	25.43	21.57
6.	Uttar Pradesh	44.82	24.93	2.15	13.49

Source: Same as for Table 5.1 (Serial Nos. 2 to 4).

A probe into the dispersal and growth of Jains at the districts level is made here by classifying all the districts according to different categories of population size. Figures presented in Table 5.4 show that not a single Jain has been enumerated in 7 districts out of 351 in 1971 and 33 districts out of 402 districts (excluding 10 districts of Assam) in 1981. Apart from these, each of the 275 districts in 1971 and 289 districts in 1981 comprised less than 10,000 population. This spurt in the number of districts in these two categories may be due to formation of new districts in 1981 out of those existing in 1971. The number of districts falling in the first three categories also increased and this increase is mostly due to the increase in the number of Jains of such districts during this decade. Whereas a decline in the number of districts in the remaining categories may be due to mobility of relatively large number of districts from this category associated with a lesser number of districts incoming from the lower category as a result of increase in the number of Jains.

Table 5.4

*Number and Percentage of Total Number of Jains Living in the Districts According to Population Size Categories, 1971 and 1981**

Category	*Population Size*	*Number of Districts*		*Percentage of Jains Living Therein*	
		1971	*1981*	*1971*	*1981*
I	10,000 and above	3	4	17.62	22.25
II	50,000–99,999	5	6	13.00	12.74
III	20,000–49,999	27	38	30.08	35.38
IV	10,000–19,999	34	32	19.26	14.06
V	Less than 10,000	275	289	20.04	15.57
VI	NIL	7	33	–	–
	Total	351	402*	100	100

*Excluding 10 districts of Assam.

Source: Same as for Table 5.1 (Serial Nos. 3 and 4).

If we look at the figure pertaining to total number of Jains living in these districts (Table 5.4), we find that little more than one-fifth are concentrated in four districts only each having more than 1 lakh population. These four districts are Greater Bombay and Kolhapur (Maharashtra), Belgaum (Karnataka) and Ahmedabad (Gujarat). These were followed by six districts falling under second category, namely, Kachchh (Gujarat), Sangli and Pune (Maharashtra), Pali and Udaipur (Rajasthan) and Delhi which accounted for 13 per cent of Jains. Of the remaining, 38 districts falling under third category comprised more than one-third of Jains and 32 districts of the fourth category accounted for 14 per cent of Jains. Thus, 70 per cent of Jains have been enumerated in 48 districts (each having more than 20,000 Jains). Moreover, if we consider all the districts having at least 10,000 Jains, we find that 80 such districts (i.e. one-fifth) of the total number of districts accounted for more than four-fifth of the total population. (Further details about the name of the districts, number of Jains and decadal per cent population change are presented in the Table 5A.1). When we compare this position of 1981 with that existed at the earlier census of 1971, we notice that the number of districts having at least 10,000 Jains increased from 69 to 80, whereas the percentage of Jains living in such districts increased from 80 to 84.

In order to analyse district level changes in the number of Jains, growth rates for all the 327 districts having Jain population at both the 1971 and 1981 censuses are computed for 1971–1981. Subsequently, these have been classified in Table 5.5 into two broad categories according to growth rate, namely, those having at least 10,000 and those having less than 10,000 Jains.[6] It is seen that 41 districts recorded 100 per cent and more growth followed by 37 having it varying from 50 to 99 per cent. In 60 districts on the other hand, there is a decline followed by 31 districts having virtual stagnation (i.e. less than 10 per cent growth). It is, however, to be noted in this connection that a large number of districts falling under both the categories (i.e. having higher growth and those having a stagnation or decline) have less than 10,000 Jains. For instance, only 1 district out of 41 districts having 100 per cent and more growth and 6 out of 60 districts having a decline had more than 10,000 Jains in 1981.

Table 5.5

Number of Districts Classified According to Different Ranges of Decadal Per cent Change in the Number of Jains, 1971–1981

Range	*Districts Having*		*All Districts*
	10,000 and More Population	*Less Than 10,000 Population*	
100 and above	1	40	41
50–99	3	34	37
25–49	35	56	91
10–24	27	40	67
0–9	8	23	31
Negative	6	54	60
Total	80	247	327

Source: Same as for Table 5.1 (Serial Nos. 3 and 4).

About the location of districts having at least 10,000 Jains and an abnormal growth, it is seen that most of them are situated in Gujarat, Karnataka and Maharashtra only (Table 5A.1). For instance three of the four such districts having relatively faster growth are situated in Karnataka and Maharashtra. These districts are Thane (158.75%), Bangalore (95.23%) and Greater Bombay (52.18%). As compared to these, following five out of six districts having decline in the number of Jains are situated in Gujarat: Banaskantha (–2.29%), Kheda (–6.28%), Rajkot (–9.08%), Jamnagar (–10.73%) and Mehsana (–11.42%).

After having analysed the patterns of population dispersal and growth of Jains, it is intended here to present a brief account of a few selected population characteristics. This is being attempted on the basis of limited data available from the 1981 census on sex composition, rural–urban distribution and number of households by religion of head of the household. It is seen from the figures presented in Table 5.6 that the decadal per cent population change is slower among Jains than Hindus, Muslims and Sikhs during 1971–1981. This slower rate in case of Jains as explained earlier is largely due to the low fertility level among them. The level of urbanization (the percentage of population living in urban areas), on the other hand, is the highest among Jains (64%) as compared to other religious communities. In other words, Jains live mostly in cities and towns, thus confirming the observation made by Sangave in his study of Jain community that 'The Jain community is essentially urban in character'.[7] The sex ratio or the number of females per 1,000 male population among Jains is comparatively higher than Hindus, Muslims and Sikhs. Lastly, the average household size or the number of persons per household is higher among Jains as compared to Hindus, Christians and Buddhists and lower than Muslims and Sikhs. When we view this higher household size in the context of the prevailing level of fertility among Jains, we notice that the TMFR is lowest among Jains as compared to other religious communities as per 1981 census as explained in the first section of this study. This fact may be regarded as an indication of the prevalence of joint family system among Jains on a large-scale despite it being one of the most urbanized community in India.

Table 5.6

Selected Population Characteristics of Jains and Other Major Religious Communities of India, 1981

Religious Community	*Growth Rate 1971–1981*	*Level of Urbanization*	*Sex Ratio*	*Average Household Size*
Jains	23.17	63.82	941	5.86
Hindus	24.14	21.94	933	5.48
Muslims	30.56	34.03	937	6.20
Christians	16.83	29.16	992	5.28
Sikhs	26.15	31.66	880	6.21
Buddhists	22.52	31.99	953	5.19

Source: Same as for Table 5.1 (Serial No. 4).

Figures on variations in these population characteristics among states and union territories are presented in Table 5.7. It is seen there from that all those four characteristics varied vastly among smaller sates and union territories owing to a very meagre number of Jains living in such areas. When we took at the position of six major states, namely, Gujarat, Karnataka, Madhya Pradesh, Maharashtra, Rajasthan and Uttar Pradesh comprising nine-tenth of the Jain population, we notice that the decadal per cent change in the number of Jains was the highest in Maharashtra as opposed to Gujarat, having hardly 4 per cent growth. The number of Jains living in urban areas is noted to be the highest in the Uttar Pradesh (74%) followed by Gujarat (70%) and the lowest in Karnataka (42%) followed by Rajasthan (approximately 50%). With regard to the sex ratio, it is seen that the female outnumbered male population in Gujarat. Of the remaining five states, in Uttar Pradesh and Madhya Pradesh, the number of females per 1,000 males is quite low (915 and 916 respectively). The number of persons per household among Jains is the highest in Uttar Pradesh (6.41) and the lowest is noted in Gujarat (5.22). A closer look at the figures on variations in the population characteristics among these states clearly shows that as a result of heavier out-migration of Jains from Gujarat, the ratio of male to female population and the average household size is adversely affected.

Table 5.7

Selected Population Characteristics of Jains by States/UTs, 1981

S. No.	*States/Union Territories*	*Decadal Per cent Change*	*Level of Urbanization*	*Sex Ratio*	*Average Household Size*
	INDIA	23.17	63.82	941	5.86
1	Andhra Pradesh	15.73	94.48	815	6.57
2	Bihar	9.64	80.29	856	7.47
3	Gujarat	3.59	69.96	1,011	5.22
4	Haryana	13.82	78.63	914	6.78

Cont'd...

...Cont'd

S. No.	*States/Union Territories*	*Decadal Per cent Change*	*Level of Urbanization*	*Sex Ratio*	*Average Household Size*
5	Himachal Pradesh	67.09	79.73	909	5.20
6	Jammu and Kashmir	37.04	94.54	972	6.79
7	Karnataka	29.99	41.76	920	6.20
8	Kerala	8.06	49.38	939	5.08
9	Madhya Pradesh	28.90	67.78	916	6.30
10	Maharashtra	33.50	66.47	924	5.84
11	Manipur	–30.75	99.18	705	9.29
12	Meghalaya	102.24	63.10	449	7.23
13	Nagaland	83.89	98.44	669	9.69
14	Orissa	1.86	66.91	862	6.72
15	Punjab	26.50	93.66	908	6.78
16	Rajasthan	21.57	49.54	990	5.66
17	Sikkim	–43.46	85.19	367	5.68
18	Tamil Nadu	20.66	76.13	906	5.94
19	Tripura	–20.80	65.99	597	5.71
20	Uttar Pradesh	13.49	74.18	915	6.41
21	West Bengal	20.06	84.86	735	6.52
22	Andaman and Nicobar Islands	–21.43	100.00	1200	3.67
23	Arunachal Pradesh	7.69	71.43	556	3.82
24	Chandigarh	85.93	98.46	865	5.57
25	Dadra and Nagar Haveli	22.77	30.38	833	4.59
26	Delhi	46.33	99.41	893	6.02
27	Goa, Daman and Diu	8.27	63.95	786	4.70
28	Mizoram	266.67	100.00	571	3.67
29	Pondicherry	16.88	98.19	787	6.93

* Excluding Assam where census was not conducted in 1981 and Lakshadweep where no Jains were enumerated in 1971 and 1981.

Source: Same as for Table 5.1 (Serial Nos. 3 and 4).

Table 5.8 gives the average position of 80 districts (which comprised four-fifth of total Jains) with respect to these population characteristics by classifying them into four population size categories. It is seen that the decadal per cent population change and the level of urbanization is the highest in the first category comprising four districts having more than 1 lakh population. Whereas the sex ratio is lower in this category than the second, third and fourth categories. In the remaining three categories, the decadal per cent population change and average household size increased and the sex ratio declined gradually in the lower categories. The level of urbanization, however, does not reveal any consistent increase or decrease among with population size.

Table 5.8

Selected Population Characteristics of Jains Living in the Districts with 10,000 and More Jains, 1981

Category	*Population Size*	*Number of Districts*	*Decadal Per cent Population Change*	*Level of Urbanization*	*Sex Ratio*	*Average Household Size*
I	1,00,000 and more	4	33.46	72.16	933	5.83
II	50,000–99,999	6	20.84	52.01	995	5.30
III	20,000–49,999	38	21.96	63.50	949	5.88
IV	10,000–19,999	32	23.22	57.56	931	5.99
	Total	80	24.83	63.09	949	5.79

Source: Same as for Table 5.1 (Serial No. 4).

A probe into the variation in these characteristics according to decadal per cent change in the number of Jains during 1971–1981 brings out that in case of 4 out of 80 districts having 50 per cent and higher growth, the average level of urbanization is the highest (Table 5.9). This level is comparatively higher again in case of districts having very slow growth (i.e. less than 10 per cent), thus implying the in- and out-migration. The lowest sex ratio of 867 females per 1,000 males as noted in the first category and the highest (1,023) noted in the fourth category may be considered as an indication of the fact that due to heavier in-migration, the ratio of females to males is unfavourable among the districts from where the Jains have moved out as revealed by the very slow pace of population growth. Lastly, the higher average household size in the first two categories may be regarded as an indication of relatively higher household congestion in the districts as a result of heavier immigration, whereas the opposite is the case in the last two categories showing a lower household size.

Table 5.9

Variations in the Population Characteristics of Jains in the Selected Districts According to Board Ranges of Decadal Per cent Population Change During 1971–1981

Category	*Range*	*Number of Districts*	*Level of Urbanization*	*Sex Ratio*	*Average Household Size*
I	50% and above	4	94.12	867	5.77
II	25–49	35	61.47	942	6.13
III	10–24	27	51.07	969	5.70
IV	Less than 10	8	63.44	1,023	5.27
V	Negative	6	60.07	1,009	5.30
	Total	80	63.09	949	5.82

Source: Same as for Table 5.1 (Serial No. 4).

To sum up, the following salient features may be noted from the foregoing analyses on dispersal, growth and selected population characteristics of Jains:

1. The decadal population growth among Jains has greatly varied during the last 100 years. In the post-independence period, it improved during 1951–1961 and 1961–1971 decades largely due to a heavier reduction in mortality rates as a result of improved living conditions. Whereas the subsequent decline during the last decade may partly be due to a reduction in the fertility rates among Jains as revealed by a decline in the TMFR during 1971–1981.

2. Three-fourth of the Jains are distributed in Maharashtra, Rajasthan, Gujarat and Madhya Pradesh followed by another 13 per cent living in Karnataka and Uttar Pradesh. Thus approximately nine-tenth of the Jains are enumerated in these six states only.
3. The number of Jains more than doubled in Maharashtra, followed by Madhya Pradesh and Karnataka out of these six states. In Gujarat, on the other hand, it remained quite slow during all the three decades.
4. About four-fifth of Jains are enumerated in one-fifth of the districts having at least 10,000 Jains. Out of these, four districts, namely, Greater Bombay, Kolhapur, Belgaum and Ahmedabad, accounted for little more than one-fifth of the Jains.
5. The decadal per cent population change during 1971–1981 is abnormal (i.e. either very fast or quite slow) in a few districts having relatively larger number of Jains, whereas majority of the districts are having a growth varying from 10 to 50 per cent only. This is in consonance with the findings of an earlier study (made by this author) about the inter-district variations in the growth rates during 1961–1971.[8]
6. With regard to variations in the selected population characteristics of Jains, it is noted that the decadal per cent population change among Jains is slower than the Hindus, Muslims and Sikhs. The level of urbanization is the highest, thus implying that Jains live mostly in cities and towns. The sex ratio is comparatively higher among Jains than the Hindus, Muslims and Sikhs, whereas the average household size is higher among Jains than the Hindus, Christians and Buddhists. This higher average household size coupled with the lowest fertility level seems to indicate that the prevalence of joint family system among Jains is still in vogue on a large-scale despite it being the most urbanized community in India.

7. At the state level, the ratio of males to females and average household size are adversely affected by the heavier out-migration of Jains in case of Gujarat out of the 6 major states as revealed by a lower growth rate. Where as, in Karnataka, the highest population growth has resulted into a lower sex ratio and a higher average household size.
8. At the district level, the decadal per cent population change and the level of urbanization is the highest in the first category comprising four districts each having more than 1 lakh population. Whereas, the sex ratio is lower in this category than the districts falling under second and third category and the average household size is lower than the third and fourth category.
9. Lastly, the higher level of urbanization is noted for both the group of districts having faster and slower growth among Jains. In other words, a higher extent of in- and out-migration among Jains is associated with the higher level of urbanization among Jains as noted in such districts. Similarly, the lowest sex ratio in the group of districts having rapid growing and the highest in the fourth category comprising districts with stagnation in Jain population may be due to in-migration in case of former and out-migration in case of latter categories. The higher average household size in case of the first two categories may also be considered as an indication of growing household congestion in the districts having relatively faster growth in the number of Jains owing to in-migrants in such areas.

Notes and References

1. Census of India, 1981, Paper No. 3 of 1984, Household Population by Religion of Head of Household (New Delhi: RGO, 1984), p. vii (figures amended as per Errata issued subsequently by this office).
2. J.P. Sharma, 'Jains as a Minority in Indian Society and History', *Jain Journal*, Vol. X, April 1976, Calcutta, pp. 137–148.

3. C.f. M.K. Jain, 'Jains in India: How Many and Where?' *Tirthankar*, Vol. 1, No. 2, 1975, pp. 8–23.
4. Total marital fertility rate (TMFR) refers to the total number of children that would have born alive per married women under the current age specific fertility rates for the entire reproductive period (in the present case for the age groups between 15 and 49.
5. Census of India, 1981, Part II Special Report and Tables Based on 5 per cent Samples Data (New Delhi: RGO, 1993), pp. 43 and 45.
6. The number of districts considered here does not tally with those reported earlier, as all those districts which have been carved out after 1971 census are clubbed together (with the districts from where, they were carved out) for the purpose of computation of growth rates as no separate population figures are available in such cases. For instance, Nalanda district of Bihar which has been carved out from Patna for this purpose.
7. V.A. Singave, *Jain Community, A Social Survey* (Bombay: Allied, 1959), p. 5
8. M.K. Jain, op. cit., p. 14.

APPENDIX

Table 5A.1

Number of Persons and Selected Population Characteristics of Jains in the Districts Having at Least 10,000 Jains, 1981

S. No.	District	Population	Growth Rate, 1971–1981	Level of Urbanization	Sex Ratio	Average Household Size
	I. Districts Having 1,00,000 and More					
1.	Greater Bombay	3,41,980	52.18	100.00	869	5.730
2.	Belgaum	1,27,306	15.59	21.32	946	5.965
3.	Kolhapur	1,21,722	30.51	23.84	1,098	6.307
4.	Ahmedabad	1,19,235	14.60	95.92	955	5.573
	II. Districts Having 50,000–99,999					
5.	Udaipur	92,093	17.31	38.27	988	5.387
6.	Delhi	73,917	46.33	99.41	893	6.017
7.	Sangli	67,304	13.20	25.92	946	5.644
8.	Pune	65,907	41.85	76.19	907	6.013
9.	Kachchh	57,454	0.61	22.98	1,271	3.987
10.	Pali	50,116	12.38	43.87	1,080	4.980
	III. Districts Having 20,000–49,999					
11.	Jaipur	47,416	26.69	74.32	917	5.792
12.	Thane	45,609	158.75	71.91	857	5.483
13.	Sagar	45,144	21.95	58.11	913	6.203
14.	Ajmer	44,263	18.82	58.43	928	5.764
15.	Jalore	41,873	20.49	27.44	1,164	5.082
16.	Bhavnagar	39,802	1.68	94.99	917	6.236
17.	Indore	39,074	49.40	94.99	917	6.236
18.	Ahmednagar	33,565	18.47	40.87	936	5.994
19.	Barmer	32,627	28.37	48.73	989	6.077
20.	Bhilwara	32,483	20.71	30.91	973	5.467
21.	Churu	31,645	22.72	77.88	1,043	6.483
22.	Banaskantha	31,028	–2.29	31.20	1,028	5.207
23.	Meerut	30,710	16.16	64.41	936	5.628
24.	Dharwad	30,629	37.44	41.74	892	6.601

Cont'd...

...Cont'd

S. No.	District	Population	Growth Rate, 1971–1981	Level of Urbanization	Sex Ratio	Average Household Size
25.	Bangalore	30,108	95.23	97.72	829	6.777
26.	Chandigarh	29,984	28.10	46.98	940	5.515
27.	Jodhpur	29,558	19.82	72.49	940	6.042
28.	Rajkot	28,973	–9.08	93.82	1,009	5.403
29.	Nasik	28,792	34.17	58.13	931	6.248
30.	Mandsaur	28,453	20.92	52.65	940	6.397
31.	Surendranagar	28,358	0.48	81.54	1,006	5.413
32.	Jabalpur	26,858	38.62	79.15	906	6.153
33.	Jamnagar	26,739	–10.73	56.46	1,034	5.336
34.	Surat	26,312	29.67	71.09	892	5.516
35.	Jalgaon	24,589	25.64	54.13	941	5.853
36.	Bikaner	24,342	9.32	78.40	1,012	6.784
37.	Sholapur	24,141	14.91	50.35	928	5.659
38.	Ratlam	24,096	26.88	80.10	932	6.308
39.	Sirohi	23,977	24.90	39.48	1,141	4.984
40.	Aurangabad	23,323	33.36	47.95	920	5.927
41.	Agra	23,179	9.05	70.92	960	5.912
42.	Nagpur	23,013	19.43	51.24	1,037	6.186
43.	Bijapur	23,011	28.04	37.79	948	6.717
44.	Madras	22,812	32.91	100.00	848	6.595
45.	Mehsana	21,347	–11.22	61.90	1,008	5.033
46.	Ujjain	20,950	20.54	81.31	924	6.224
47.	Calcutta	20,487	8.19	100.00	726	6.632
48.	Guna	20,265	27.42	63.52	903	6.775
	IV. Districts Having 10,000–19,999					
49.	Vadodara	19,062	9.59	84.27	971	5.314
50.	Tonk	19,041	27.65	39.79	934	6.290
51.	Damoh	18,639	23.40	33.31	929	5.723
52.	Dhule	17,073	30.97	48.98	908	6.438
53.	Nagpur	16,853	42.33	85.53	940	5.754
54.	Akola	16,720	10.24	58.66	937	5.921

Cont'd...

...Cont'd

S. No.	District	Population	Growth Rate, 1971–1981	Level of Urbanization	Sex Ratio	Average Household Size
55.	Kheda	16,242	–6.28	64.23	994	5.366
56.	Lalitpur	16,234	30.04*	51.56	830	9.161
57.	Bhind	15,778	31.45	70.95	883	6.807
58.	Sawai Madhopur	15,719	59.12	36.65	932	5.798
59.	Banswara	14,667	40.48	25.36	937	5.774
60.	Muzaffarnagar	14,138	16.35	71.46	936	6.707
61.	Sabarkantha	13,857	14.12	49.53	1,045	5.261
62.	Valsad	13,725	22.62	70.12	900	5.492
63.	Vidisha	13,683	26.27	69.13	921	6.007
64.	South Kannada	13,646	14.22	15.77	1,027	5.140
65.	Kota	13,106	28.88	80.39	891	5.756
66.	Dungarpur	11,972	23.00	31.30	954	5.555
67.	Jaipur	11,474	43.41	84.91	906	7.299
68.	Sitara	11,293	26.07	58.79	934	5.689
69.	Gwalior	11,248	27.78	88.37	930	6.636
70.	Buldhana	11,168	8.38	48.22	957	5.953
71.	Yavatmal	11,124	28.84	46.15	924	5.923
72.	Osmanabad	11,113	33.57	39.72	951	6.073
73.	Parbhani	11,100	–7.37	51.76	922	5.701
74.	Tikamgarh	11,029	36.23	47.07	901	5.729
75.	Shajapur	10,973	17.21	66.97	940	6.417
76.	Durg	10,835	39.72**	73.02	877	6.751
77.	Bhopal	10,721	29.76***	97.17	914	5.634
78.	Amravati	10,447	4.80	63.44	927	5.638
79.	Dhar	10,339	11.89	56.19	943	6.398
80.	Alwar	10,321	30.50	48.78	932	6.236

*Relates to Lalitpur and Jhansi districts together in 1981 as no separate population figures are available from 1971 census.

**For Durg and Rajnandgaon together in 1981 as population figures for each of these are not available from 1971 census.

***Growth rate computed by clubbing Bhopal and Sehore districts of 1981 together as no separate figures are available for them in 1971.

6

Jains in the Censuses of 1991 and 2001

Prakash C. Jain

This chapter analyses the major population characteristics of the Jains as per the 1991 and 2001 censuses of India. The 1991 census data are based on the *C-9 Religion Table* which gives data for persons, males and females, separately for each of the six major religious communities, namely, Hindus, Muslims, Christians, Sikhs, Buddhists and Jains and combined figures for 'other religions and persuasions' and 'religion not stated' by total, rural and urban for India, states and union territories.[1] The 2001 census data are derived from *Census of India 2001*: *The First Report of Religion Data* (2004).[2] The 1991 and 2001 census tables correspond to Table C-VII-Religion of 1961, 1971 and Table HH-15 of 1981,[3] the only difference being that the figures of religion for 1961, 1971, 1991 and 2001 were based on the religion of the individual, whereas the figures presented in 1981 were based on religion of head of the household.

Population Size

In modern times, the Jains have been a minority and the smallest religious community in India (Jain, 1975; Sharma, 1976). Exactly how small has been the Jain community in recent times was not known until 1881 when the first systematic census of Indian population was undertaken. In 1881, the total Jain population was enumerated at 12,21,896 or 0.48 per cent of the total Indian population. Since then the Jains have seldom constituted more than half a per cent of the total population of India (See Table 6.1; also Figures 6.1 and 6.2). With the enumeration of 4.2 million (0.4%) Jains in the 2001 census of India, they still constitute the smallest religious community in the country. The corresponding figures for other religious communities are Hindus 827 million (81.4%), Muslims 138 million (12.4%), Christians 24 million (2.3%), Sikhs 19 million (1.9%), Buddhists 7.9 million (0.8%) and other religious communities 6.6 million (0.7%).

In the 1991 census, Hindus were enumerated as the largest religious community (82%) followed by Muslims (12.12%), Christians (2.34%), Sikhs (1.94%), Buddhists (0.76%) and Jains (0.4%). As can be seen in Table 6.2, the religious composition of the Indian society in the census year 2001 continued to remain more or less the same as in 1991 with minor variations. The average decadal growth rate was found to be 21.5 per cent. Against this only Hindus (20.0%) and Sikhs (16.9%) showed less than average growth rate during 1991–2001, whereas Muslims (29.3%), Christians (22.1%), Buddhists (23.2%) and Jains (26.0%) grew at higher than average rate (Figure 6.3). Other important religious communities enumerated in the 1991 census were Jews (5,271), Zoroastrians (76,382) and Bahais (5,575). About a quarter of a million people were listed as unclassified. In the 2001 census, only 69,601 (33,949 males and 35,652 females) Parsis/Zoroastrians were enumerated.

Table 6.1

Variations in the Number of Jains since 1891

Census	*Number of Jains (in 000s)*	*Percentage of Total Population*	*Decadal Per cent Change in the Number of Jains*
1881	1,222	0.49	–
1891	1,417	0.51	15.94
1901	1,334	0.47	–5.83
1911	1,248	0.41	–6.47
1921	1,177	0.39	–5.26
1931	1,251	0.37	6.28
1941	1,440	0.37	15.81
1951	1,618	0.45	11.67
1961	2,027	0.46	25.17
1971	2,605	0.47	28.48
1981*	3,193	0.48	23.17
1991**	3,352	0.4	4.42
2001	4,225	0.4	26

*Excluding Assam where census was not held in 1981 owing to disturbed conditions.

**Excluding Jammu and Kashmir where 1991 census was not held.

Sources: 1. Kingsley Davis, *Population of India and Pakistan* (New York: Russell and Russell), 1951, pp. 178–179.
2. Census of India, 1961, Paper No. 1 of 1963, Religion (New Delhi: RGO, 1963), pp. ii–viii.
3. Census of Indian, 1971, Paper No. 2 of 1972, Religion (New Delhi: RGO, 1972), pp. 2–5.
4. Census of India, 1981, Paper No. 4 of 1984, Household Population by Religion of Head of Household (New Delhi: RGO, 1984), p. 26 (figures amended as per Errata issued subsequently by this office).
5. Census of India, 1991, Paper No, 1 of 1995, Religion (New Delhi: RGO, 1995).
6. Census of India, 2001, First Report of Religion Data (New Delhi: RGO, 2004).

Figure 6.1

Variation of Jain Population in India 1881–2001

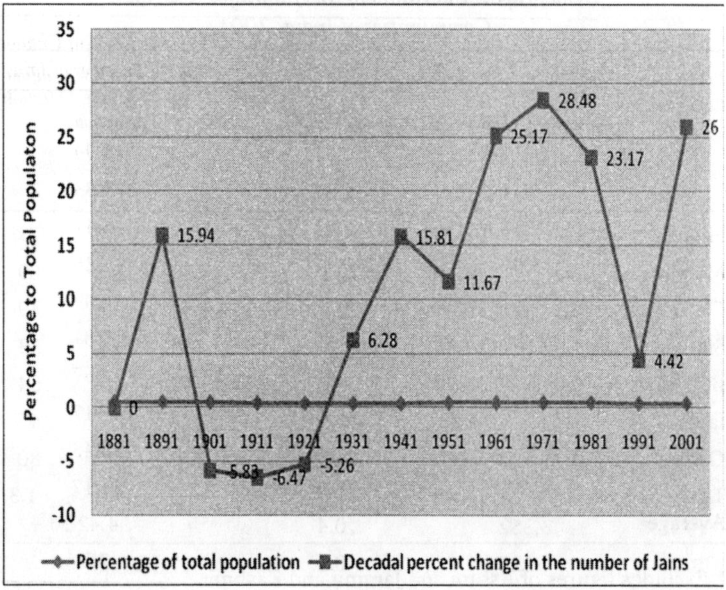

Figure 6.2

Number of Jains (in 000s) in India, 1881–2001

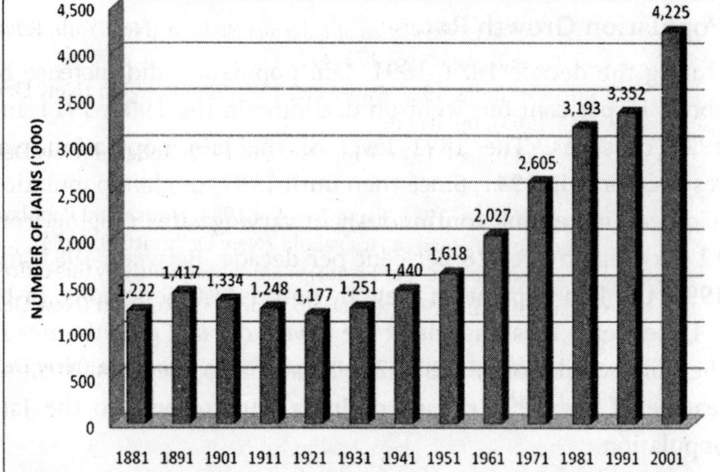

Table 6.2

Demographic Indicators of the Six Major Religious Communities of India, 2001

Religious Communities	*Percentage of Total Population*	*Population Growth (1981–1991)**	*Population Growth (1991–2001)*	*Sex Ratio*	*Sex Ratio (0–6)*	*Proportion of Child Population in Age Group (0–6)*	*Infant Mortality*
Hindus	81.4	22.78	20.0	931	925	15.6	77
Muslims	12.4	32.76	29.3	936	950	18.7	69
Christians	2.3	16.89	22.1	1,009	964	13.5	49
Sikhs	1.9	25.48	16.9	893	780	12.8	53
Buddhists	0.8	35.98	23.2	953	942	14.4	54
Jains	0.4	4.42	26.0	940	870	10.6	47
Others	0.7	NA	111.3	992	976	18.0	80
Total/ Average	100.0	23.05	21.5	933	927	15.9	61.3

* Excludes figures of Assam and Jammu and Kashmir.

Sources: 1. Census of India, 2001.

2. Infant mortality data are based on National Family Health Survey (NFHS-2), 1998–99, *Indian Express*, Delhi, 18 November 2001.

Population Growth Rate

During the decade 1881–1891, Jain population did increase by about 16 per cent but went on declining in the 1901, 1911 and 1921 censuses. The 1891 level of the Jain population was restored only in 1941. Since then until 1981, the Jain population had been increasing continuously at varying rates ranging from 12 per cent to over 28 per cent per decade. Between 1981 and 1991, the Jain population grew by only 1,41,065 persons, or by 4.42 per cent. This was one of the lowest decadal growth rates in the Jain population since 1921. This is also the most striking feature of the 1991 census of India with respect to the Jain population.

Figure 6.3

A Comparison of Decadal Population Growth of Various Religious Communities during 1981–1991 and 1991–2001

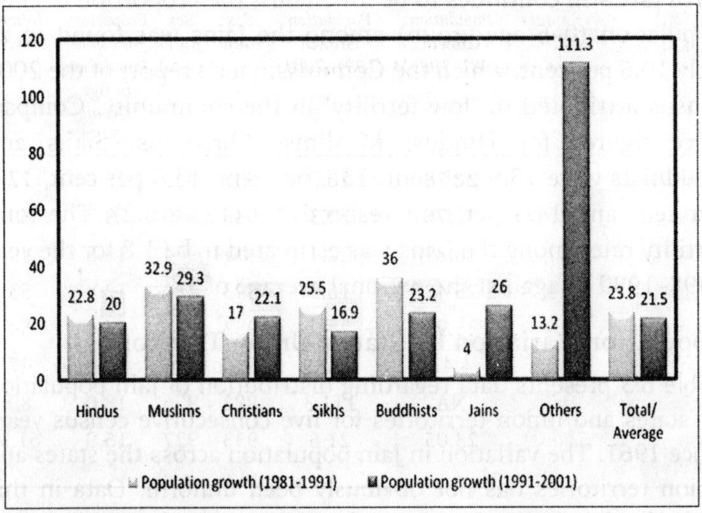

The slow growth in Jain population can be attributed to the decline in fertility rate due to affluence among the Jains and their upper middle class status. When most demographers were expecting less than 4 per cent population growth rate of Jains in the 2001 census, they were surprised to discover that it turned out to be over 26 per cent during the decade 1991–2001. This time around census procedural check on 'drift' coupled with 'ethnic revivalism' is considered to be the main cause of population growth among the Jains. According to the Indian Census officials, the

> respondents were allowed to look at the information collected from them by enumerators and sign the forms after verifying that they were to their satisfaction in 2001 census. This was the first time this procedure was followed. Earlier, many of the enumerators might have recorded Jains as Hindus. But with the respondents verifying and signing the form, they would have insisted on being registered as separate, as Jains and not Hindus. This could be one of the reasons for the jump in Jain growth figures.[4]

In spite of this second highest decadal growth rate among Jains in the 120-year-old history of census enumeration, their birth rate still continues to be low. Thus, the proportion of child population (0–6 age group) among the Jains was found to be only 10.6 per cent, which the Commissioner's report of the 2001 census attributed to 'low fertility' in the community. Comparative figures for Hindus, Muslims, Christians, Sikhs and Buddhists were 15.9 per cent, 15.6 per cent, 13.5 per cent, 12.8 per cent and 14.4 per cent respectively (Table 6.2). The total fertility rate among the Jains was estimated to be 1.8 for the year 1998–1999 as against the national average of 2.7.

Population Variation by States/Union Territories

Table 6.3 presents data regarding distribution of Jain population by states and union territories for five consecutive census years since 1961. The variation in Jain population across the states and union territories has not obviously been uniform. Data in this table clearly suggest that as per the 1991 census data, in 14 states and five union territories there was varying increase in Jain population over the 1981 figures. These states and union territories are Andhra Pradesh, Arunachal Pradesh, Goa, Gujarat, Himachal Pradesh, Karnataka, Kerala, Madhya Pradesh, Maharashtra, Manipur, Nagaland, Tamil Nadu, Tripura and Uttar Pradesh, Andaman and Nicobar Islands, Dadra and Nagar Haveli, Daman and Diu, Delhi and Pondicherry. In the 2001 census, however, all the states and union territories showed varying percentage of increase in the Jain population. No Jains were reported in Lakshadweep in any census year. There was no census taking in Assam in 1981 and in Jammu & Kashmir in 1991.

As per 1991 census, in nine states and one union territory, Jain population varyingly had declined during the decade 1981–1991. These states and the union territory along with per cent decrease in population are listed as follows: Bihar (–16.53), Haryana (–0.52), Meghalaya (–17.90), Mizoram (–63.64), Orissa (–5.12), Punjab (–23.24), Rajasthan (–9.85), Sikkim (–62.96), West Bengal (–11.14) and Chandigarh (–18.95). It is remarkable, however, that no decline of Jain population was registered in any state and union territory in India between 1991 and 2001. It must be pointed out here that during the 1990s, there was a vigorous campaign in the Jain ethnic media to the effect that during the census enumerations they should return themselves as 'Jains' and not 'Hindus'. The media exhorted them to write their surnames as 'Jain' in addition to, or in place of using caste, sub-caste, clan or family names.

Table 6.3

Total Population of Jains, 1961–2001 (India, States and Union Territories)

India/States/ Union Territories	*1961*	*1971*	*1981*	*1991*	*2001*
India	20,27,281	26,04,646	32,06,038	33,52,706	42,25,053
Jammu & Kashmir	1,427	1,150	1,576	*	2,518
Himachal Pradesh	95	626	1,046	1,206	1,408
Punjab	48,754	21,383	27,049	20,763	39,276
Chandigarh	**	1,016	1,889	1,531	2,592
Uttaranchal	$	$	$	7,870	9,294
Haryana	**	31,173	35,482	35,296	57,167
Delhi	29,595	50,513	73,917	94,672	1,55,122
Rajasthan	4,09,417	5,13,548	6,24,317	5,62,806	6,50,493
Uttar Pradesh	1,22,108	1,24,728	1,41,549	1,68,389	2,07,111
Bihar	17,598	25,185	27,613	11,332	16,085
Sikkim	19	–	108	40	183
Arunachal Pradesh	14	39	42	64	216
Nagaland	263	627	1,153	1,202	2,093
Manipur	778	1,408	975	1,337	1,461
Mizoram	***	–	11	4	179
Tripura	195	375	297	301	477
Meghalaya	***	268	542	445	772
Assam	9,468	12,917	*	20,645	23,957

Cont'd...

...Cont'd

India/States/ Union Territories	*1961*	*1971*	*1981*	*1991*	*2001*
West Bengal	26,940	32,203	38,663	34,355	55,223
Jharkhand	$$$	$$$	$$$	11,717	16,301
Orissa	2,295	6,521	6,642	6,302	9,154
Chhattisgarh	$$	$$	$$	43,213	56,103
Madhya Pradesh	2,47,927	3,45,211	4,44,960	4,47,111	5,45,446
Gujarat	4,09,754	4,51,578	4,67,768	4,91,331	5,25,305
Daman and Diu	+	223	140	212	268
Dadra and Nagar Haveli	120	303	372	529	864
Maharashtra	4,85,672	7,03,664	9,39,392	9,65,840	13,01,843
Andhra Pradesh	9,012	16,108	18,642	26,564	41,846
Karnataka	1,74,366	2,18,862	2,97,974	3,26,114	4,12,659
Goa	68	333	462	487	820
Lakshadweep	–	–	–	–	–
Kerala	2,967	3,336	3,605	3,641	4,528
Tamil Nadu	28,350	41,097	49,564	66,900	83,359
Pondicherry	76	237	277	470	952
Andaman and Nicobar Islands	3	14	11	17	23

*No census conducted, **Included under Punjab, ***Included under Assam, $ Included under Uttar Pradesh, $$ Included under Madhya Pradesh, $$$ Included under Bihar, + Included under Goa.

Sources: 1. The Census 2001 population figures for India and Manipur exclude those of Mao Maram, Paomata and Purul sub-divisions of Senapati district of Manipur.

2. In 1991, figures for Uttaranchal, Uttar Pradesh, Jharkhand, Bihar, Chhattisgarh and Madhya Pradesh have been recasted as per the Jurisdiction in 2001 census.

3. All religious communities include 'Religion not stated'.

4. Population figures for 1961 are as per 'Social and Culture Tables' part-II-C (i), Census of India 1971, 1981 as per 'Religion', Paper 2 of 1972, Census of India 1971, 1981 as per 'Household population by religion of head of household', Paper 4 of 1984, Census of India 1981 and 1991 as per 'Religion' Part IV B (ii) Census of India, 1991.

If by some definition or devise India could be divided into eastern and western halves, then it can very well be established that at least 90 per cent of total Jain population lives in western half of the country and only less than 10 per cent in the eastern half. Incidentally, as per 1991 census figures, in the seven north-eastern states only about 24,000 Jains were enumerated. Of these over 20,000 lived in Assam alone. The corresponding figures for the census year 2001 were about 29,000.

Among the union territories, the largest number of Jains lived in Delhi: about 74,000 in 1981, a little over 94,600 in 1991 and 1,55,122 in 2001. In other union territories, Chandigarh had 1,531 Jains in 1991 followed by Dadra and Nagar Haveli (529), Pondicherry (470), Daman and Diu (212) and Andaman and Nicobar Islands (17). Corresponding figures for the census year 2001 for Chandigarh, Dadra and Nagar Haveli, Pondicherry, Daman and Diu and Andaman and Nicobar Islands were 2,592, 864, 952, 268 and 23. No Jains have been reported in Lakshadweep in any census year since 1951 (Table 6.3).

Concentration in Seven States/Union Territories

Table 6.4 presents data about variations in the number and percentage of Jains and decadal per cent population change among them in seven major states/union territories, namely Gujarat, Karnataka, Rajasthan, Maharashtra, Madhya Pradesh, Uttar Pradesh and Delhi (see also Fig. 6.4). In 1951, Gujarat had the largest number of Jains followed by Rajasthan and Maharashtra. In 1961, however Maharashtra became the number one state to have the largest number of Jains, followed by Gujarat and then Rajasthan. Since then Maharashtra has been continuing to have this distinction with ever increasing concentration of the Jain population within its boundaries. Thus, in the 1991 census report there were 9,65,840 Jains in Maharashtra followed by 5,62,806 in Rajasthan and 4,91,331 in Gujarat. The corresponding figures in the 2001 census were Maharashtra 13,01,843, Rajasthan 6,50,491, and Gujarat 5,25,305. Meanwhile in the 2001 census, Madhya Pradesh with 5,45,446 Jains emerged as the state supporting the third largest Jain population after Maharashtra and

Rajasthan. These four states, together with Karnataka, Uttar Pradesh, and Delhi accounted for about 90 per cent of the total Jain population in India in 2001. The varying pace of population growth can be attributed mainly to inter-state migration, ethnic revivalism and natural increase.

Table 6.4

Variations in the Number and Percentage of Jains and Decadal Per cent Population Change in Seven Major States since 1961

States	*1961*	*1971*	*1981*	*1991*	*2001*
			Number of Jains		
Maharashtra	4,85,672	7,03,664	9,39,392	9,65,840	13,01,843
Rajasthan	4,09,417	5,13,548	6,24,317	5,62,806	6,50,493
MP	2,47,927	3,45,211	4,44,960	4,90,324	5,45,446
Gujarat	4,09,754	4,51,578	4,67,508	4,91,331	5,25,305
Karnataka	1,74,366	2,18,862	2,84,508	3,26,114	4,12,659
UP	1,22,108	1,24,728	1,41,549	1,76,259	2,07,111
Delhi	29,595	50,513	73,917	94,672	1,55,122
			Percentage of Total Number of Jains		
Maharashtra	23.96	27.02	29.42	28.98	30.81
Rajasthan	20.22	19.72	19.56	16.89	15.39
MP	12.23	13.25	13.94	13.35	12.91
Gujarat	20.21	17.34	14.65	14.75	12.43
Karnataka	8.60	8.40	8.91	9.79	9.76
UP	6.02	4.79	4.43	5.29	4.90
Delhi	0.07	1.20	1.74	2.24	3.67
			Per cent Population Change During		
	1951–1961	*1961–1971*	*1971–1981*	*1981–1991*	*1991–2001*
Maharashtra	43.87	44.88	33.50	2.82	34.78
Rajasthan	13.80	25.43	21.57	–9.85	15.58
MP	36.73	39.24	28.90	10.20	12.75
Gujarat	9.30	10.21	3.59	5.04	6.90
Karnataka	24.66	25.52	29.99	14.62	26.53
UP	24.93	2.15	13.49	24.52	17.50
Delhi	–	70.68	46.33	28.08	63.85

Source: As in Table 6.1.

Figure 6.4

Percentage of Total Number of Jains in Seven Major States in India, 1961–2001

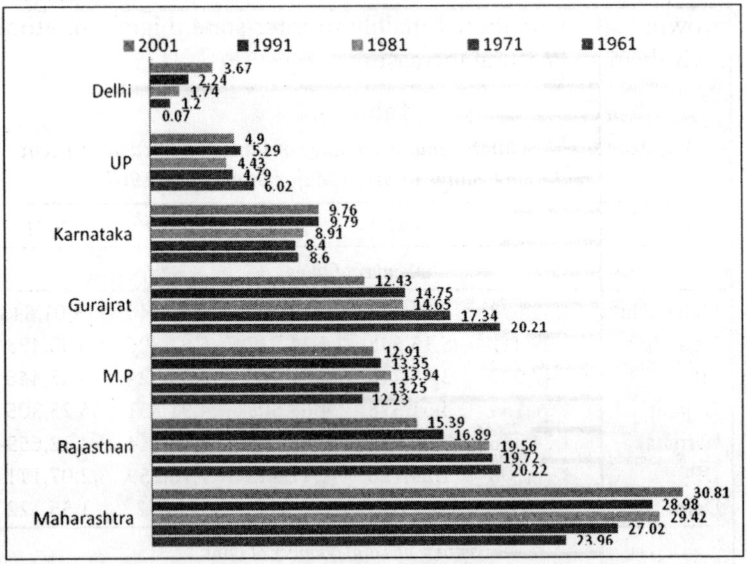

In some of these states a number of districts are there where the Jains constitue the third largest religious community in 2001 census. Data for these districts are presented in Table 6.12 Districts where the Jains constitute the third largest religious group having populatin more than 20,000 are shown in Figure 6.5. Decadal percentage change in total population of Jains and the rural-urban breakup in seven major states are presented in Figures 6.6 and 6.7 respectively.

Urbanization

A highly significant population characteristic of the Jains in India is their high degree of urbanization. Thus, as per 2001 census, 32,15,706 lived in urban areas, whereas only 10,09,347 lived in rural areas. About 64 per cent of the Jains lived in cities and towns in 1981. This figure increased to about 71 per cent in the 1991 census and to about 75 per cent in the 2001 census. Thus, today Jains are the most urbanized religious community in India.

Figure 6.5

Districts Where Jains Constitute the Third Largest Religious Group Having Population More Than 20,000

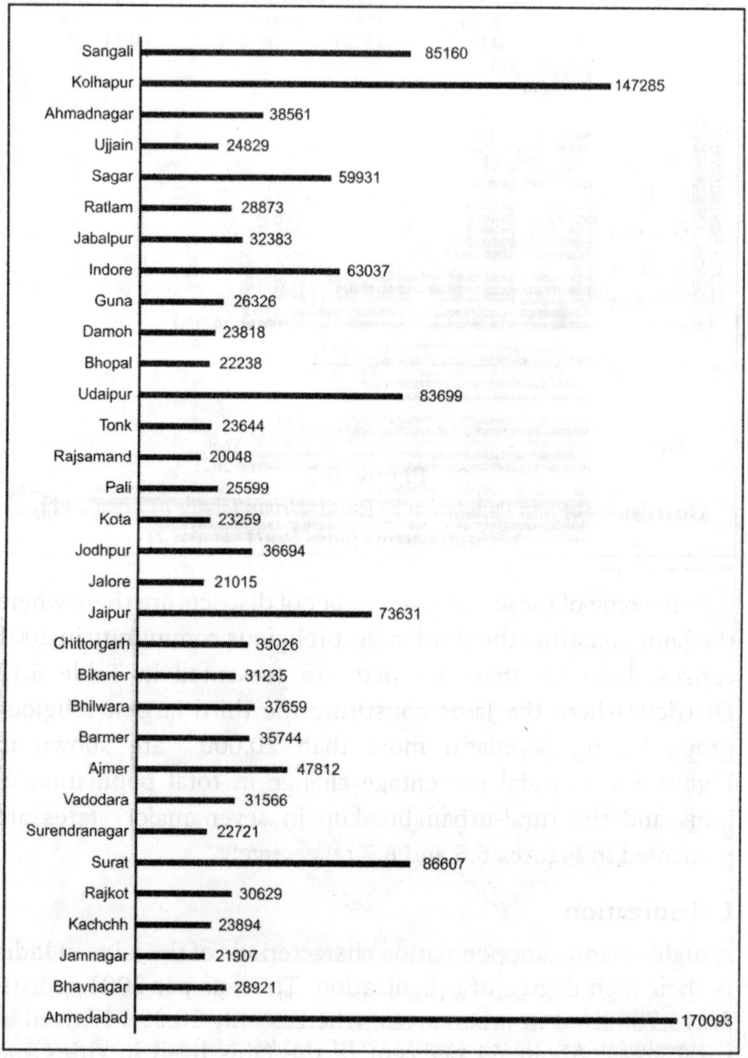

Figure 6.6

Decadal percentage Change of Population of Jains in Seven Major States

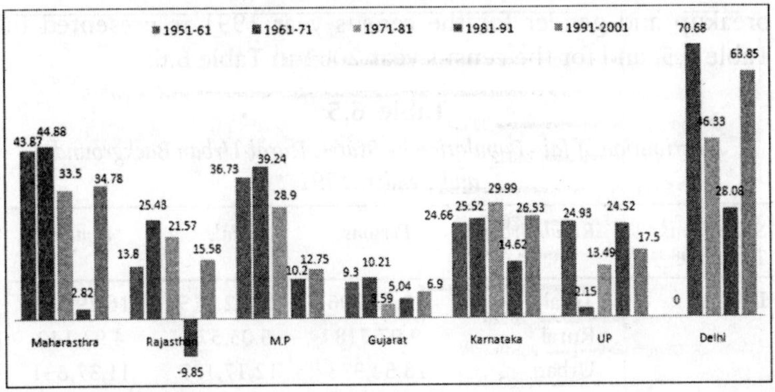

Figure 6.7

Distribution of Jain Population by Rural–Urban Divide in Seven Major States across India, 2001

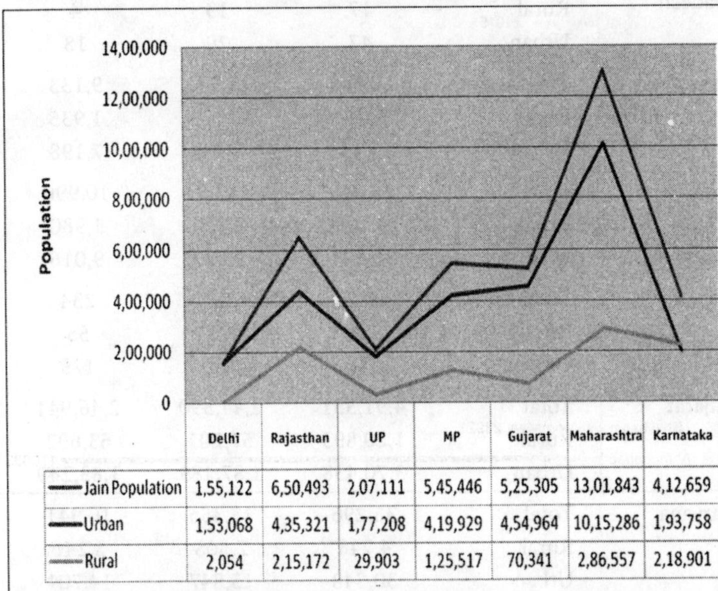

	Delhi	Rajasthan	UP	MP	Gujarat	Maharashtra	Karnataka
Jain Population	1,55,122	6,50,493	2,07,111	5,45,446	5,25,305	13,01,843	4,12,659
Urban	1,53,068	4,35,321	1,77,208	4,19,929	4,54,964	10,15,286	1,93,758
Rural	2,054	2,15,172	29,903	1,25,517	70,341	2,86,557	2,18,901

Apparently this has been so for over a century now. State-wise distribution of the Jain population in terms of rural–urban breakup and gender for the census year 1991 is presented in Table 6.5, and for the census year 2001 in Table 6.6.

Table 6.5

Distribution of Jain Population by States, Rural/Urban Background and Gender, 1991

States/Union Territories	*Rural/Urban*	*Persons*	*Male*	*Female*
INDIA	Total	33,52,706	17,22,715	16,29,991
	Rural	9,97,718	5,05,578	4,92,140
	Urban	23,54,998	12,17,137	11,37,851
States				
Andhra Pradesh	Total	26,564	14,103	12,461
	Rural	1,092	594	498
	Urban	25,472	13,509	11,963
Arunachal Pradesh	Total	64	42	22
	Rural	17	13	4
	Urban	47	29	18
Assam	Total	20,645	11,512	9,133
	Rural	4,512	2.577	1,935
	Urban	16,133	8,935	7,198
Bihar	Total	23.049	12.053	10,996
	Rural	4,208	2,228	1,980
	Urban	18.841	9,825	9,016
Goa	Total	487	253	234
	Rural	128	73	55
	Urban	359	180	179
Gujarat	Total	4,91,331	2,44,390	2,46,941
	Rural	1,20,893	57,201	63,692
	Urban	3,70,438	1,87,189	1,83,249
Haryana	Total	35,296	18,355	16,941
	Rural	4,748	2,508	2,240
	Urban	30,548	15,847	14,701

Cont'd...

...Cont'd

States/Union Territories	*Rural/Urban*	*Persons*	*Male*	*Female*
Himachal Pradesh	Total	1,206	640	566
	Rural	121	62	59
	Urban	1,085	578	507
Karnataka	Total	3,26,114	1,68,824	1,57,290
	Rural	1,88,389	96,328	92,061
	Urban	1,37,725	72,496	65,229
Kerala	Total	3,641	1,837	1,804
	Rural	1,499	742	751
	Urban	2,142	1,095	1,047
Madhya Pradesh	Total	4,90,324	2,55,189	2,35,135
	Rural	1,28,049	66,843	61,206
	Urban	3,62,275	1,88,346	1,73,229
Maharashtra	Total	9,65,840	4,99,729	4,66,111
	Rural	2,63,514	1,36,377	1,27,137
	Urban	7,02,326	3,63,352	3,38,974
Manipur	Total	1,337	706	631
	Rural	27	11	16
	Urban	1,310	695	615
Meghalaya	Total	445	254	191
	Rural	49	26	23
	Urban	396	228	161
Mizoram	Total	4	4	–
	Rural	–	–	–
	Urban	4	4	–
Nagaland	Total	1,202	690	512
	Rural	12	9	3
	Urban	1,190	681	509
Orissa	Total	6,302	3,328	2,974
	Rural	1,938	1,011	927
	Urban	4,364	2,317	2,047

Cont'd...

...Cont'd

States/Union Territories	*Rural/Urban*	*Persons*	*Male*	*Female*
Punjab	Total	20,763	10,662	10,101
	Rural	1,327	675	652
	Urban	19,436	9,987	9,449
Rajasthan	Total	5,62,806	2,84,198	2,78,658
	Rural	2,20,718	1,08,905	1,11,813
	Urban	3,42,088	1,75,243	1,66,845
Sikkim	Total	40	26	14
	Rural	–	–	–
	Urban	40	26	14
Tamil Nadu	Total	66,900	34,882	32,018
	Rural	12,415	6,148	6,267
	Urban	54,485	28,734	25,751
Tripura	Total	301	181	120
	Rural	85	57	28
	Urban	216	124	92
Uttar Pradesh	Total	1,76,259	91,999	84,260
	Rural	37,406	19,727	17,679
	Urban	1,38,853	72,272	66,581
West Bengal	Total	34,355	18,326	16,029
	Rural	5,223	2,744	2,479
	Urban	29,132	15,582	13,550
Union Territories				
Andaman and Nicobar Island	Total	17	8	9
	Rural	13	6	7
	Urban	4	2	2
Chandigarh	Total	1,531	804	727
	Rural	47	27	20
	Urban	1,484	777	707
Dadra and Nagar Haveli	Total	529	267	262
	Rural	290	140	150
	Urban	239	127	112

Cont'd...

...Cont'd

States/Union Territories	*Rural/Urban*	*Persons*	*Male*	*Female*
Daman & Diu	Total	212	115	97
	Rural	9	8	1
	Urban	203	107	96
Delhi	Total	94,672	49,120	45,552
	Rural	989	538	451
	Urban	93,683	48,582	45,101
Lakshadweep	Total	–	–	–
	Rural	–	–	–
	Urban	–	–	–
Pondicherry	Total	470	268	202
	Rural	–	–	–
	Urban	470	268	202

Source: Adapted From Census of India, 1991; Paper I of 1995, Religion, Registrar-General and Census Commissioner, New Delhi, 1995, pp. 6, 10 and 14.

Table 6.6

Distribution of Jain Population by Rural–Urban Background, 2001

States/Union Territories	*Total Population*	*Jain Population*	*Urban*	*Rural*
INDIA	1,02,86,10,328	42,25,053	32,15,706	10,09,347
Jammu and Kashmir	1,01,43,700	2,518	2,040	478
Himachal Pradesh	60,77,900	1,408	1,148	260
Punjab	2,43,58,999	39,276	37,265	2,011
Chandigarh	9,00,635	2,592	2,570	22
Uttaranchal	84,89,349	9,249	8,167	1,082
Haryana	2,11,44,564	57,167	50,829	6,338
Delhi	1,38,50,507	1,55,122	1,53,068	2,054
Rajasthan	5,65,07,188	6,50,493	4,35,321	2,15,172
Uttar Pradesh	16,61,97,921	2,07,111	1,77,208	29,903

Cont'd...

...Cont'd

States/Union Territories	*Total Population*	*Jain Population*	*Urban*	*Rural*
Bihar	8,29,98,509	16,085	12,903	3,182
Sikkim	5,40,851	183	126	57
Arunachal Pradesh	10,97,968	216	130	86
Nagaland	19,90,036	2,093	1,984	109
Manipur	21,66,788	1,461	1,369	92
Mizoram	8,88,573	179	45	134
Tripura	31,99,203	477	287	190
Meghalaya	23,18,822	772	432	340
Assam	2,66,55,528	23,957	20,354	3,603
West Bengal	8,01,76,197	55,223	45,869	9,354
Jharkhand	2,69,45,829	16,301	11,688	4,613
Orissa	3,68,04,660	9,154	6,038	3,116
Chhattisgarh	2,08,33,803	56,103	45,837	10,266
Madhya Pradesh	6,03,48,023	5,45,446	4,19,929	125,517
Gujarat	5,06,71,017	5,25,305	4,54,964	70,341
Daman and Diu	1,58,204	268	212	56
Dadra and Nagar Haveli	2,20,490	864	601	263
Maharashtra	9,68,78,627	13,01,843	10,15,286	286,557
Andhra Pradesh	7,62,10,007	41,846	39,856	1,990
Karnataka	5,28,50,562	4,12,659	1,93,758	218,901
Goa	13,47,668	820	721	99
Lakshadweep	60,650	–	–	–
Kerala	3,18,41,374	4,528	2,328	2,200
Tamil Nadu	6,24,05,679	83,359	72,427	10,932
Pondicherry	9,74,345	952	928	24
Andaman and Nicobar Islands	3,56,152	23	18	5

Source: Census of India (2001).

Sex Ratio and Child Sex Ratio

The 1991 census data reveal that of the 33,52,706 Jains, 17,22,715 were males and 16,29,991 females. The sex ratio (females per 1,000 males) thus comes to 946 which suggest a slight improvement over that for the census year 1981 that is 941. The sex ratio among the Jains was thus found to be better vis-à-vis Hindus (925), Muslims (930) and Sikhs (888) but worse than that among the Christians (994) and Buddhists (952) (Figure 6.8). Unfortunately, this gain was wiped out in the 2001 census in which case there were only 20,47,655 females for 21,77,398 males. Thus, the sex ratio among the Jains in 2001 declined to only 940.

Among the major states Kerala has returned the highest sex ratio of 996 for Jains. In Gujarat and Rajasthan also sex ratio of Jains is high at 969 and 966 respectively. In twenty states Jain population has sex ratio between 901 and 950.[5]

Figure 6.8

Sex Ratio and Child Sex Ratio among Various Religious Communities, 2001

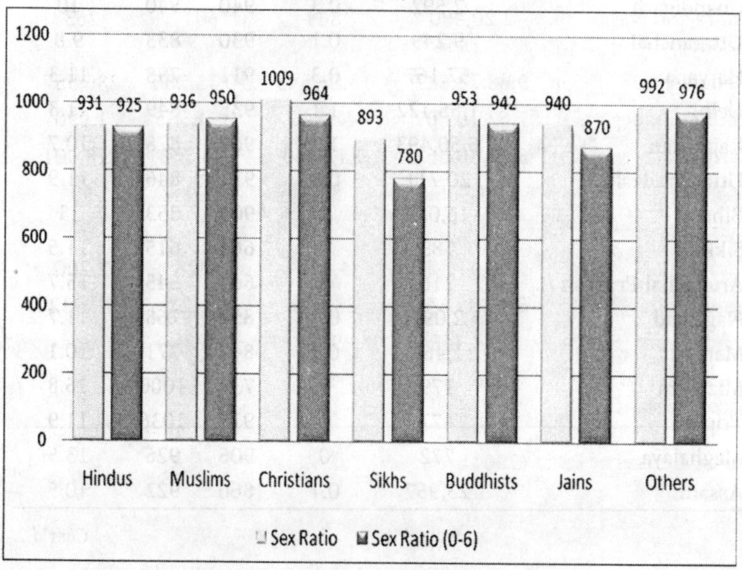

Even more alarming aspect of sex ratio among the Jains is the sharp decline of sex ratio in the 0–6 age group which is only 870 compared to 927 for all religious communities in India, 925 for Hindus and 950 for Muslims (Figure 6.8). In terms of state-wise distribution, 16 states and union territories had a child sex ratio below 850 among the Jains.[6] Among the major states having large Jain population sex ratio in the age group 0–6 is low at 832 in Gujarat, 878 in Rajasthan and 906 in Madhya Pradesh (Table 6.7).

Table 6.7

Sex Ratio among the Jains, 2001

States/ Union Territories	*Jain Population*	*Proportion of Jain Population*	*Sex Ratio*	*Sex Ratio (0–6)*	*Proportion of Child Population in the Age Group 0–6 Years*
INDIA	42,25,053	0.4	940	870	10.6
Jammu and Kashmir	2,518	0	856	887	10.9
Himachal Pradesh	1,408	0	877	644	10.5
Punjab	39,276	0.2	914	758	10.2
Chandigarh	2,592	0.3	940	940	10
Uttaranchal	9,249	0.1	930	833	9.8
Haryana	57,167	0.3	911	798	11.3
Delhi	1,55,122	1.1	935	849	11.3
Rajasthan	6,50,493	1.2	960	878	10.7
Uttar Pradesh	20,711	0.1	911	846	11.9
Bihar	16,085	0	904	853	11
Sikkim	183	0	664	615	11.5
Arunachal Pradesh	216	0	662	545	15.7
Nagaland	2,093	0.1	852	768	11.7
Manipur	1,461	0.1	842	771	10.1
Mizoram	179	0	738	1000	16.8
Tripura	477	0	916	1036	11.9
Meghalaya	772	0	906	926	13.5
Assam	23,957	0.1	866	922	10.5

Cont'd...

...Cont'd

States/ Union Territories	*Jain Population*	*Proportion of Jain Population*	*Sex Ratio*	*Sex Ratio (0–6)*	*Proportion of Child Population in the Age Group 0–6 Years*
West Bengal	55,223	0.1	929	920	9.6
Jharkhand	16,301	0,1	928	852	11.1
Orissa	9,154	0	933	895	10.8
Chhattisgarh	56,103	0.3	922	922	11.7
Madhya Pradesh	5,45,446	0.9	925	906	11.3
Gujarat	5,25,305	1	969	832	9.2
Daman and Diu	268	0.2	1,000	1,071	10.8
Dadra and Nagar Haveli	864	0.4	895	831	13.8
Maharashtra	13,01,843	1.3	942	862	10.1
Andhra Pradesh	41,846	0.1	936	912	11.3
Karnataka	4,12,659	0.8	926	892	12
Goa	820	0.1	885	867	11.5
Lakshadweep	–	–	–	–	–
Kerala	4,528	0	996	845	9.7
Tamil Nadu	83,359	0.1	933	889	10.8
Pondicherry	952	0.1	900	692	11.6
Andaman and Nicobar Islands	23	0	917	500	13

Source: Census of India (2001).

On another measure, that is, the proportion of child population in the age group 0–6 years to the total population, the Jains are again lagging behind all other religious communities in India (Table 6.7). Thus, Jains had the lowest proportion of child population (10.6%) compared with the national average (15.9%), Hindus (15.6%), Muslims (18.7%), Christians (13.5%), Sikhs (12.8%) and Buddhists (14.4%).

The proportion of population in the age group 0–6 among the Jains reveals that among the major states Karnataka accounts for highest proportion of 12 percent which is far below the national average. Gujarat has the lowest proportion of 9.2 percent. Low fertility trend among the Jains is evident from the fact that except two states all other states have child population proportion below 14 percent. Jains have reported the lowest child population 9.2 percent in Gujarat followed by West Bengal (9.6%) among the major states.[7]

In the absence of any study on the subject, the causes of declining sex ratio among the Jains are not easy to find. Apparently the prevalence of female foeticide could be one factor in this regard. Female child *diksha* and discouragement of widow remarriage in the community could also be the contributing factors (See Sangave, 1980: 29–30). Needless to say, this decline in sex ratio has begun to give rise to a number of marital and social problems among the Jains that in turn have been contributing factors in lowering the sex ratio – a vicious circle indeed.

Literacy, Work Participation and Occupation

Literacy-wise, in 2001 Jains with a figure of 94.1 per cent were the most literate community, followed by Christians at 80.3 per cent, Buddhists 72.7 per cent, Sikhs 69.4 per cent, Hindus 65.1 per cent and Muslims 59.1 per cent (Table 6.8 and Figure 6.9). It

Table 6.8

Literacy, Female Literacy and Work Participation Rate in India by Religious Communities

Religious Communities	*Literacy Rate*	*Female Literacy Rate*	*Work Participation*
Hindus	65.1	53.2	40.4
Muslims	59.1	50.1	31.3
Christians	80.3	76.2	39.7
Sikhs	69.4	63.1	37.7
Buddhists	72.7	61.7	40.6
Jains	94.1	90.6	32.9
Others	47.0	–	48.4
Total/Average	64.4	–	39.1

Source: Census of India, 2001.

Figure 6.9

Literacy, Female Literacy and Work Participation Rate in India by Religious Communities, 2001

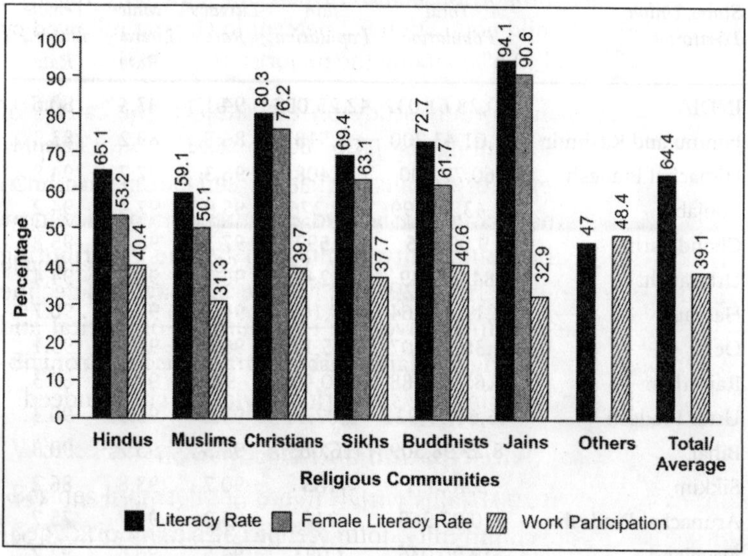

must be noted that in as many as 29 states of India, the literacy rate among the Jains is above 90 per cent. The national average for literacy is 64.8 per cent. In all the religious communities, female literacy was found to be lower than the male literacy by about 11 percentage points. It stood at 53.7 per cent. In female literacy too, the Jains take the lead with a figure of 90.6 per cent, followed by Christians (76.2%), Sikhs (63.1%), Buddhists (61.7%), Hindus (53.2%) and Muslims (50.1%). In 29 states and union territories, the female literacy among the Jains is 80 per cent or above (Table 6.9). According to the report of the Registrar General and Census Commissioner of India, 'the Jains are likely to reach the goal of universal literacy for the total population any time now'.[8]

Along with the highest literacy rate, the work participation rate (WPR) or percentage of workers to total population is also highest among the Jain males (55.2%) followed by Sikhs (53.3%)

Table 6.9

Literacy Rate among the Jains by States/Union Territories, 2001

States/Union Territories	*Total Population*	*Jain Population*	*Literacy Rate*	*Male Literacy Rate*	*Female Literacy Rate*
INDIA	10,28,61,032	42,25,053	94.1	97.4	90.6
Jammu and Kashmir	1,01,43,700	2,518	86.5	89.2	83.3
Himachal Pradesh	60,77,900	1,408	96.3	97.7	94.8
Punjab	2,43,58,999	39,276	95.9	97.4	94.2
Chandigarh	9,00,635	2,592	97.3	98.7	95.8
Uttaranchal	84,89,349	9,249	96.3	98.2	94.4
Haryana	2,11,44,564	57,167	94.2	97.4	90.7
Delhi	1,38,50,507	1,55,122	96.8	98.5	95.1
Rajasthan	5,65,07,188	6,50,493	94	98.6	89.3
Uttar Pradesh	16,61,97,921	2,07,11	93.2	95.9	90.3
Bihar	8,29,98,509	16,085	93.3	95.7	90.8
Sikkim	5,40,851	183	90.7	93.8	86.2
Arunachal Pradesh	10,97,968	216	85.2	91.7	75.7
Nagaland	19,90,036	2,093	94.5	96.6	92.2
Manipur	21,66,788	1,461	94.5	95.4	93.5
Mizoram	8,88,573	179	61.7	65.9	55.7
Tripura	31,99,203	477	82.9	86.9	78.4
Meghalaya	23,18,822	772	69.9	74.1	65.3
Assam	2,66,55,528	23,957	95.3	97.2	93
West Bengal	8,01,76,197	55,223	92.8	96.5	88.9
Jharkhand	2,69,45,829	16,301	90.9	95.6	86
Orissa	3,68,04,660	9,154	93.3	96.6	89.6
Chhattisgarh	2,08,33,803	56,103	96.8	98.7	94.8
Madhya Pradesh	6,03,48,023	5,45,446	96.2	98.5	93.6
Gujarat	5,06,71,017	5,25,305	96	98.4	93.5
Daman and Diu	1,58,204	268	94.6	97.5	91.6
Dadra and Nagar Haveli	2,20,490	864	94.4	97.7	90.7
Maharashtra	9,68,78,627	13,01,843	95.4	98.3	92.3
Andhra Pradesh	7,62,10,007	41,846	93.2	96.5	89.6
Karnataka	5,28,50,562	4,12,659	84.3	90.9	77.2

Cont'd...

...Cont'd

States/Union Territories	*Total Population*	*Jain Population*	*Literacy Rate*	*Male Literacy Rate*	*Female Literacy Rate*
Goa	13,47,668	820	95.7	96.3	95.2
Lakshadweep	60,650	–	–	–	–
Kerala	3,18,41,374	4,528	95.5	97.6	93.4
Tamil Nadu	6,24,05,679	83,359	92.2	95.8	88.4
Pondicherry	9,74,345	952	96.3	98.9	93.6
Andaman and Nicobar Islands	3,56,152	23	100	100	100

Source: Census of India, 2001.

and Hindus (52.4%); the WPR for all religious communities being 39.1 per cent in the 2001 census (Table 6.10). The lowest WPR for the male population is found among the Muslim males (47.5%). In spite of the highest literacy rate among the Jain females however, their WPR in 2001 census was the lowest (9.2%) preceded by Muslims (14.1%) and Hindus (27.5%). Thus, there exists a sharp gender gap in regard to WPR among the Jains.

Table 6.10

Distribution of Category of Workers by Religious Communities, 2001

Religious Communities	*Cultivators*	*Agricultural Labourers*	*Household Industry Workers*	*Others*	*Total*
Hindus	33.1	27.6	3.8	35.5	100
Muslims	20.7	22.0	8.1	49.1	100
Christians	29.2	15.3	2.7	52.8	100
Sikhs	32.4	16.8	3.4	47.3	100
Buddhists	20.4	37.6	2.9	39.2	100
Jains	11.7	3.3	3.3	81.7	100
Others	49.9	32.6	3.2	14.3	100
Average	31.7	26.5	4.2	37.6	100

Source: Census of India, 2001.

Figure 6.10

Religious Communities and Their Occupations, 2001

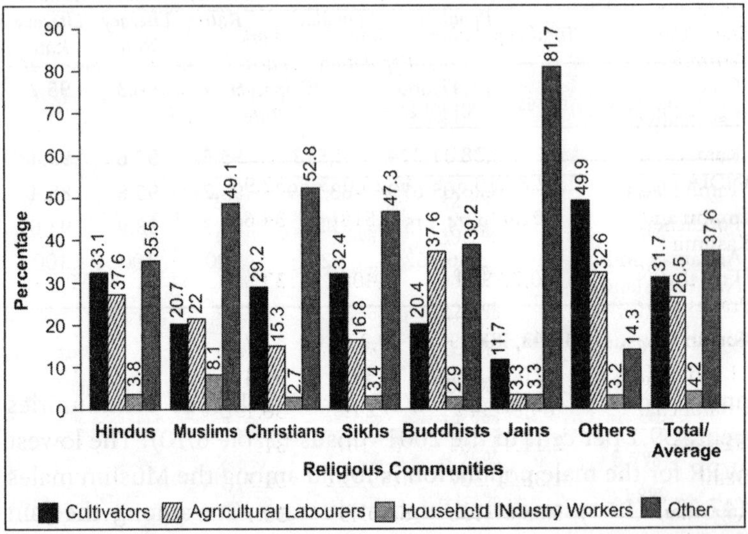

Distribution of the Jain population in terms of the four work participation categories, namely, cultivators, agricultural labourers, household industry workers and other workers was heavily skewed in favour of the last category which included workers in trade and commerce, banking and allied activities, and employees in government and private sectors. In this category, 81.7 per cent Jains were employed, whereas 11.7 per cent were engaged as cultivators, 3.3 per cent as agricultural labourers, and less than 3.0 per cent as household industry workers (Table 6.10; Figure 6.10). Thus, the business class character of the Jain community is evident from the 2001 census data.

Conclusion

The Jains have always been a minority community in India in modern times. Since the 1881 census, the Jains seldom constituted more than half a per cent of the total population of India. In 2001 census the population of Jains is estimated

Table 6.11

Work Participation Rate among the Jains by States, 2001

States/Union Territories	*Total Population*	*Jain Population*	*Work Participation Rate*	*Male Work Participation Rate*	*Female Work Participation Rate*
INDIA	1,02,86,10,328	42,25,053	32.9	55.2	9.2
Jammu and Kashmir	1,01,43,700	2,518	34.6	55.9	9.8
Himachal Pradesh	60,77,900	1,408	33.8	54.5	10.2
Punjab	2,43,58,999	39,276	32.7	56.1	7.2
Chandigarh	9,00,635	2,592	34.4	54.5	13
Uttaranchal	84,89,349	9,249	30.1	51.1	7.4
Haryana	2,11,44,564	57,167	31.1	52.6	7.4
Delhi	1,38,50,507	1,55,122	31.2	54.4	6.3
Rajasthan	5,65,07,188	6,50,493	30.1	52	7.3
Uttar Pradesh	16,61,97,921	2,07,11	28.8	50.1	5.5
Bihar	8,29,98,509	16,085	29.9	53.2	4.2
Sikkim	5,40,851	183	38.3	54.5	13.7
Arunachal Pradesh	10,97,968	216	42.6	55.4	23.3
Nagaland	19,90,036	2,093	33.7	57.5	5.6
Manipur	21,66,788	1,461	37.6	55.6	16.3
Mizoram	8,88,573	179	60.9	69.9	48.7
Tripura	31,99,203	477	41.1	64.3	15.8
Meghalaya	23,18,822	772	48.1	63	31.6
Assam	2,66,55,528	23,957	32.9	57.1	5
West Bengal	8,01,76,197	55,223	32.9	56.5	7.5
Jharkhand	2,69,45,829	16,301	30.5	52.4	6.8
Orissa	3,68,04,660	9,154	30.5	54.1	5.2
Chhattisgarh	2,08,33,803	56,103	30.7	54.1	5.4
Madhya Pradesh	6,03,48,023	5,45,446	31.4	53.7	7.4
Gujarat	5,06,71,017	5,25,305	31.9	56.2	6.8
Daman and Diu	1,58,204	268	36.9	66.4	7.5

Cont'd...

...Cont'd

States/Union Territories	*Total Population*	*Jain Population*	*Work Participation Rate*	*Male Work Participation Rate*	*Female Work Participation Rate*
Dadra and Nagar Haveli	2,20,490	864	35.8	59.4	9.3
Maharashtra	9,68,78,627	13,01,843	34.5	57	10.6
Andhra Pradesh	7,62,10,007	41,846	30.4	55.3	3.9
Karnataka	5,28,50,562	4,12,659	39.3	58.2	18.8
Goa	13,47,668	820	37.1	60	11.2
Lakshadweep	60,650	–	–	–	–
Kerala	3,18,41,374	4,528	36	59.7	12.3
Tamil Nadu	6,24,05,679	83,359	32.3	55.3	7.7
Pondicherry	9,74,345	952	32	55.5	6
Andaman and Nicobar Islands	3,56,152	23	30.4	58.3	–

Source: Census of India, 2001.

Table 6.12

Districts Where the Jains Constitute the Third Largest Religious Group, 2001

States/Districts	*Jain Population*	*States/Districts*	*Jain Population*
Gujarat	**5,25,305**	**Madhya Pradesh**	**5,45,448**
Ahmedabad	1,70,093	Bhopal	22,238
Amreli	2,309	Chhatarpur	9,766
Banaskantha	18,544	Damoh	23,818
Bhavnagar	28,921	Dewas	6,767
Gandhinagar	7,769	Dhar	12,397
Jamnagar	21,907	Guna	26,326
Junagarh	4,291	Harda	1,505
Kachchh	23,894	Indore	63,037
Mehsana	7,122	Jabalpur	32,3838
Navsari	13,575	Katni	5,307
Panchmahal	4,382	Mandsaur	19,519
Patan	5,136	Morena	7,177

Cont'd...

...Cont'd

States/Districts	*Jain Population*	*States/Districts*	*Jain Population*
Porbandar	589	Narsinghpur	8,178
Rajkot	30,629	Neemuch	14,626
Sabarkantha	11,198	Panna	4,534
Surat	86,607	Raisen	10,459
Surendranagar	22,721	Rajgarh	1,854
Vadodara	31,566	Ratlam	28,873
Rajasthan	6,50,493	Sagar	59,931
Ajmer	47,812	Satna	3,162
Banswara	18,406	Sehore	5,936
Barmer	35,744	Shajapur	13,536
Bhilwara	37,659	Shivpuri	12,093
Bikaner	31,235	Tikamgarh	14,604
Bundi	13,186	Ujjain	24,829
Chittorgarh	35,026	Vidisha	17,757
Churu	13,882	West Nimar	6,273
Dausa	3,908	**Maharashtra**	13,01,843
Dungar	12,542	Ahmednagar	38,561
Dholpur	2,685	Kolhapur	147,285
Jaipur	73,631	Sangli	85,160
Jalore	21,015	**Uttar Pradesh**	2,07,111
Jhalawar	11,759	Agra	18,463
Jodhpur	36,694	Baghpat	17,929
Karauli	3,760	Banda	884
Kota	23,259	Etawa	3,176
Nagaur	17,478	Firozabad	19,237
Pali	25,599	Jhansi	7,620
Rajsamand	20,048	Lalitpur	19,797
Sawai Madhopur	10,660	**Delhi**	No district is qualified
Sikar	3,957		
Sirohi	12,427	**Karnataka**	No district is qualified
Tonk	23,644		
Udaipur	83,699		

Source: Census of India, 2001.

around 4.2 million. They are heavily concentrated in the western half of India, particularly Maharashtra, Rajasthan, Madhya Pradesh, Gujarat, Karnataka, Uttar Pradesh and Delhi. About 2,50,000 Jains are in diaspora, mainly in North America, the United Kingdom and East Africa. Close to 75 per cent of Jains live in urban areas. Other demographic features include very high level of literacy, the lowest infant mortality rate and the medium level of sex ratio (940 in 2001 compared to 931 for Hindus and 950 for Muslims). During the 1981–1991 decade, the Jain population had increased very slowly, that is, at the rate of only 4.42 per cent compared to 23.17 per cent for the previous decade. This confirmed the urban middle class character of the community.

Two major demographic challenges that the Jain community in India is facing today are the very low rate of population growth and the declining sex ratio not only among the adults but also among the younger generation. Both these trends are quite evident from the data available from the 1991 and 2001 census reports. Although due to ethnic revivalism, the decadal growth rate of the Jain population during the 1991–2001 decade has jumped to 26 per cent, in all probability it will come down to around 4.0 per cent by the next census year in 2011. The sex ratio among the Jains is also likely to further drop slightly by that time.

Notes and References

1. Census of India, 1991, Paper No, 1 of 1995, Religion (New Delhi: RGO, 1995).
2. Census of India, 2001, First Report of Religion Data (New Delhi: RGO, 2004).
3. Census of India, 1961, Paper No. 1 of 1963, Religion (New Delhi: RGO, 1963), pp. ii–viii; Census of India, 1971, Paper No. 2 of 1972, Religion (New Delhi: RGO, 1972), pp. 2–5; Census of India, 1981, Paper No. 4 of 1984, Household Population by Religion of Head of Household (New Delhi: RGO, 1984), p. 26

(figures amended as per Errata issued subsequently by this office).

4. Rema Nagarajan, 'How, or Why Hindus Are Losing the Races?', *The Hindustan Times*, 9 September 2004.
5. Census of India, 2001, op. cit., p. xviii.
6. Ibid.
7. Ibid., p. xx.
8. Ibid., p. xxi.

7

Jain Population and Demography, 2011

Prakash C. Jain

Based on the 2011 census data, this chapter mainly focusses on the Jain demography of the first decade of the twenty-first century. In much of the analysis of the 2011 data, a comparative account with 2001 data therefore has been necessary. The chapter also serves to highlight historical and/or long range trends of certain population characteristics. Efforts have also been made to provide as much data as possible in order to facilitate a better demographic understanding of the Jain community. As in 1991 and 2001 censuses, the 2011 census data on religion too are based on the response of individual members of the household and not on the response of the head of the household as in the case of 1981 census.

Population Size

As per census of India 2011, the total geographical area of India is 32,87,469 sq km consisting of 21,01,199.82 sq km as rural and

Table 7.1

Jains: Variations in the Number, Decadal Per cent Change, Urbanization and Sex Ratio Since 1881

Census	*Number of Jains (in 000s)*	*Percentage of Total Population*	*Decadal Per cent Change in the Number of Jains*	*Urbanization (%)*	*Sex Ratio*
1881	1,222	0.49	–	–	–
1891	1,417	0.51	15.94	–	–
1901	1,334	0.47	–5.83	30	929
1911	1,248	0.41	–6.47	29.6	940
1921	1,177	0.39	–5.26	33.9	931
1931	1,251	0.37	6.28	34.6	940
1941	1,440	0.37	15.81	41.4	930
1951	1,618	0.45	11.67	–	927
1961	2,027	0.46	25.17	53.9	924
1971	2,605	0.47	28.48	59.8	940
1981*	3,206	0.48	23.17	64	941
1991**	3,352	0.4	4.42	71	946
2001	4,225	0.4	26	75	940
2011	4,451	0.37	5.4	79.7	954

*Excluding Assam where census was not held in 1981 owing to disturbed conditions.

**Excluding Jammu and Kashmir where 1991 census was not held.

Sources: 1. Kingsley Davis, *Population of India and Pakistan* (New York: Russell and Russell, 1951), pp. 178–179.

2. Census of India, 1961, Paper No. 1 of 1963, Religion (New Delhi: RGO, 1963), pp. ii–viii.

3. Census of Indian, 1971, Paper No. 2 of 1972, Religion (New Delhi: RGO, 1972), pp. 2–5.

4. Census of India, 1981, Paper No. 4 of 1984, Household Population by Religion of Head of Household (New Delhi: RGO, 1984), p. 26 (figures amended as per Errata issued subsequently by this office).

5. Census of India, 1991, Paper No. 1 of 1995, Religion (New Delhi: RGO, 1995).

6. Census of India, 2001, First Report of Religion Data (New Delhi: RGO, 2005).

7. Most 2011 census data in this chapter are taken from Dheeraj Jain (2017).

1,02,526.18 sq km urban area. With a population of 1,21,08,54,977 in 2011, the density of population per square kilometre is 382.

In 1881, the total Jain population was enumerated at 12,21,896 or 0.48 per cent of the total Indian population. Since then the Jains have seldom constituted more than half a per cent of the total population of India (See Table 7.1). With the enumeration of 4.45 million (0.37%) Jains in the 2011 census of India, they still constitute the smallest religious community in the country. The corresponding figures for other religious communities are Hindus 966.62 million (79.80%), Muslims 172.2 million (14.23%), Christians 27.80 million (2.3%), Sikhs 20.8 million (1.72%), Buddhists 8.44 million (0.7%) and other religious communities 10.8 million (0.89%). Distribution of the population of the Jains and other religious communities by rural-urban break up and gender, is prsented in Tables 7.2 and 7.3 respectively.

Table 7.2

Population of India by Religious Communities and Rural–Urban Distribution, 2011

Religion	*Total Population*	*% of Total*	*Rural*	*% of Rural*	*Urban*	*% of Urban*
Total	1,21,08,54,977	100	83,37,48,852	68.86	37,71,06,125	31.14
Hindu	96,62,57,353	79.80	68,40,93,951	70.80	28,21,63,402	29.20
Muslim	17,22,45,158	14.23	10,35,04,739	60.09	6,87,40,419	39.91
Christian	2,78,19,588	2.30	1,66,57,065	59.88	1,11,62,523	40.12
Sikh	2,08,33,116	1.72	1,49,30,792	71.67	59,02,324	28.33
Buddhist	84,42,972	0.70	48,14,849	57.03	36,28,123	42.97
Jain	44,51,753	0.37	9,04,809	20.32	35,46,944	79.68
Other*	79,37,734	0.66	71,99,007	90.69	7,38,727	9.31
Religion not stated	28,67,303	0.23	16,43,640	57.32	12,23,663	42.68

*Other religions and persuasions.

Table 7.3

Population of India by Religious Communities and Gender

Religion	*Total Population*	*% of Total*	*Male*	*% of Male*	*Female*	*% of Female*
Total	1,21,08,54,977	100	62,32,70,258	100.00	58,75,84,719	100
Hindu	96,62,57,353	79.80	49,83,06,968	79.95	46,79,50,385	79.64
Muslim	17,22,45,158	14.23	8,82,73,945	14.16	8,39,71,213	14.29
Christian	2,78,19,588	2.30	1,37,51,031	2.21	1,40,68,557	2.39
Sikh	2,08,33,116	1.72	1,09,48,431	1.76	98,84,685	1.68
Buddhist	84,42,972	0.70	42,96,010	0.69	41,46,962	0.71
Jain	44,51,753	0.37	22,78,097	0.37	21,73,656	0.37
Other*	79,37,734	0.66	39,52,064	0.63	39,85,670	0.68
Religion not stated	28,67,303	0.24	14,63,712	0.23	14,03,591	0.24

*Other religions and persuasions.

Population Growth Rate

Since at least the 1931 census, the Jain population has been growing at varying rates ranging from 4.4 per cent during 1981–1991 decade to 28.48 per cent during 1961–1971 decade. In spite of these however, 1991 and 2011 growth rate data clearly reveal the lowest population growth rate among the Jains vis-à-vis other communities (Table 7.5). The jump in the Jain population in 2001 census as explained in the previous chapter was a short-term phenomenon.[1] The 2011 population growth rate clearly confirms the middle class character of the Jain community.

However, the birth rate still continues to be low among the Jains. Thus, the proportion of child population (0–6 age group) among the Jains was found to be only 10.6 per cent in 2001 and 8.89 per cent in 2011, which the Commissioner's report of the 2001 census attributed to 'low fertility' in the community.[2] Comparative figures for the year 2001 for Hindus, Muslims, Christians, Sikhs and Buddhists were 15.9 per cent, 15.6 per cent,

13.5 per cent, 12.8 per cent and 14.4 per cent respectively. The total fertility rate (TFR) among the Jains was estimated to be 1.6 for the year 2011 as against the national average of 2.17.

Population Variation by States/Union Territories

Table 7.4 presents data regarding distribution of Jain population by states and union territories for six consecutive census years since 1961. The variation in Jain population across the states and union territories has not obviously been uniform. Data in this table clearly suggest that in the 2001 census all the states and union territories showed varying percentage of increase in the Jain population. The same cannot be said about the 2001–2011 period as the Jain population has decreased in eight states and union territories mainly Rajasthan, Haryana, Jharkhand, Uttarakhand, Kerala, Jammu and Kashmir, Chandigarh and Meghalaya. It must be noted however that for the first time in 2011 census, the Jain population has been recorded in all the states and union territories of India (Table 7.4).

As in previous censuses, in 2011 census too, a vast majority of Jain population continues to live in western half of the country. Among the union territories, the largest number of Jains lived in Delhi: about 94,600 in 1991, 1,55,122 in 2001 and 1,66,231 in 2011. In other union territories, namely Chandigarh, Dadra and Nagar Haveli, Pondicherry, Daman and Diu, Andaman and Nicobar Islands and Lakshadweep only 4,675 Jains were enumerated in 2011 census (Table 7.4).

Concentration in Ten States/Union Territories

Table 7.4 presents data about variations in the number of Jains in all the states/union territories, in India. In 2011 census, the top ten states/union territories with largest concentration of Jain population were as follows: Maharashtra, Rajasthan, Gujarat, Madhya Pradesh, Karnataka, Uttar Pradesh, Delhi, Tamil Nadu, Chhattisgarh and West Bengal. About 95 per cent of the total Jain populations is concentrated in these 10 states/union territories.

Table 7.4

Distribution of Jain Population by States/Union Territories, 1961–2011

States/Union Territories	*1961*	*1971*	*1981*	*1991*	*2001*	*2011*
INDIA	20,27,281	26,04,646	32,06,038	33,52,706	42,25,053	44,51,753
Maharashtra	4,85,672	7,03,664	9,39,392	9,65,840	13,01,843	14,00,349
Rajasthan	4,09,417	5,13,548	6,24,317	5,62,806	6,50,493	6,22,023
Gujarat	4,09,754	4,51,578	4,67,768	4,91,331	5,25,305	5,79,654
Madhya Pradesh	2,47,927	3,45,211	4,44,960	4,47,111	5,45,446	5,67,028
Karnataka	1,74,366	2,18,862	2,97,974	3,26,114	4,12,659	4,40,280
Uttar Pradesh	1,22,108	1,24,728	1,41,549	1,68,389	2,07,111	2,13,267
NCT of Delhi	29,595	50,513	73,917	94,672	1,55,122	1,66,231
Tamil Nadu	28,350	41,097	49,564	66,900	83,359	89,265
Chhattisgarh	$$	$$	$$	43,213	56,103	61,510
West Bengal	26,940	32,203	38,663	34,355	55,223	60,141
Andhra Pradesh	9,012	16,108	18,642	26,564	41,846	53,849
Haryana	**	31,173	35,482	35,296	57,167	52,613
Punjab	48,754	21,383	27,049	20,763	39,276	45,040
Assam	9,468	12,917	*	20,645	23,957	25,949
Bihar	17,598	25,185	27,613	11,332	16,085	18,914
Jharkhand	$$$	$$$	$$$	11,717	16,301	14,974

Cont'd...

...Cont'd

States/Union Territories	*1961*	*1971*	*1981*	*1991*	*2001*	*2011*
Odisha	2,295	6,521	6,642	6,302	9,154	9,420
Uttarakhand	$	$	$	7,870	9,249	9,183
Kerala	2,967	3,336	3,605	3,641	4,528	4,489
Nagaland	263	627	1,153	1,202	2,093	2,655
Jammu and Kashmir	1,427	1,150	1,576	*	2,518	2,490
Chandigarh	**	1,016	1,889	1,531	2,592	1,960
Himachal Pradesh	95	626	1,046	1,206	1,408	1,805
Manipur	778	1,408	975	1,337	1,461	1,692
Puducherry	76	237	277	470	952	1,400
Dadra and Nagar Haveli	120	303	372	529	864	1,186
Goa	68	333	462	487	820	1,109
Tripura	195	375	297	301	477	860
Arunachal Pradesh	14	39	42	64	216	771
Meghalaya	***	268	542	445	772	627
Mizoram	***	–	11	4	179	376
Sikkim	19	–	108	40	183	314

Cont'd...

...Cont'd

States/Union Territories	*1961*	*1971*	*1981*	*1991*	*2001*	*2011*
Daman and Diu	+	223	140	212	268	287
Andaman and Nicobar Islands	3	14	11	17	23	31
Lakshadweep	–	–	–	–	–	11

* No Census conducted,
** Included under Punjab,
***Included under Assam,
$ Included under Uttar Pradesh,
$$ Included under Madhya Pradesh,
$$$ Included under Bihar,
+ Included under Goa.

Sources: 1. The Census 2001 population figures for India and Manipur exclude those of Mao Maram, Paomata and Purul subdivisions of Senapati district of Manipur.

2. In 1991, figures for Uttaranchal, Uttar Pradesh, Jharkhand, Bihar, Chhattisgarh and Madhya Pradesh have been recasted as per the Jurisdiction in 2001 census.

3. All religious communities include 'Religion not stated'.

4. Population figures for 1961 are as per 'Social and Culture Tables', Part II C (i), Census of India 1971, 1981 as per 'Religion', Paper 2 of 1972, Census of India 1971, 1981 as per 'Household population by religion of head of household', Paper 4 of 1984, Census of India 1981 and 1991 as per 'Religion', Part IV B and (ii) Census of India 1991.

Table 7.5

Decadal Growth Rate of Population in India by Religious Communities, 1961–2011

Decade	*India*	*Hindu*	*Muslim*	*Christian*	*Sikh*	*Buddhists*	*Jains*
1961–1971	24.75	23.67	30.84	32.58	32.28	17.08	28.48
1971–1981	21.41	21.29	22.95	13.65	26.01	23.8	23.09
1981–1991	26.05	25.08	34.54	21.5	24.33	35.33	4.57
1991–2001	22.66	20.35	36.02	22.61	18.18	24.54	26.02
2001–2011	17.72	16.76	24.65	15.53	8.42	6.13	5.37

Districts with Major Concentration of Jain Population

In 1981 census, there were only four districts in India each with 1,00,000+ Jain population: Greater Bombay (3,41,980), Belgaum (1,27,306), Kolhapur (1,21,722) and Ahmedabad (1,19,235). The combined population of Jains in these four districts was 7,10,243, that is about 22 per cent of the country's total Jain population.[3] This situation changed significantly in 2011 census with the doubling of the number of districts in this category to 8 and the Jain population to 14,64,581, or 32.9 per cent of the total Jain population (Table 7.6a).

The number of districts in 2011 with more than 50,000 and less than 1,00,000 Jains was 7. These districts hosted 5,16,656 Jains, or 11.6 per cent of the total Jain population (Table 7.6b). The third category of districts numbering 24 with Jain population between 25,000 and 49,999 had 14.5 per cent (6,44,839) of the total Jain population (Table 7.6c). Thus, in 2011 about 59 per cent of the total Jain population lived in 39 districts where the concentration of the Jain population ranged from 25,005 in Damoh district to 343,639 in Mumbai Suburban.

Table 7.6a

Districts with Jain Population >1 Lakh

Name of District	*Population of Jains as per Census 2011*		
	Total	*Male*	*Female*
Mumbai Suburban	3,43,639	1,72,042	1,71,597
Ahmedabad	2,09,287	1,06,152	1,03,135
Belgaum	1,78,310	91,671	86,639
Thane	1,72,052	87,903	84,149
Mumbai	1,66,000	82,950	83,050
Kolhapur	1,54,882	80,024	74,858
Pune	1,27,786	65,560	62,226
Surat	1,12,835	58,575	54,260

These eight districts together constitute 32.9 per cent, that is around one-third of total Jain population.

Table 7.6b

Districts with Jain Population >50,000 and <1 Lakh

Name of District	*Population of Jains as per Census 2011*		
	Total	*Male*	*Female*
Sangli	87,453	45,284	42,169
Bangalore	83,090	42,383	40,707
Jaipur	81,079	41,785	39,294
Udaipur	78,647	40,221	38,426
Indore	71,667	36,462	35,205
Sagar	62,992	32,691	30,301
Chennai	51,708	26,519	25,189

Table 7.6c

Districts with Jain Population >25,000 and <50,000

Name of District	*Population of Jains as per Census 2011*		
	Total	*Male*	*Female*
East Delhi	46,927	24,108	22,819
Ajmer	45,614	23,231	22,383
North West Delhi	43,460	22,513	20,947

Cont'd...

...Cont'd

Name of District	*Population of Jains as per Census 2011*		
	Total	*Male*	*Female*
Ahmednagar	38,718	19,776	18,942
Nashik	38,212	19,548	18,664
Jodhpur	36,697	18,555	18,142
Bhilwara	35,149	17,775	17,374
Barmer	34,010	17,453	16,557
Jabalpur	33,728	17,345	16,383
Rajkot	33,591	16,820	16,771
Aurangabad	30,981	15,920	15,061
Bikaner	30,850	15,500	15,350
Ratlam	29,353	14,891	14,462
Dharwad	29,037	14,895	14,142
Solapur	28,134	14,635	13,499
Vadodara	27,650	13,993	13,657
Jalgaon	27,404	14,205	13,199
Bhavnagar	26,974	13,613	13,361
Bhopal	25,950	13,145	12,805
Chittaurgarh	25,843	13,139	12,704
Kota	25,742	13,396	12,346
Kachchh	25,312	12,387	12,925
Bagalkot	25,198	12,939	12,259
Damoh	25,005	13,180	11,825

More demographic data of 2011 census in terms of total Jain population, gender-wise distribution, sex ratio, child sex ratio, literary rate and work participation rate (WPR) for top 10 districts in 18 major states/union territories are provided in Tables 7A.1–7A.18 of this chapter.

Urbanization

A highly significant population characteristic of the Jains in India is their high degree of urbanization. This has been so since the very beginning of the twentieth century. As early as in the 1901 census, about 30.0 per cent of the Jain population was living in urban areas that declined slightly to 29.6 per cent in 1911, but continued to rise since 1921 (33.9%) to reach a figure of 59.8 per cent in 1971 and 75.0 per cent in 2001. As per 2011 census, about 79.68 per cent Jains lived in urban areas.

Age and Gender Structure

Age structure of Jain population in India as per 2011 census data is shown in Table 7.7. It is clear from the data that about 20.6 per of Jain population is below 15 years of the age, 66.6 per cent under 60 years and about 12.8 per cent over 60 years of age. The proportion of females is more than that of males in the elderly Jain population indicating better life expectancy of women.

Table 7.7

Age Structure of Jain Population by Gender, 2011

Age Group	*Population of Jain*					
	Total	*%*	*Male*	*%*	*Female*	*%*
All ages	44,51,753	100	22,78,097	100	21,73,656	100
0–4	2,74,333	6.16	1,44,653	6.35	1,29,680	5.97
5–9	3,06,113	6.88	1,63,359	7.17	1,42,754	6.57
10–14	3,40,952	7.66	1,82,042	7.99	1,58,910	7.31
15–19	3,59,137	8.07	1,90,812	8.38	1,68,325	7.74
20–24	3,81,590	8.57	1,95,758	8.59	1,85,832	8.55
25–29	3,85,662	8.66	1,94,577	8.54	1,91,085	8.79
30–34	3,65,817	8.22	1,84,013	8.08	1,81,804	8.36
35–39	3,48,301	7.82	1,72,807	7.59	1,75,494	8.07
40–44	3,26,049	7.32	1,64,292	7.21	1,61,757	7.44
45–49	3,09,203	6.95	1,57,792	6.93	1,51,411	6.97
50–54	2,66,819	5.99	1,37,519	6.04	1,29,300	5.95
55–59	2,18,824	4.92	1,12,463	4.94	1,06,361	4.89
60–64	1,85,827	4.17	93,486	4.10	92,341	4.25
65–69	1,35,810	3.05	66,840	2.93	68,970	3.17
70–74	1,01,862	2.29	49,667	2.18	52,195	2.40
75–79	64,173	1.44	31,213	1.37	32,960	1.52
80+	66,090	1.48	29,094	1.28	36,996	1.70
Age not stated	15,191	0.34	7,710	0.34	7,481	0.34

The age structure of a community or society further reveals major population characteristics, that is, dependency ratio which can be defined as the number of young and old for every 1,000 persons in 15–59 age group. The dependency ratios for various religious communities for 2001 and 2011 census years are given in Table 7.8. The total dependency ratio for 2001 was 752 and for 2011 it was 652. Across all religious communities this ratio for Jains was the lowest at 597 and the highest for Muslims at 748. Given the fact that both children and elderly are dependent on the able and adult population, demographers also make a distinction between young dependency and the old dependency ratio which can be defined as the number of children aged up to 15, or the number of elderly 60 years or above, dependent on every 1,000 persons in 15–59 age group respectively. As per census data, whereas the young dependency ratio in India has declined from 621 in 2001 to 510 in 2011, the old dependency ratio has increased from 131 in 2001 to 142 in 2011.[4]

Table 7.8

Dependency Ratio by Religious Communities 2001 and 2011

Religious Community	*2001*	*2011*
Hindus	737	640
Muslims	887	748
Christians	636	598
Sikhs	692	565
Buddhists	723	572
Jains	544	597
Others	823	741
All/Average	752	652

Source: Subodh Varma (2016).

Jain Elderly Population

Compared to other religious communities the Jains have the largest percentage of population in 65+ age group (8.60%) and the Muslims the lowest (3.99%). In the case of the Jains the proportion of the elderly population is about 50 per cent higher than the national average (Table 7.9). Relatively more elderly (65+) people of all religious communities (including Jains), except Christians, are found to live in rural than urban areas (Table 7.10).

Table 7.9

Percentage of 65+ Populations by Religious Communities and Gender

	India	*Hindus*	*Muslims*	*Christians*	*Sikhs*	*Buddhists*	*Jains*
Female	5.75	5.97	4.12	6.74	7.65	6.79	8.79
Male	5.19	5.36	3.86	5.96	7.51	5.74	7.76
Total	5.47	5.65	3.99	6.36	7.57	6.26	8.26

Source: Census of India (2011).

Table 7.10

Percentage of 65+ Populations by Religious Community and Rural–Urban Background, 2011

	India	*Hindu*	*Muslim*	*Christian*	*Sikh*	*Buddhist*	*Jain*
Total	5.47	5.65	3.99	6.36	7.57	6.26	8.26
Rural	5.64	5.81	4.12	6.07	7.85	7.42	9.29
Urban	5.09	5.27	3.78	6.79	6.88	4.71	8.00

Sex Ratio

Sex ratio in India is defined as the number of females per 1,000 males in the population. It is expressed as 'number of females per 1,000 males'. Historical demographic analysis of sex ratio amongst Jains suggests that there has been a clear deficiency of females during the twentieth century. The sex ratio in the Jain population ranges from 924 in 1961 to 946 in 1991, and averages to about 935 for the twentieth century. The sex ratio among the Jains in 2001 declined to 940, but considerably improved in 2011 census with 954 females per 1,000 males (See Table 7.1).

According to 2011 census as against the average sex ratio of 954 for Jains, more than average sex ratio among the Jains was found in Kerala (1,018), Manipur (968), Gujarat (966), Maharashtra (964), Andhra Pradesh (960), Rajasthan (958),

West Bengal (958) and Tamil Nadu (957). On the other hand, the following states have less than average sex ratio: Karnataka (952), Madhya Pradesh (942), Delhi (942), Bihar (941), Haryana (923), Uttar Pradesh (921), Assam (916), and Punjab (912) (See Table 7.11).

Table 7.11

Jain Literacy Rate, Sex Ratio and Work Participation Rate by State, 2011

India/States/ Union Territories	*Literacy Rate*			*Sex Ratio*	*Sex Ratio (0–6)*	*Work Participation Rate*		
	Person	*Male*	*Female*			*Person*	*Male*	*Female*
INDIA	94.88	96.78	92.91	954	889	35.53	57.71	12.27
Maharashtra	95.35	96.66	93.99	964	887	36.77	58.63	14.08
Rajasthan	95.14	97.97	92.21	958	859	33.68	56.10	10.29
Gujarat	96.98	97.93	96.01	966	872	34.15	58.29	9.16
Madhya Pradesh	96.23	97.58	94.79	942	939	34.59	56.79	11.03
Karnataka	88.33	92.94	83.51	952	902	39.39	59.35	18.42
Uttar Pradesh	94.05	95.81	92.16	921	882	33.45	54.35	10.76
NCT of Delhi	97.77	98.76	96.72	942	853	34.22	57.37	9.63
Tamil Nadu	94.51	97.44	91.46	957	939	34.94	59.13	9.67
Chhattisgarh	97.24	98.17	96.26	947	880	33.95	58.33	8.19
West Bengal	93.51	95.96	90.96	958	906	35.76	59.37	11.11
Andhra Pradesh	91.94	95.22	88.55	960	933	34.56	56.47	11.75
Haryana	95.87	97.47	94.15	923	866	34.36	55.75	11.19
Punjab	95.28	96.09	94.39	912	831	35.86	58.81	10.69
Assam	96.13	97.67	94.46	916	891	35.55	60.47	8.33
Bihar	85.36	88.57	81.92	941	987	31.15	49.11	12.06
Jharkhand	93.45	96.14	90.56	929	882	33.97	56.65	9.55
Odisha	92.92	95.83	89.79	928	918	35.25	57.85	10.92
Uttarakhand	96.84	98.14	95.47	934	801	34.22	54.43	12.58
Kerala	97.08	98.65	95.57	1,018	822	38.16	57.71	18.95
Nagaland	92.14	93.5	90.69	934	917	37.66	57.61	16.30

Cont'd...

...Cont'd

India/States/ Union Territories	Literacy Rate			Sex Ratio	Sex Ratio (0–6)	Work Participation Rate		
	Person	Male	Female			Person	Male	Female
Jammu and Kashmir	93.46	95.57	91.15	901	779	37.39	59.31	13.05
Chandigarh	98.51	99.02	97.97	966	1,027	38.32	56.87	19.11
Himachal Pradesh	95.23	95.31	95.15	910	851	40.17	57.88	20.70
Manipur	91.51	93.23	89.74	963	908	40.13	60.09	19.40
Puducherry	96.22	98.24	94.19	994	1,000	30.93	53.56	8.17
Dadra and Nagar Haveli	97.55	98.76	96.18	877	824	35.58	57.91	10.11
Goa	95.58	97.71	93.22	912	1,018	40.04	58.45	19.85
Tripura	88.49	92.54	84.2	898	625	38.60	54.97	20.39
Arunachal Pradesh	60.62	72.7	50	1,078	806	42.93	50.94	35.50
Meghalaya	85.82	86.35	85.2	833	714	39.55	58.19	17.19
Mizoram	72.33	79.64	63.16	808	854	36.70	38.46	34.52
Sikkim	89.64	91.98	86.44	735	789	49.36	59.67	35.34
Daman and Diu	96.17	98.5	93.75	952	857	39.72	65.31	12.86
Andaman and Nicobar Islands	96.3	100	92.86	1,214	3,000	35.48	57.14	17.65
Lakshadweep	87.5	100	75	833	500	–	–	–

Child sex ratio is another indicator of gender equality in a community or society. Child sex ratio (0–6 years) has been defined as the number of females in the age group 0–6 years per 1,000 males in the same age group in the population. It is expressed as number of female children aged (0–6) years per 1,000 male children aged (0–6) years. Among the Jains, the child sex ratio was 879 in 2001 compared to 927 for all religious communities in India. It was 925 for Hindus and 950 for Muslims. In 2011, the child sex ratio was 889 which is an appreciable improvement over the 2001 figure (Table 7.12).

Table 7.12

Sex Ratio and Child Sex Ratio by Religious Communities, 2011

	Total	*Hindu*	*Muslim*	*Christian*	*Sikh*	*Buddhist*	*Jain*
Sex Ratio	943	939	951	1,023	903	965	954
Sex Ratio (0–6)	918	913	943	958	828	933	889

Source: Census of India (2011).

In spite of significant changes in sex and child sex ratios in the Jain population however, the causes and consequences of these phenomena continue to more or less remain the same as discussed in the previous chapter.

Also, notwithstanding the improvement in sex and child sex ratios, a large number of districts with 500 or more Jain population suffer from worst sex and child sex ratios. The data about these districts are presented in Tables 7.13 and 7.14. Needless to say, sociological surveys are required to ascertain the causes and consequences of the two phenomena.

Table 7.13

Jain Population: Districts with Worst Sex Ratio, 2011

Sex Ratio	*Districts**
Less than 800	Jhunjhunu (740),
800–850	Darrang, Sonbhadra, Mirzapur, Mewat, Malda, Nalbari, Dakshin Bastar or Dantewada
850–870	Bardhaman, Mathura, Sundargarh, Anantapur, Surguja, Sonitpur, Famangara, Jorhat, Moga, Hardwar, Bhagalpur, Pratapgarh, Rewari, Narayanpur, Morena
870–890	Rampur, Ramgarh, Dhaulpur, Karauli, Sirsa, Muktsar, Mansa, Jind, North Goa, Dadra and Nagar Haveli, Dindori, Tinsukia, Allahabad, Hoshiarpur, Darjeeling, Jalpaiguri, Dhubri, Firozabad, Kheda, Dibrugarh, Mahendragarh
890–900	Bhind, Tarn Taran, Ambala, Mandla, Udham Singh Nagar, Gadchiroli, Anuppur, Tapi, Palwal, Solan, Kapurthala, Janjgir-Champa, Faridkot, Bhiwani, Banda, Damoh, Amritsar, Kamrup, Dausa, Patiala, Mainpuri, Balangir, Fatehabad

*Only districts with 500 or more Jain population have been taken into consideration.

Table 7.14

Jain Population: Districts with Worst Child Sex Ratio, 2011

Child Sex Ratio	*Districts**
Less than 600	SAS Nagar, Y.S.R.
600–700	Kamrup, Jalpaiguri, Mirzapur, Nalbari, Mahendragarh, Chamarajanagar, Mewat, Bongaigaon Giridih, Mathura, Udham Singh Nagar, Rampur, Solan, Ratnagiri, Jhunjhunu, Kheda, Darjeeling, Bhiwani
700–750	Ramgarh, Tapi, Hoshangabad, Korba, Muktsar, Panchkula, Dakshin Bastar, Dantewada, Mansa, Kabirdham, Thanjavur, Yamunanagar, Sundargarh, Dibrugarh, Balangir
750–800	Mahasamund, North Delhi, Hoshiarpur, Bijnor, Mandla, Sindhudurg, Bid, Dehradun, Buldhana, Raichur, Dungarpur, South Goa, Barwani, Sangli, Muzaffarnagar, Janjgir-Champa, Dausa, Jhajjar, Moradabad, Dewas, Anantapur, Jammu, Wayanad, Madurai, Rewari, Central, Bangalore Rural

*Only districts with 500 or more Jain population have been taken into consideration.

Marital Status

The 2011 census data clearly show that the median as well as mean age at the time of marriage in India has increased across categories of people and genders. The reason for this upswing is the increased socio-economic changes in the country. It is particularly noticeable among mobile and migratory workers who happen to be relatively free from the restrictions of a traditional social setup. Additionally the higher level of school enrolment could also be a contributory factor.

According to census 2011 data, more than 17 lakh Jains (38.92%) have reported as 'Never married'. The 'Currently Married' constitute about 55.87 per cent of the total Jain population. The widowed/divorced and separated constitute about 5 per cent of the total Jain population as shown in the Table 7.15.

Table 7.15

Marital Status of Jain Population by Gender, 2011

Sex	*Never Married*	*Currently Married*	*Widowed*	*Divorced/ Separated*	*Total*
Male	9,88,224	12,34,743	48,641	6,489	22,78,097
(%)	(43.38%)	(54.20%)	(2.14%)	(0.28%)	(100.00%)
Female	7,44,292	12,52,526	1,67,872	8,966	21,73,656
(%)	(34.24%)	(57.62%)	(7.72%)	(0.41%)	(100.00%)
Total	17,32,516	24,87,269	2,16,513	15,455	44,51,753
(%)	(38.92%)	(55.87%)	(4.86%)	(0.35%)	(100.00%)

Among those who have attained the marriageable age, that is, 21 years for men and 18 years for women, 18 per cent Jain males and 14 per cent Jain females are never married as against the national average of 16 per cent and 11 per cent respectively (see Table 7.16). Comparable figures for Hindus are 16 per cent and 10 per cent and for Muslims 7 per cent and 13 per cent respectively. In other words, 82 per cent of Jain males and 86 per cent of Jain females of marriageable ages got married as per 2011 census data.

Age at Marriage: The mean age at marriage amongst Jains is 24.8 years for males and 21.2 years in case of females. Age group wise distribution of Jain ever-married population revealed that out of the total 14,29,364 ever married female Jain population, about 83.8 per cent of females got married after attaining 18 years or more, while 8.6 per cent female reported to have married between 16 and 17 years followed by 7.6 per cent females in the age less than 15 years. While in case of ever married male Jain population of 12,89,873, about 92.7 per cent reportedly got married after attaining the age 20 years. Male (4.6%) reported to have married between 16 and 19 years followed by 2.7 per cent males in the age less than 15 years.[5]

According to 2011 census data, divorce and separation rates (2.6 and 3.1 per 1,000 married people respectively) are the lowest among Jains. Polygamy and widowhood were two conspicuous features of the Jain family life until about the middle of the twentieth century.[6] This situation has almost reversed now. With 79.6 widows per 1,000 married people, the widowhood rate in 2011 was on the lower side among the Jains vis-à-vis Sikhs, Hindus, Christians and Buddhists (Table.7.16).

Table 7.16

Marital Status by Religious Communities, 2011

Religion	*Widowed*	*Separated*	*Divorced*	*Never Married People of Marriageable Age* (%)*	
				M	*F*
Hindu	88.3	5.5	1.8	16	10
Muslim	72.7	4.8	3.4	17	13
Christian	97.0	9.4	3.9	21	18
Sikh	88.2	4.2	2.8	17	14
Buddhist	100.3	9.5	4.3	21	14
Jain	79.6	3.1	2.6	18	14
All Religion	16	11	–	–	–

Male 21+ years and females 18+ years

Source: Subodh Varma, 'Triple Talaq Effect?: 5 in 1,000 Women Divorced', *Times of India*, New Delhi, 24 August 2016.

Table 7.17

Mean Age at Marriage by Religious Communities and Gender, 2011

Mean Age at Marriage	*Total*	*Hindu*	*Muslim*	*Christian*	*Sikh*	*Buddhist*	*Jain*
Male	23.3	23.2	23.4	26.3	24.0	24.1	24.8
Female	19.3	19.2	19.1	22.0	21.2	19.6	21.2

Total Fertility Rate (TFR)

TFR is defined as the number of children which a woman of hypothetical cohort would bear during her life time if she were to bear children throughout her life at the rates specified by the *age specific fertility rate* for the particular year if none of them dies before crossing the age of reproduction.

As can be seen in Table 7.18, TFR during 2001–2011 has gone down across all communities as well as at the national level. The TFR was lowest for the Jains and the highest for Muslims in the previous two censuses. The Buddhist, Sikh and Christian communities have been closely following the Jains in this regard.

Table 7.18

Total Fertility Rate among Jains and Other Communities, 2001 and 2011

	Total	*Hindu*	*Muslim*	*Christian*	*Sikh*	*Buddhist*	*Jain*
2011	2.17	2.11	2.66	1.89	1.81	1.76	1.46
2001	2.52	2.47	3.06	2.06	1.86	2.29	1.50

Period Fertility

As per 2011 census of India data, for the first time in the recorded history of India, more than half the families (54%) had two or less children. Corresponding figure in 2001 census was 46.6 per cent. In terms of absolute numbers, about 34 crore married women had about 92 crore children – averaging to about 2.69 children per woman. Besides a trend towards smaller families, there is also a tendency towards deferring child birth to later years. Thus, about 35 per cent women in the age group 20–24 and 16 per cent in the age group 25–29 had no children.

> As a result of these changes, the period fertility rate – the average number of children that a women in the age group 45–49 years has ever borne – has decline by a drastic 16% between 2001 and 2011 (Table 7.19). The fertility rate of women between 45 and 49 years, that is, when their child bearing days are over, is considered a standard measure by demographers for defining average fertility.[7]

Table 7.19

Period Fertility Rate by Religious Communities, 2001 and 2011

Communities	*2001*	*2011*	*Decline (2001–2011)*
Hindus	3.37	3.17	16%
Muslims	4.92	4.24	14%
Christians	3.32	2.79	16%
Sikhs	3.45	2.79	18%
Buddhists	3.87	3.15	19%
Jains	2.49	2.38	22%
All	3.88	3.27	16%

Source: Subodh Varma (2016).

Survival Ratio

The survival ratio is highest among Jains (0.93). This is mainly due to high literacy rate. It also implies better health facilities available to them (Table 7.20).

Table 7.20

Survival Ratio among Jains and Other Communities, 2001 and 2011

	Total	*Hindu*	*Muslim*	*Christian*	*Sikh*	*Buddhist*	*Jain*
2011	0.896	0.895	0.898	0.911	0.913	0.897	0.929
2001	0.879	0.877	0.883	0.902	0.905	0.874	0.924

Literacy and Education

Literacy rate of a population is defined as the percentage of literates to the total population aged 7 years and above. Literacy-wise, in 2011 Jains with a figure of 94.88 per cent were the most literate community, followed by Christians (84.5%), Buddhists (81.29%), Sikhs (75.39%), Hindus (73.27%) and Muslims (68.54%) (Table 7.21). The national average for literacy is 72.98 per cent. In all the religious communities, female literacy was found to be lower than the male literacy by about 16 percentage points. It stood at 64.63 per cent in 2011. In the case of female literacy too, the Jains take the lead with a figure of 92.91 per cent, followed by Christians, Buddhists, Sikhs, Hindus and Muslims. In 33 states and union territories, the female literacy among the Jains is 80 per cent or above (Table 7.11).

Table 7.21

Sex Ratio, Literacy and Work Participation Rate by Religious Communities and Gender

Community	*Sex Ratio*	*Sex Ratio (0–6)*	*Literacy Rate*			*Work Participation Rate*		
			Total	*Male*	*Female*	*Total*	*Male*	*Female*
Total	943	918	72.98	80.88	64.63	39.80	53.26	25.52
Hindu	939	913	73.27	81.7	64.34	41.04	53.91	27.35
Muslim	951	943	68.54	74.73	62.04	32.57	49.51	14.77
Christian	1,023	958	84.53	87.7	81.47	41.91	52.90	31.16
Sikh	903	828	75.39	80.03	70.31	36.32	55.43	15.16
Buddhist	965	933	81.29	88.31	74.04	43.15	53.39	32.54
Jain	954	889	94.88	96.78	92.91	35.53	57.71	12.27

Source: Census of India (2011).

Jains are not only the most literate religious community, they are also the most educated one as is evident from Table 7.22. Thus, over 25 per cent of all the literate Jains have graduation and above educational qualification – a significant improvement over 2001 census figure of 18 per cent. Likewise matriculation or secondary (15.48%) and senior secondary levels (14.08%) of education are also highest among the Jains vis-à-vis the other religious communities. Ironically, however according to 2011 census data, about 2,07,000 'Jains of age 7 years and above are still counted as illiterate. Out of these, 87% are in 6 States viz. Maharashtra (59,752), Karnataka (46,229), Rajasthan (27,510), Madhya Pradesh (19,459), Gujarat (16,107), Uttar Pradesh (11,394)'.[8] More than 50 per cent of these illiterate Jains are concentrated in 20 districts.

Table 7.22

Educational Status by Religious Communities, 2011

	Literate without Edu. Level	*Below Primary*	*Primary*	*Middle*	*Matric/ Sec.*	*Senior Sec.*	*Non-Tech. Diploma*	*Tech. Diploma*	*Graduate and Above*
Hindu	2.88	11.83	15.11	11.27	9.00	6.62	0.07	0.61	5.98
Muslim	2.90	14.32	16.08	9.73	6.33	4.44	0.17	0.27	2.76
Christian	3.53	11.95	14.65	12.35	10.08	10.32	0.18	2.23	8.85
Sikh	2.15	8.04	15.66	11.19	14.78	8.25	0.08	0.79	6.40
Buddhist	3.46	14.32	14.37	13.04	10.93	8.61	0.04	0.47	6.18
Jain	3.29	7.36	10.29	8.82	15.48	14.05	0.19	1.10	25.65

Edu.: Educational, Sec.: Secondary, Tech.: Technical

Work Participation and Occupation

Besides literacy rate, the WPR or percentage of workers to total population was also highest among the Jain males (57.71%); the WPR for all religious communities being 39.8 per cent in the 2011 census (Table 7.21). The lowest WPR for the male population was found among the Muslim males (49.51%). In spite of the highest literacy rate among the Jain females however, their WPR in 2011 census was the lowest (12.27%) preceded by Muslims (14.77%) and Hindus (27.35%). This suggests that gender gap in regard to WPR continues to remain sharp among the Jains. Apparently, education and talent among the Jain women is not being properly utilized. It is likely that most Jain women spend their time either in performing religious activities or in doing household chores. It is also very likely that they do not feel the need for gainful employment given the fact that the Jains are economically a better off community. But these are only just hypotheses which require sociological validation through fieldwork in different parts of India.

Table 7.23

Distribution of the Working Population of India by Religious Communities and Economic Sectors (%), 2011

Occupation (%)	*Total*	*Hindu*	*Muslim*	*Christian*	*Sikh*	*Buddhist*	*Jain*
Cultivators	24.65	25.81	15.70	25.86	28.97	15.37	9.03
Agricultural Labourers	29.95	31.26	24.85	15.51	18.40	38.42	3.66
Household Industry	3.81	3.43	6.99	2.39	3.64	2.09	4.61
Others	41.59	39.50	52.46	56.24	48.99	44.12	82.69

In terms of the four broad categories of workers, namely cultivators, agricultural labourers, household industry workers and other workers (this last category includes workers in tertiary sector, such as service, manufacturing, trade and commerce and allied activities), the distribution of Jain population in 2001 census was heavily skewed in favour of the 'industry and service sectors' (81.7%). With about 11.7 per cent of the Jain population being engaged as cultivators, 3.3 per cent as agricultural labourers, about 3.3 per cent as household industry workers.[9] As per 2011 census, 9.03 per cent Jains were engaged as cultivators, 3.66 per cent as agricultural labourers, 4.61 per cent as household industry workers and 82.69 per cent as workers in trade, industry and service sector (Table 7.23). Thus, the business and service class character of the Jain community is clearly evident from the 2011 census data. But again, systematic sociological studies are needed to ascertain the precise nature of the economic and occupational structure of the Jain community in India.

Working population aged between 15 and 59 years can be divided into three categories: (a) main workers, that is, those who work for the most part of the year, (b) marginal workers, those who are not getting work for more than six months and (c) non-workers, include mainly women. In this context, a comparison between 2001 and 2011 census data indicates that whereas the share of main workers has declined, the proportions of marginal and non-workers have increased across all communities over a 10-year period. As far as the Jains are concerned, they have the lowest share of marginal workers, but the highest proportion of non-workers. The latter is mainly due to the lowest WPR of Jain women which is only about 12 per cent. Also with the marginal exception of Jains and Christians, the proportion of people in each religious community seeking or available for work too has gone up (Table 7.24).

Table 7.24

Types of Workers as Share of Working Age Population (15–59 years) (in %)

	Main	*Marginal*	*Non-workers*	*Seeking Work*	
				2011	*2001*
India	44	14	42	15	11
Hindu	45	14	40	14	11
Muslim	39	12	49	16	11
Christian	47	12	40	16	16
Sikh	42	7	50	11	8
Buddhist	51	10	40	12	11
Jain	44	3	53	6	6
Other	40	35	25	28	13

Source: Subodh Varma, '"Main Workers" Across Religion See a Dip', *The Times of India*, New Delhi, 8 June 2016.

Caste Categories

As per 2011 census data, Jain population has also been divided into the usual caste categories of scheduled castes (SCs), scheduled tribes (STs), other backward classes (OBCs) and general castes (general). The relevant data are provided in Table 7.25 which clearly suggest that an overwhelming majority of Jain population (94%) belongs to the general category of Jain castes. The Jain community does not have any scheduled castes member. Only 2.6 per cent of its population belongs to STs and 3 per cent to OBCs (Table 7.25).

Table 7.25

Distribution of Population of Each Religion by Caste Categories, 2011

Religion/Caste	*SCs*	*STs*	*OBCs*	*Forward Caste/Others*
Hinduism	22.2%	9%	42.8%	26%
Islam	0.8%	0.5%	39.2%	59.5%
Christianity	9.0%	32.8%	24.8%	33.3%
Sikhism	30.7%	0.9%	22.4%	46.1%
Jainism	0.0%	2.6%	3.0%	94.3%
Buddhism	89.5%	7.4%	0.4%	2.7%
Zoroastrianism	0.0%	15.9%	13.7%	70.4%
Others	2.6%	82.5%	6.25%	8.7%
Total	19.7%	8.5%	41.1%	30.8%

Conclusion

As per the 2011 census data, the Jain community vis-à-vis other religious communities in India can distinctly be characterized by the smallest population-base (about 4.5 million), the lowest decadal population growth rate (5.37%), the highest level of urbanization (80%), the highest literacy rate (95%), a little more than average sex ratio and less than average child sex ratio (954 and 889 respectively), the lowest fertility rate (1.6%), and the highest proportion of elderly population in the 65+ age group (8.26%). This profile comfortably puts the community into the category of an urban middle and/or upper middle class.

It can well be hypothesized that this demographic profile of the community is the direct outcome of its relative economic affluence that accrues to it mainly due to its traditional engagement in trade, commerce and banking, and now additionally and increasingly in modern professions. Historically, the evolution of the Jain community as followers of the soteriological religion of cultured professional monks inculcates in Jains the 'Protestant ethic'-like socio-economic norms and values that help them in acquiring worldly success.

Given the above economic and socio-demographic profile, the Jain community in India appears to be the foremost and the fitting case of zero population growth in near future, followed by phases of population stagnation and then progressive population decline.

Notes and References

1. Prakash C. Jain, *Jains in India and Abroad* (New Delhi: International School for Jain Studies, 2011).
2. Jayant K. Banthia, 'Introduction', Census of India 2001, First Report of Religion Data (New Delhi: RGO, 2004).
3. See M.K. Jain, 'A Demographic Analysis on Jains in India', *Jain Journal*, 1986, p. 48.
4. Subodh Varma, 'Now Majority of Families Have 2 or Less Kids', *The Times of India*, New Delhi, 2 March 2016.
5. See Dheeraj Jain, *Population of Jains in India: A Perspective from the Census 2011* (New Delhi: International School for Jain Studies, 2017), pp. 7–8. See also, 'Median Marriage Age Up: Census Data', *The Hindu*, New Delhi, 29 June 2016.
6. Subodh Varma, op. cit. See also V.A. Sangave, *Jain Community: A Social Survey* (Bombay: Popular Prakashan, 1980), Chapter 1.
7. Ibid.
8. Dheeraj Jain, op. cit., p. 4.
9. See Prakash C. Jain, op. cit., pp. 67–80.

APPENDIX

States/Districts–Wise Data at a Glance, 2011

Dheeraj Jain

This section presents district level data on Jain population and demography in 18 major states and union territories. From each state/UT, 10 districts with highest concentration of Jain population have been selected for computation in terms of size and other population characteristics such as sex and child sex ratios, literacy and work participation rate. The data are based on 2011 census report.

Table 7A.1

Select Population Characteristics of Jains in Top 10 Districts of Maharashtra, 2011

District	*Total*	*Male*	*Female*	*Sex Ratio*	*Child Sex Ratio*	*Literacy Rate*	*Work Participation Rate*
Mumbai Suburban	3,43,639	1,72,042	1,71,597	997	933	97.07	36.52
Thane	1,72,052	87,903	84,149	957	917	95.41	36.13
Mumbai	1,66,000	82,950	83,050	1,001	937	96.15	36.83
Kolhapur	1,54,882	80,024	74,858	935	813	91.57	38.95
Pune	1,27,786	65,560	62,226	949	912	96.05	37.16
Sangli	87,453	45,284	42,169	931	778	91.79	39.89
Ahmednagar	38,718	19,776	18,942	958	878	96.48	35.11
Nashik	38,212	19,548	18,664	955	854	97.4	34.39
Aurangabad	30,981	15,920	15,061	946	860	95.34	34.49
Solapur	28,134	14,635	13,499	922	854	95	36.3

Table 7A.2

Select Population Characteristics of Jains in Top 10 Districts of Rajasthan, 2011

District	*Total*	*Male*	*Female*	*Sex Ratio*	*Child Sex Ratio*	*Literacy Rate*	*Work Partici-pation Rate*
Jaipur	81,079	41,785	39,294	940	834	97.62	35.11
Udaipur	78,647	40,221	38,426	955	848	95.12	35.47
Ajmer	45,614	23,231	22,383	963	808	96.14	31.89
Jodhpur	36,697	18,555	18,142	978	926	95.01	32.93
Bhilwara	35,149	17,775	17,374	977	901	94.52	34.44
Barmer	34,010	17,453	16,557	949	877	90.84	31.63
Bikaner	30,850	15,500	15,350	990	884	95.46	30.21
Chittaurgarh	25,843	13,139	12,704	967	896	95.12	35.39
Kota	25,742	13,396	12,346	922	847	97.13	33.25
Banswara	22,613	11,579	11,034	953	838	96.2	39.02

Table 7A.3

Select Population Characteristics of Jains in Top 10 Districts of Gujarat, 2011

District	*Total*	*Male*	*Female*	*Sex Ratio*	*Child Sex Ratio*	*Literacy Rate*	*Work Partici-pation Rate*
Ahmedabad	2,09,287	1,06,152	1,03,135	972	845	97.64	35.29
Surat	1,12,835	58,575	54,260	926	883	97.07	33.21
Rajkot	33,591	16,820	16,771	997	966	97.99	33.3
Vadodara	27,650	13,993	13,657	976	833	97.22	33.67
Bhavnagar	26,974	13,613	13,361	981	891	97.06	32.92
Kachchh	25,312	12,387	12,925	1,043	923	92.7	32.01
Surendranagar	22,992	11,798	11,194	949	823	97.88	32.71
Jamnagar	18,856	9,472	9,384	991	940	95.99	35.46
Valsad	13,809	6,978	6,831	979	809	97.05	34.89
Navsari	13,386	6,860	6,526	951	959	97.4	32.98

Table 7A.4

Select Population Characteristics of Jains in Top 10 Districts of Madhya Pradesh, 2011

District	*Total*	*Male*	*Female*	*Sex Ratio*	*Child Sex Ratio*	*Literacy Rate*	*Work Participation Rate*
Indore	71,667	36,462	35,205	966	917	97.07	36.51
Sagar	62,992	32,691	30,301	927	966	96.8	33.65
Jabalpur	33,728	17,345	16,383	945	972	97.21	34.58
Ratlam	29,353	14,891	14,462	971	950	97.07	34.41
Bhopal	25,950	13,145	12,805	974	994	96.15	35.13
Damoh	25,005	13,180	11,825	897	917	95.41	36.17
Ujjain	24,622	12,464	12,158	975	964	97.05	34.47
Bhind	19,950	10,554	9,396	890	958	92.66	29.54
Mandsaur	19,029	9,703	9,326	961	953	96.65	37.03
Vidisha	18,490	9,547	8,943	937	957	95.71	35.22

Table 7A.5

Select Population Characteristics of Jains in Top 10 Districts of Karnataka, 2011

District	*Total*	*Male*	*Female*	*Sex Ratio*	*Child Sex Ratio*	*Literacy Rate*	*Work Participation Rate*
Belgaum	1,78,310	91,671	86,639	945	863	84.03	41.43
Bangalore	83,090	42,383	40,707	960	925	95.54	36.32
Dharwad	29,037	14,895	14,142	949	895	88.06	40.05
Bagalkot	25,198	12,939	12,259	947	829	75.63	37.33
Mysore	14,419	7,387	7,032	952	968	94.2	35.52
Dakshina Kannada	10,397	5,245	5,152	982	933	96.77	42.11
Haveri	9,834	5,119	4,715	921	926	87.95	46.88
Shimoga	9,234	4,646	4,588	988	1,084	88.22	46.21
Bijapur	8,665	4,360	4,305	987	987	88.05	37.56
Bellary	8,044	4,118	3,926	953	998	93	32.14

Table 7A.6

Select Population Characteristics of Jains in Top 10 Districts of Uttar Pradesh, 2011

District	*Total*	*Male*	*Female*	*Sex Ratio*	*Child Sex Ratio*	*Literacy Rate*	*Work Participation Rate*
Agra	21,508	11,259	10,249	910	841	92.66	33.5
Lalitpur	20,390	10,636	9,754	917	879	96.21	34.32
Firozabad	19,077	10,121	8,956	885	826	93.97	33.72
Meerut	18,544	9,554	8,990	941	940	96.31	34.36
Ghaziabad	16,412	8,409	8,003	952	902	95.67	36.9
Muzaffarnagar	16,345	8,563	7,782	909	779	96.64	32.08
Baghpat	16,139	8,490	7,649	901	860	95.53	31.58
Saharanpur	10,208	5,345	4,863	910	893	96.58	33.78
Jhansi	7,328	3,798	3,530	929	884	96.68	33.58
Kanpur Nagar	5,710	2,895	2,815	972	884	95.22	33.71

Table 7A.7

Select Population Characteristics of Jains in 9 Districts of Delhi, 2011

District	*Total*	*Male*	*Female*	*Sex Ratio*	*Child Sex Ratio*	*Literacy Rate*	*Work Participation Rate*
East	46,927	24,108	22,819	947	872	98.03	33.37
North West	43,460	22,513	20,947	930	804	97.83	33.95
North East	24,673	12,767	11,906	933	899	96.93	31.8
North	13,049	6,721	6,328	942	752	98.03	35.42
West	11,322	5,828	5,494	943	942	97.88	35.34
South	11,020	5,561	5,459	982	870	97.76	38.52
South West	9,215	4,747	4,468	941	885	97.52	35.47
Central	5,886	3,042	2,844	935	796	98.28	36.58
New Delhi	679	318	361	1,135	1,000	97.21	47.86

Table 7A.8

Select Population Characteristics of Jains in Top 10 Districts of Tamil Nadu, 2011

District	*Total*	*Male*	*Female*	*Sex Ratio*	*Child Sex Ratio*	*Literacy Rate*	*Work Participation Rate*
Chennai	51,708	26,519	25,189	950	921	94.89	34.2
Tiruvannamalai	7,898	3,951	3,947	999	933	93.09	39.11
Kancheepuram	4,962	2,540	2,422	954	973	95.73	34.44
Viluppuram	4,032	2,003	2,029	1,013	1,138	93.87	39.34
Thiruvallur	3,693	1,935	1,758	909	913	94.15	35.53
Vellore	3,514	1,780	1,734	974	1,069	95.43	32.13
Coimbatore	3,284	1,669	1,615	968	976	96.11	33.47
Madurai	1,532	780	752	964	793	95.39	32.83
Cuddalore	1,280	649	631	972	831	95.87	33.67
Thanjavur	1,256	629	627	997	726	87.9	38.77

Table 7A.9

Select Population Characteristics of Jains in Top 10 Districts of Chhattisgarh, 2011

District	*Total*	*Male*	*Female*	*Sex Ratio*	*Child Sex Ratio*	*Literacy Rate*	*Work Participation Rate*
Durg	17,209	8,810	8,399	953	870	97.78	33.23
Raipur	17,137	8,767	8,370	955	920	97.98	34.49
Rajnandgaon	8,187	4,168	4,019	964	913	97.38	33.19
Dhamtari	3,612	1,856	1,756	946	838	96.63	33.42
Bastar	3,466	1,784	1,682	943	946	96.04	34.56
Bilaspur	2,357	1,203	1,154	959	991	96.91	35.17
Mahasamund	1,495	780	715	917	750	98.01	33.38
Kabirdham	1,167	611	556	910	722	93.99	35.05
Koriya	1,155	600	555	925	943	97.81	33.07
Uttar Bastar Kanker	1,071	553	518	937	885	96.55	33.52

Table 7A.10

Select Population Characteristics of Jains in Top 10 Districts of West Bengal, 2011

District	Total	Male	Female	Sex Ratio	Child Sex Ratio	Literacy Rate	Work Partici-pation Rate
Kolkata	21,178	10,508	10,670	1,015	972	96	37.78
Haora	9,699	5,014	4,685	934	846	96.35	32.98
North Twenty Four Parganas	4,452	2,222	2,230	1,004	1,005	94.98	35.78
Puruliya	3,052	1,589	1,463	921	865	85.22	34.8
Murshidabad	3,037	1,567	1,470	938	871	95.41	34.51
Bankura	2,904	1,515	1,389	917	823	75.11	36.16
Hugli	2,160	1,136	1,024	901	830	94.65	35.6
Koch Bihar	1,869	952	917	963	1,153	97.08	36.06
Darjeeling	1,840	977	863	883	694	94.58	35.16
Barddhaman	1,674	903	771	854	947	91.68	34.71

Table 7A.11

Select Population Characteristics of Jains in Top 10 Districts of Andhra Pradesh, 2011

District	Total	Male	Female	Sex Ratio	Child Sex Ratio	Literacy Rate	Work Partici-pation Rate
Hyderabad	19,560	9,922	9,638	971	902	95.17	36.49
Krishna	6,320	3,221	3,099	962	949	93.07	33.18
East Godavari	4,149	2,139	2,010	940	945	94.37	31.74
Ranga Reddy	3,536	1,828	1,708	934	1,022	89.65	35.63
Guntur	3,282	1,707	1,575	923	960	90.53	35.47
Sri Potti Sriramulu Nellore	2,610	1,339	1,271	949	993	93.09	32.57
Visakhapatnam	2,316	1,154	1,162	1,007	1,023	92.12	31.91
Kurnool	2,235	1,158	1,077	930	825	87.24	34.9
West Godavari	1,578	819	759	927	891	93.01	32
Anantapur	1,417	762	655	860	788	85.7	36.06

Table 7A.12

Select Population Characteristics of Jains in Top 10 Districts of Haryana, 2011

District	Total	Male	Female	Sex Ratio	Child Sex Ratio	Literacy Rate	Work Participation Rate
Gurgaon	7,451	3,769	3,682	977	903	98.01	39.15
Sonipat	6,033	3,144	2,889	919	892	95.02	32.97
Faridabad	4,883	2,491	2,392	960	920	96.48	36.99
Ambala	4,845	2,562	2,283	891	879	97.48	38.06
Panipat	4,647	2,394	2,253	941	925	95.12	31.57
Hisar	3,620	1,895	1,725	910	848	94.84	31.85
Rohtak	3,491	1,817	1,674	921	804	96.88	32.37
Jind	2,594	1,383	1,211	876	934	93.61	31.88
Sirsa	2,256	1,204	1,052	874	914	94.89	33.33
Panchkula	1,626	833	793	952	720	97.06	37.95

Table 7A.13

Select Population Characteristics of Jains in Top 10 Districts of Punjab, 2011

District	Total	Male	Female	Sex Ratio	Child Sex Ratio	Literacy Rate	Work Participation Rate
Ludhiana	19,620	10,192	9,428	925	831	97	35.89
Jalandhar	4,011	2,108	1,903	903	860	96.25	37.45
Sangrur	3,222	1,688	1,534	909	938	95.64	35.29
Jalandhar	3,203	1,681	1,522	905	866	96.67	38
Amritsar	3,152	1,662	1,490	897	856	86.83	36.07
Hoshiarpur	2,034	1,080	954	883	755	97.72	37.91
Patiala	1,914	1,008	906	899	820	95.9	35.11
Mansa	1,577	841	736	875	721	94.54	35.76
Bathinda	1,266	660	606	918	814	91.92	34.44
Sahibzada Ajit Singh Nagar	1,257	658	599	910	564	97.75	34.69

Table 7A.14

Select Population Characteristics of Jains in Top 10 Districts of Assam, 2011

District	*Total*	*Male*	*Female*	*Sex Ratio*	*Child Sex Ratio*	*Literacy Rate*	*Work Participation Rate*
Kamrup Metropolitan	9,250	4,740	4,510	951	899	97.63	35.26
Dhubri	1,846	980	866	884	952	96.67	35.16
Cachar	1,673	872	801	919	924	97.96	34.55
Kamrup	1,330	701	629	897	621	96.47	33.68
Nagaon	1,162	611	551	902	817	95.63	34.42
Dibrugarh	1,055	559	496	887	742	95.35	39.53
Nalbari	1,004	546	458	839	630	96.72	34.06
Sonitpur	1,003	539	464	861	804	93.04	37.99
Bongaigaon	871	439	432	984	646	96.72	32.84
Tinsukia	837	445	392	881	1,000	94.98	36.68

Table 7A.15

Select Population Characteristics of Jains in Top 10 Districts of Bihar, 2011

District	*Total*	*Male*	*Female*	*Sex Ratio*	*Child Sex Ratio*	*Literacy Rate*	*Work Participation Rate*
Patna	2,151	1,129	1,022	905	924	86.35	32.26
Araria	1,910	985	925	939	865	94.92	31.52
Gaya	1,723	864	859	994	1,080	82.68	39
Kishanganj	1,476	755	721	955	892	96.44	32.45
Bhojpur	1,472	739	733	992	1,064	91.55	30.57
Purnia	1,450	738	712	965	1,135	90.63	30.34
Bhagalpur	1,050	563	487	865	810	92.49	32.57
Aurangabad	775	373	402	1,078	1,439	92.3	30.32
Nalanda	561	276	285	1,033	962	81.84	31.02
Supaul	546	282	264	936	923	92.14	30.4

Table 7A.16

Select Population Characteristics of Jains in Top 10 Districts of Jharkhand, 2011

District	*Total*	*Male*	*Female*	*Sex Ratio*	*Child Sex Ratio*	*Literacy Rate*	*Work Partici-pation Rate*
Ranchi	2,733	1,403	1,330	948	947	96.77	34.1
Bokaro	2,045	1,066	979	918	958	84.93	31.93
Hazaribagh	1,676	881	795	902	913	98.56	32.82
Purbi Singhbhum	1,670	860	810	942	935	97.16	33.95
Giridih	1,503	790	713	903	656	97.49	34.53
Dhanbad	1,268	645	623	966	1,023	94.24	33.6
Kodarma	980	508	472	929	857	95.73	32.65
Jamtara	783	419	364	869	829	90.4	40.1
Ramgarh	537	287	250	871	700	97.74	32.96
Palamu	284	144	140	972	923	93.82	36.97

Table 7A.17

Select Population Characteristics of Jains in Top 10 Districts of Odisha, 2011

District	*Total*	*Male*	*Female*	*Sex Ratio*	*Child Sex Ratio*	*Literacy Rate*	*Work Partici-pation Rate*
Balangir	2,225	1,171	1,054	900	746	95.26	33.66
Kalahandi	1,225	639	586	917	984	95.18	34.12
Cuttack	1,180	606	574	947	850	97.38	35.08
Nuapada	905	463	442	955	978	95.83	36.13
Sundargarh	721	388	333	858	742	94.6	37.86
Koraput	491	252	239	948	1,000	92.62	37.88
Khordha	476	235	241	1,026	1,700	95.97	34.66
Nabarangapur	325	171	154	901	1,000	92.88	36.31
Baleshwar	201	102	99	971	692	92.74	34.33
Malkangiri	195	103	92	893	1,083	88.24	38.46

Table 7A.18

Select Population Characteristics of Jains in Top 10 Districts of Uttarakhand, 2011

District	*Total*	*Male*	*Female*	*Sex Ratio*	*Child Sex Ratio*	*Literacy Rate*	*Work Partici-pation Rate*
Dehradun	5,117	2,605	2,512	964	764	98.1	34.53
Hardwar	2,501	1,342	1,159	864	858	96.66	33.43
Udham Singh Nagar	738	390	348	892	679	90.76	33.2
Nainital	356	174	182	1,046	800	95.63	33.15
Garhwal	212	106	106	1,000	1,300	96.83	35.38
Tehri Garhwal	91	46	45	978	750	94.05	41.76
Uttarkashi	74	40	34	850	750	92.54	41.89
Almora	31	15	16	1,067	–	85.19	38.71
Champawat	28	13	15	1,154	–	100	32.14
Pithoragarh	13	5	8	1,600	–	92.31	23.08

8

Some Notes on the Jain Diaspora

Prakash C. Jain

During the past four decades, a significant number of Jains have been settled abroad which can now collectively be referred to as Jain diaspora. Lately, the Jain diaspora has acquired its own identity and profile – independent of Hindu diaspora. Diaspora literally means dispersal – dispersal of a population group. More specifically it refers to any population group settled abroad but maintaining close links with its homeland. As such diasporas can be defined as 'ethnic minority groups of migrant origins residing and acting in host countries but maintaining strong sentimental and material links with countries of origin – homelands'.[1] In this definition, two major characteristics of a diaspora group are highlighted: maintaining one's cultural identity on the one hand and maintaining strong sentimental and material relations with homeland on the other.

In terms of the above definition, the Jains cannot be said to have existed in diaspora during the ancient and early medieval periods as there is no evidence of their organized settlement abroad. The earliest proof of Jains' diasporic settlement relates to West Asia where Ormuz is reported to have in 1549 CE, 'a small colony of the Jains and Hindus who were described as complete vegetarians and worshippers of cows'.[2] In short, with perhaps this exception, the Jain diaspora did not exist in ancient and medieval periods. Even if it did, it could not survive and continue up to the present times.[3]

Modern Jain Diaspora

Modern Indian diaspora is about 200 years old – largely a creation of British colonialism in India and some other countries of Asia, Africa, Oceania and the West Indies. This is evident from the fact that the vast majority of Indians migrated to the British colonies only (two major exceptions being Surinam and Reunion Islands – then Dutch and French colonies respectively).

Whereas the expanding capitalist plantation economies in the overseas British colonies created a great demand for labour and other occupational groups (especially traders, artisans and government servants), in India a combination of the following factors led to the exodus of Indians abroad: decline of handicraft industry, increase in land revenue, famines in the second half of the nineteenth century, sluggish and enclavist industrialization and mass illiteracy.

Historically, the following five patterns of Indian emigration have been identified by scholars: (a) indentured labour emigration, (b) *kangani/maistry* labour emigration, (c) passage or 'free' emigration, (d) 'brain/drain' type emigration, and (e) emigration to West Asia. These patterns which are briefly discussed below varyingly contributed to the formation and growth of the India diaspora.

Indian migration overseas began with the export of indentured, contract or 'coolie' labour in the 1830s when following the abolition of slavery in the British Empire, labour was needed to work on the sugar plantations in various British colonies. Until the Second World War, Indians emigrated mainly as indentured or contract labourers to British Guiana, Trinidad, Surinam, South Africa, Fiji, Mauritius and Reunion; and as *kangani* or *maistry* labourers to Burma, Malaysia, Singapore and Sri Lanka.[4] Along with these, the migration of traders also took place, especially to Burma, Malaysia, Fiji, Kenya, Uganda, Tanzania and South Africa. Such migration, however, was proportionately very small. This form of emigration is known as 'free' or 'passage' emigration – the nomenclature being derived from the fact that the emigrants paid their own passage and were free in all respects.[5]

Following the Second World War, Indian migration to the advanced industrialized countries of Europe and North America had also begun to gain momentum. The post-war economic expansion in these countries created heavy demand for skilled labour and professionals. Simultaneously, immigration laws were also relaxed in Canada and the United States. This form of overseas Indian migration of skilled and educated personnel, popularly known as the 'brain drain', thus resulted in the formation of sizeable Indian communities in Britain, Canada, Australia and the United States.[6] Since the early 1970s, Indians have also been migrating to the oil-rich Persian Gulf and other West Asian countries.[7] Some Indians have settled down permanently in these countries.

Of the five major historical patterns of emigration discussed above, whereas the first three forms of migration were colonial phenomena, the last two are the results of the inherent contradictions of the post-colonial socio-economic development in India. The current global Indian diaspora population is estimated at about 30 million. With this brief account of Indian diaspora, we now return back to our theme of Jain diaspora.

Jains emigrated mostly in relation to trade, business or commerce or as professionals and semi-professionals. Thus, for example, as 'passage' or 'free' emigrants, they migrated to South Africa, Eastern African countries of Kenya, Tanzania and Uganda, Fiji and Hong Kong.[8] The Jains also migrated to Britain, Canada, the United States, Australia, New Zealand and many European countries. Lately they have also been migrating to oil-rich Persian Gulf countries and to Israel. It is against this general background of the world-wide Indian diaspora that the various Jain diasporic communities in different parts of the world are briefly discussed in the following sections.

East Africa

Although India's trade relations with East Africa go back to antiquity, the sizeable Indian and particularly the Jain diaspora could emerge only after the consolidation of the British colonial rule in East Africa. Thus, a beginning was made in 1899 when a couple of Jains migrated to settle in Mombasa. Their descendants can still be found in Kenya.[9] The Jains as a community in East Africa grew slowly during the inter-war period, and rather rapidly after the Second World War. In 1930, there were about 2,000 Jains in East Africa: about 1,000 in Nairobi, 500 in Mombasa, 100 in Dar-es-Salaam and the rest elsewhere. By the late 1940s, their total number was estimated at 7,400: 6,000 in Kenya, 1,000 in Tanzania and 400 in Uganda.[10]

> In 1963 the total for East Africa was estimated at 32,000, with a possible 25,000 in Kenya (including 8,000 in Nairobi and 4,000 in Mombasa). The group in Uganda was rather small with a few families in Kampala and some scattered in the smaller townships. In Tanganyika, as well as scattered settlers, there were an estimated 850 Jains in Dar-es-Salaam, and 850 in Zanzibar.[11]

Almost all the Jains in East Africa have been Shvetambars originating from western India, particularly Saurashtra, Gujarat, Kutch and Maharashtra. These can be further divided into two main groups: (a) the Visa Oshwals, also known as Halari Jains and (b) the Kutchi Jains. 'In Kenya, Uganda and Tanganyika, the majority of Jains were Visa Oswals, and it was only in Zanzibar that approximately half of the community were Kutchi Jains and the other half Sthanakvasis'.[12] A great majority of Jains had been *Dukawalas* or traders, settled in urban areas.[13] With the advancement in education in the East African countries, in due course of time some of their descendants also diversified into other vocations such as engineering, medicine, law, teaching, business management and information technology.

Being mostly traders and professionals, the members of the Indian diaspora including the Jains formed a 'middleman minority' in East Africa. They faced racial discrimination in East African countries not only from the White settlers but also from the native Africans, particularly during the latter phase of their national independence movements. Consequently, many Indians chose to migrate to Britain, Canada, the United States and other countries. In 1972, the Ugandan dictator Idi Amin expelled about 70,000 Indians. Unfortunately we do not know precisely as to how many Jains were affected by these moves and where and when they migrated. A report had suggested that there were at least 13,000 Jains living in Kenya in 2003; the vast majority being concentrated in the capital city Nairobi and the rest living in Mombasa, Kisumu, Thika, Eldoret, Nakuru and Kitale. Although there are different sects of Jains living in Kenya (Shvetambara Murtipujaks, Sthanakvasis, Digambaras and a few who follow Shrimad Rajchandra), strong sectarianism is absent.[14] Digambars in Kenya who constitute a tiny minority have a temple called Digambar Jain Chaityalaya in Nairobi that was constructed in 1980. A Shvetambar Jain temple already existed in Nairobi since 1926 and one in Mombasa since 1963.[15] Prominent Jain associations in Kenya and Tanzania are: Young Jains Nairobi; Veerayatan Kenya and Veerayatan Nairobi; Shree Sthanakvasi Jain Mandal (Jain Bhavan, Forest Road, Nairobi); Jain Shvetambar Derawasi (Langoni Road, Mombasa); Visa Oshwal Community, Thika; Jain Sangh of Tanzania, Dar-Es-Salaam. Young Jains Nairobi (YJN), a non-sectarian Jain organization, has been active in Kenya since 1996. Inspired and modelled after Young Jains UK, the YJN has undertaken a large number of projects in the fields of ecology, education, health care and other aspects of community services in Kenya.

Elsewhere in Africa, Sudan hosts a small community of Jains who are of Gujarati origin and are settled in older part of the capital city. There are also small number of Jains in Ethiopia, Eritrea, South Africa, Mozambique, Zambia and Zimbabwe – perhaps not more than 100 in each country. Lusaka (Zambia) has an association called Jain Association.

West Asia

A very small number of Jains have been migrating to the West Asian countries, particularly to countries and territories in the Persian Gulf/Red Sea region since the second half of the nineteenth century when the region came under the British influence and/or administration, and economic opportunities were made available in pearl financing and general trade. Aden, Muscat and Dubai were particularly important in this regard. Subsequent to oil-price hike during the 1970s, the Jains have been migrating as professionals as well as traders in significant numbers to all the Gulf countries.

In fact we do not have much information about the Jains in different Gulf countries. In the United Arab Emirates, approximately 500 families/individuals were reported to have been living. In Kuwait, the reported figure of total Jain families/individuals is about 70–80. Elsewhere there must be a sizeable Jain community in Oman, and much smaller communities in Bahrain, Qatar, Yemen and Saudi Arabia. In Kuwait and the United Arab Emirates, there are branches of the Jain Social Group, a Mumbai-based Jain sociocultural association. Sthanakvasi Shvetambar Jain association, Veerayatan run by Sadhwi Chandanaji, is also active in Dubai.

International trade in gems and diamonds has led some Jains to settle in Israel as well as Belgium, South Africa, the

United Kingdom and the United States. In Israel, there are about 30 Jain families consisting of about 150 individuals. Almost all of them are Gujarati Shvetambar Jains tracing their origin to Palanpur and are involved in diamond business. 'The Gujarati community is socially active and, by and large, well respected in Israel. It has set up an informal association called the Gujarati Indian Association that celebrates major cultural festivals' (*High Level Committee*, 2001: 115).

South and Southeast Asia

We do not have information about the population of Jains in various South Asian countries, except Nepal in which case there were about 21,500 Jains in the late 1990s.[16] Current population could be estimated at about 30,000. There is also a Jain Temple situated at Bhagwan Mahavir Jain Niketan in Kathmandu. It serves all the major sects of the Jain community. There are about half a dozen Jain associations in Nepal. The major ones being: Nepal Jain Parisad. Nepal Swetamber Terapanthi Sabha, Shri Digamber Jain Parisad, Nepal Jain Mahila Mandal, Terapanthi Mahila Mandal, Nepal Jain Yuvak Parisad and others.

During the British period, a number of Jains migrated to Southeast Asian countries of Burma, Malaya, Singapore, Hong Kong and Japan. In Burma, the capital city of Rangoon hosted about 10,000 Jains. In 1956, a Jain temple was constructed there. A military coup in 1958 compelled a majority of them to migrate elsewhere. The Jain population in Myanmar is presently estimated at about 2,000. In Malaysia, Singapore and Hong Kong, a considerable number of Jains have been residing for a couple of generations.

Malaysia hosts about 3,000 Jains. Almost all of them belong to the Shvetambar sect. 'They are mostly ethnic Gujaratis, with a lineage in Malaysia of several generations. It is possible that some of the early Jains arrived way back in the fifteenth and sixteenth centuries in Malacca, which today has a strong Jain community'. There is also a Jain temple located at First Garden,

Ipoh. It was built by a Jain businessman Bharat Jasani. The Temple houses the idol of Parshvanath, and now serves as a pilgrimage place as well as a cultural centre. It is managed by a charitable trust called Shantiniketan Foundation. The temple is designed after a famous one in Tithal in India. Another Jain temple is located at Kuala Lumpur.

The Jains have been living in Singapore for more than a century now. Although only a few Jains had settled in Singapore during the 1920s and 1930s, their number and organized activities increased only after the Second World War. Until 1965, these activities were carried out at 79 Waterloo Street, and since 1978 at 18 Jalan Yasin off Jalan Eunos. The two storey-building named 'Jain Sthanak' consisted of a big hall, kitchen, store, parking lots on the ground floor, and an office, a library, and a hall used for religious functions on the second floor. In 1995, a new building with modern amenities was constructed with a donation of Singapore $5,00,000 by Shrimati Nirmalaben Doshi in loving memory of her husband, Shri Chandulal Doshi, Society's founder trustee and former president. Now the building is named Shrimati Nirmalaben Chandulal Doshi Jain Sthanak.

Presently there are about 1,000 Jains in Singapore, about 95 per cent of them being from the states of Gujarat and Rajasthan. Singapore Jain Religious Society has been running a 'Jain *shala* (school) every Sunday morning. A chartered bus shuttles the children from their homes to the Sthanak and back. The Society library has religious and cultural books in Gujarati, Hindi and English. Ladies have their *satsang* every week. The members also use the Sthanak premises for marriages and other social activities' (http://www.sjrs.org.sg/history.html). Besides the Singapore Jain Religious Society, there are three more Jain associations in Singapore, namely Jain Sangh of Singapore at 54 Arab Street; Jain Sangh in Katong and Singapore Jain Society on 150 South Bridge Road. The society is managed by a committee which is elected annually at a general body meeting.

In Hong Kong, there are about 500 Jains, mainly Gujarati and Rajasthani. Most of them migrated to Hong Kong in 1980s and are mainly engaged in diamond trading business. The Hong Kong Jain Sangh had founded a Jain temple in 1996. The Jain Center of Hong Kong Ltd. (4–B, 4/F Wealthy Heights, 35–37 Macdonnell Road) and the Jain International (38a, Macdonnell Road, 4th Floor) are two more Jain associations in Hong Kong.

In Japan, the Jain community is relatively small consisting of about 50 families, but a Mahavir Swami Jain Temple exists in Kobe since 1984. The idol of Bhagwan Mahavir was flown from Bombay in 1984 and the *panch kalyanak pratishtha* was held in April month of the same year. However, the formal opening ceremony of the temple was held on 1 June 1885. The temple is located at Ijinkan quarters of Kitano-cho, Chou-Ku-Kobe, Japan.

Thailand hosts a major Jain community in Southeast Asia. It consists of 500 families of which about 100 families belong to the Digambar Jain sect and the rest to the Shvetambar sect. The Digambar Jains have got an association called the Digambar Jain Federation, Bangkok, whereas the Shvetambars are organized through an association named Bangkok Jain Sangh. Most of the Jains in Thailand are reportedly doing business in gems and jewellery. A majority of them lives in Bangkok which now boasts of two Jain temples – one each for Shvetambars and Digambars. Whereas the three-storey Digambar Jain temple called Shri 1008 Mahavir Digambar Jain Mandir came into existence in 2006, the Shvetambar Jain temple was constructed a few years ago. Interestingly, a periodic Jain pilgrimage tourism from India to Thailand and some other countries of the region has also begun to take place in recent years. Jakarta, Indonesia, also hosts a small Jain community of about 80 families with an association Jain Social Group.

In other countries of the Asia-Pacific region, New Zealand had only 207 adherents of Jainism in its 2013 census. In Australian census, the Jains are now listed separately and there were 4,047 Jains in 2016 census. Small communities of Jains are there in Canberra, Melbourne, Adelaide, Perth and Sydney. There is a Jain temple in Canberra since March 2000, and another had come up in Melbourne in April 2008. In Melbourne, an association called Melbourne Shwetambar Jain Sangh is active since 2002. Jain Society of Sydney is located at 38 Ourimbah Road, Mosman, Sydney.

United Kingdom

Barrister Champat Rai Jain was perhaps the first Jain to have gone to England for getting a degree in law during 1862–1867. Subsequently he visited Europe several times, studied Christianity and wrote a few books on comparative religion (e.g. *Science, Jainism and Christianity*, and *Confluence of Opposites*). The next Jain scholar to have visited Britain in 1896 and again in 1901 was Virchand R. Gandhi, who was instrumental at that time in getting a few Christians converted to Jainism in the United States and the United Kingdom. One such convert Mr Herbert Warren wrote a book called *Jainism in Western Garb* (1912). In 1905, J.L. Jaini, a prominent Jain scholar, visited Britain where he wrote and published his well-known book *Outlines of Jainism*.

Besides these scholars, a very few Jains immigrated to England either from India or East Africa until the mid-1960s. Since the late 1960s, a small number of Jains began to migrate to the United Kingdom individually under the Commonwealth Immigrants Quota System. About the same time, Jains from East Africa also began to settle in England, particularly following the introduction of the Voucher System by the British Government. The policy of Africanization pursued by the newly independent East African states that culminated in the expulsion of Asians from Uganda in 1972 was the major push factor for the Jains as well to get out of East Africa.[17] Some Jains also immigrated to Britain from Ethiopia, Sudan and Yemen during the 1960s and 1970s due to adverse political situations there. Thus of the estimated total population of about 20,000 Jains in Britain in the mid-1990s, about 5,000 were from India and about 15,000 from East Africa and elsewhere.[18] By the late 1990s, there were 30,000 Jains in the United Kingdom – 25,000 in London, 1,000 in Leicester, 500 in Manchester and 500 in Birmingham. Presently, the Jain population in the United Kingdom is estimated at around 50,000.

Jains' sociocultural and religious needs in Britain are being looked after by about half a dozen temples and more than 30 associations. Major Jain temples are Jain Temple, Leicester; Kailash Giri Jain Temple, London; Shree Parshwanath Digambar Jain Mandir, London; and Bhagwan Mahaveer Jain Temple, Middlesex. The Jain Temple of Leicester is located at a converted church which was bought by the Jains in 1980 with the blessings of Shri Chitrabhanuji. The *pratishtha mahotsav* was held in 1988 under the guidance of H.H. Shri Charukeerthi Bhattarak Maharaj of Shravanabelagola. The temple has the idol of Bhagwan Chandraprabhu as the main deity. A 10 feet high idol of Bhagwan Bahubali in a *kayotsrga*, goddess Padmavati and other Jain idols are also in the temple. The temple premises also have three *sanctum sanctorums* dedicated to the Shvetambar sect, besides a big hall, a school and a library, the boarding and lodging facilities are also available in the temple complex.

Of the numerous Jain sociocultural associations in the United Kingdom, the following three are the most important ones: the Jain Samaj Europe, the Oshwal Association of the United Kingdom and the Navnat Vanik Association (UK).

> The Jain Samaj Europe has established a Jain Centre in the city of Leicester. This centre is a major symbol of Jain unity, the first centre of its kind to embody co-operation among Jain groups by including in one building a Shvetambar temple, a Digambar temple, a Guru Gautam mandir, a Sthanakvasi *upashraya* and a Shrimad Rajchandra *Jnana Mandir*. Its fine Jain architecture, including elaborate interior and exterior carvings, has made it a major tourist attraction and place of pilgrimage

for the Jains. The Jain Samaj Europe has published books and a journal on Jainism. Jains in Europe are seeking to widen their activities through the creation of 'inter-faith' links such as the Jain-Christian Association, the Jain-Jewish Association and the Leicestershire Ahimsa Society for the Care of Nature.[19]

A major initiative taken by the Jains in United Kingdom was the establishment of Institute of Jainology. The institute, conceived in 1983 at the first International Jain Conference in London, has campuses in Greenford (Middlesex, UK) and Ahmedabad (Gujarat, India). It is a charitable trust registered in 1986. One of the major achievements of the institute has been the finalization of *Jain Declaration on Nature* which was incorporated by the World Wide Fund (WWF) on nature in October 1990 as official entry of the Jain faith into the WWF Network on conservation and religion. The preparation of this document involved about 30 scholars from different countries including late Dr L.M. Singhvi, a prominent jurist, a Jain scholar, Indian parliamentarian and a former Ambassador of India to United Kingdom who had prepared the final draft.

Besides United Kingdom, Belgium hosts a well-organized Jain community consisting of about 400 families, numbering about 1,500 persons. They have been there since about the middle of the twentieth century. The majority of the Jains lives in Antwerp, and they are engaged in the diamond business. A Jain temple and a meditation centre (*upashray*) exist in Wilrijk (near Antwerp) which was completed in August 2010. There are two cultural associations in Belgium: one is called Jain Cultural Center and is located at Hoveniersstraat 2, Room 345, 2018 Antwerp, and the other is Jain Ashram located at 15 Ahornenlaan, Wilrijk, Antwerp.

United States

Sri Virchand R. Gandhi is credited as the first Jain visitor to North America when he attended the Parliament of World Religions in Chicago in 1893. He stayed with the Howard family for two years and lectured extensively on Jainism. His next visit to the United States occurred in 1896. Another Jain to have visited the United States was Barrister Champat Rai Jain. He addressed the World Fellowship of Faiths in Chicago on 30 August 1933. A third name often mentioned in this context is that of Sri J.L. Jaini of the World Jain Mission of Aliganj, Etah, India, who had travelled to the United States, the United Kingdom, Germany and some other European countries.

The first Jain settlers in United States had arrived in 1944. For the next 30 years, a very small number of Jains continued to immigrate and settle in the United States. Meanwhile, two Shvetambar Jain monks Shri Chitrabhanuji and Muni Sushil Kumarji did considerably towards propagating Jainism in North America and Europe. The former first visited North America in 1971 and had established many Jain meditation centres and contributed substantially through his discourses and publications. Similarly Muni Sushil Kumarji who first visited North America in 1975 was instrumental in establishing the International Mahavir Jain Mission (IMJM) at Blairstown in New Jersey in 1991, and its numerous branches in the United States., Canada and other parts of the world. The Blairstown IMJM also known as *Siddhachalam* (*The Jain Tirth*) has emerged as a major Jain pilgrimage centre in North America. The Canadian headquarter of the IMJM is located at Scarborough, Ontario.

Until 1950s, there was no Jain diasporic community worth the name in the United States. From 1960s onwards, a considerable number of professionals, academics and students began to settle in North America. During mid-1960s, the Jain population in North America was estimated at about 15,000; a majority of them being Gujaratis. By the early 1980s, this figure increased to '20,000 plus', constituting about one-fourth of the total Jain diasporic population.[20]

A statistical profile of the Jain community given in the *1986 Directory of Jains* shows that the majority of the respondents were either engineers (33.1%) or in the medical field (19.8%); 'even though Jains are known as businessmen in India, a small percentage (12.1%) are self-employed in the United States'.[21] By 1990s, the population of Jains in the United States had increased to about 50,000 and presently it is estimated at 1,60,000. In the United States, 80 per cent of Jains live in 10 states, dominated by New Jersey (16%), California (15%) and New York (12%), with significant representation in Maryland, Massachusetts, Pennsylvania, Michigan, Ohio, Illinois and Texas.

By the mid-1990s, there were 55 Jain sociocultural associations/societies/centres in the United States catering to a wide variety of community needs. Currently such associations may number more than 100. In order to coordinate the activities of a certain number of these associations, the Federation of Jain Associations in North America (JAINA) was formed in 1981 'which had more than 6,000 participants in their ninth biannual convention in 1997'.[22]

JAINA was initiated at the first Jain Convention in 1981 in Los Angeles under the guidance of Shri Chitrabhanuji and the late Acharya Sushil Kumarji and formed at the second Jain Convention in New York in 1983. Since that time JAINA has striven to foster brotherhood, friendship and unity among various Jain communities and to preserve, protect and promote Jain heritage. JAINA has also been very active in forging relationships with interfaith and multi-faith organizations. JAINA headquarters are located in Getzville, New York, but Jain centres can be found in over half of the 50 states. JAINA functions through more than 300 volunteers from all corners of North America.

Diasporic Jains are particularly keen to pass on their social values and cultural heritage to the next generation. Towards this end, the JAINA had established in July 1991 a 'committee' called Young Jain Association (YJA) that puts emphasis on projects relating to Jain youth between the ages 14 and 29. The mission of the YJA is to be recognized as a national and international umbrella youth organization for establishing a network to share Jain heritage through young people.

The Jain community in North America has been slowly moving towards institutional completeness in terms of building temples, establishing sociocultural associations, attempting to socialize the new generation in the Jaina way of life and increasingly continuing marriages within the community. More than 5,500 Jain youth regularly attend Jain *Päthashäläs* (schools) once a month on Sundays in about 70 Jain centres of North America.

The current phase of Jain diaspora in North America is being dominated by socially informed second generation. Often distancing themselves from considerations of sects, castes and excessive rituals rooted in Indian Jainism,

> they seek to adapt the principles of care for organisms, plants, animals, and all people inherent in their tradition to a public stance on vegetarianism (and increasingly veganism), environmental advocacy, meditation, civic and gender equality, interfaith alliances, and community service.[23]

A document 'Jain Vision 2020' prepared by the JAINA's Long Range Planning Committee is eloquent testimony to the adaptability and transformation of Jainism from a moksha marg ideology to a socially concerned religion. To quote Donaldson again,

> with a historic base in industries such as banking, engineering, education, and medicine, and recent involvement in technology and politics, it is reasonable to anticipate that modern Jainism will adapt itself to new challenges in global financing, scientific and technological innovation, corporate accountability, communication, and bioethics.[24]

Canada

Jains in Canada are often hyphenated with their US counterparts. Most Jain activities are also tied up with those of the US

Jain communities. In the case of Canada, it is difficult to say who migrated first to Canada and when. In all probability, the first Jains must have migrated to Canada after India's independence, particularly from the 1950s onwards. Since then a large number of Jains have migrated to Canada first under the Quota system and subsequently under the Point system. These were joined by a small number of East African Jain refugees who were expelled from Uganda by Idi Amin Dada in 1972. As per Canadian Census data, there were 1,410 Jains in 1991 and 2,455 in 2001. It is difficult to reconcile these figures with an estimate that suggested that in the early 1990s there were about 10,000 Jains in Canada.[25] According to the same source, all Canadian provinces except Saskatchewan, Prince Edward Island, Yukon and North West Territories had Jain residents. Ontario was the host to the majority of Jains followed by Quebec and British Columbia. This trend of geographical distribution still holds good. As in the United States, in Canada too a majority of Jains reside in urban and industrial centres and happen to be professionals.

Concluding Remarks

The modern Jain diaspora was mainly formed during the past four decades, though its history can be traced back to the late nineteenth century. It made a small beginning in the last decade of the nineteenth century in East Africa and has been continuing to flourish there in spite of two World Wars, the Great Depression, Africanization and the expulsion of Indians from Uganda. In countries other than East Africa, the Jain diaspora could not emerge until the last quarter of the twentieth century when the Jains began to emigrate to the industrially developed countries in Europe and North America, Australia, New Zealand and the Persian Gulf countries. Unlike in India where the Jains continue to remain overwhelmingly a trading community, the diasporic Jains have emerged mainly as communities of professionals.

With the increase in their numerical strength over the years, the Jain diaspora has acquired an independent identity – independent of the Hindu diaspora. Everywhere they are consolidating their distinct identity and life style by forming sociocultural or religious associations, building Jain temples and promoting vegetarianism and so on.

Of the total diasporic population estimated at about quarter-of-a-million, about 90 per cent of the Jains abroad live in just five countries, namely the United States (1,60,000+), the United Kingdom (50,000+), Nepal (25,000), Kenya (15,000) and Canada (5,000). For the past few years, the small diasporic Jain population has been exerting a significant amount of influence on the Jains in India through a number of associations. Making people aware about Jainism as a world religion and spreading its messages of *ahimsa,* peaceful co-existence and vegetarianism appear to be high on the agenda of the Jain diasporic pro-activism.

Notes and References

1. Sheffer, Gabriel (ed.), *Modern Diasporas in International Politics* (London: Croom Helm, 1986), p. 3.
2. Lach, Donald, *Asia in the Making of Europe*. Vol. 1. (Chicago: University of Chicago Press, 1965).
3. A number of scholars however have been attempting to prove that during the ancient period Jainism was spread practically all over the world. This is suggested on the ground that the key Jain doctrines, particularly *ahimsa* and vegetarianism, were prevalent in most countries of the world, and that the world famous temples such as Borobudur in Java and the Angkor Wat in Cambodia were basically the Jain temples. See Gokul Prasad Jain, *Videshon mein Jain Dharma,* Lucknow: Shri Bharatvarshiya Digambar Jain Mahasabha, 2012; J.D. Jain, *Jaina Archeology Outside India,* Lucknow: Shri Bharatvarshiya Digambar Jain Mahasabha, 2011.
4. Sandhu, Karnail Singh, *Indians in Malaysia Some Aspects of Immigration and Settlement 1786-1967* (Cambridge: University, London, 1969); Tinker, Hugh, *A New System of Slavery: The Export*

of Indian Labour Oversea, 1830–1920 (London: Oxford University Press, 1974).

5. Jain, Prakash C., *Racial Discrimination against Overseas Indians: A Class Analysis* (New Delhi: Concept Publishing Company, Delhi, 1990); Mangat, J.S., *A History of Asians in East Africa* (Oxford: Clarendon Press, 1969).
6. Helweg, A.W., *Sikhs in England: The Development of a Migrant Community* (Delhi: Oxford University Press, 1987); Helweg, Arthur W. and Usha M. Helweg, *An Immigrant Success Story: East Indians in America* (Delhi: Oxford University Press, 1990).
7. Jain, Prakash C., *Indian Diaspora in West Asia: A Reader* (Delhi: Manohar Books, 2007).
8. Jain, *Racial Discrimination against Overseas Indians*; Mangat, *A History of Asians in East Africa*; Ramchandani, R.R., *Uganda Asians: The End of an Empire* (Bombay: United Asian Publication, 1976); Vaid, K.N., *The Overseas Indian Community in Hong Kong* (Hong Kong: University of Hong Kong, 1972).
9. Shah, Sneh, 'Who are the Jains?', *New Community*, Vol. 7, 1977, p. 371.
10. Mangat, *A History of Asians in East Africa*, p. 142.
11. Shah, 'Who Are the Jains?', p. 372.
12. Ibid.
13. Jain, *Racial Discrimination against Overseas Indians*, Chapter 4.
14. Shah, Vina, 'Nairobi Revival', *Jain Spirit*, No. 14, 2003, p. 4.
15. Dundas, Paul, *The Jains* (London: Routledge, 1992), p. 233.
16. Gall, Thomothy L., *Worldmark Encylopedia of Culture and Daily Life*, Vol. 3 (Cleveland: Eastwood Publications, 1998), pp. 565 and 567.
17. Ramchandani, *Uganda Asians*.
18. Shah, 'Who Are the Jains?', p. 371.
19. Shah, Natubhai, *Jainism: The World of Conquerors*, Vol. 1 (Brighton: Sussex Academic Press, 1998), p. 80.
20. Paul Dundas, *The Jains* (London/New York: Routledge, 1992), p. 232.
21. Williams, Raymond Body, *Religions of Immigrants from India and Pakistan* (Cambridge: Cambridge University Press, 1988), p. 64.
22. Shah, Natubhai, *Jainism*, p. 82.

23. Donaldson, Brianne, 'The Socially-informed Second Generation Jains in America', 2015, p. 2. www.patheos.com/topics/jains-in-america-brianne-donaldson-7-1-2015-aspx-p.=2
24. Ibid.
25. Bhuvanendra Kumar, *Jainism in North America* (Mississagua, Ontario: Humanities Press, 1996).

9

Jain Population Predicament

Need to Learn from the Parsi and Jewish Situations

Sulekh C. Jain and Yashwant K. Malaiya

A few religious communities of the world such as Parsis and Jews have identified the threat to their existence. The Parsis have managed to survive after arriving in India. However, today they are raising very few children and are on the verge of extinction.[1] Half the Jewish population in United States marry outside their community. Studies show that most grandchildren of Jewish–non-Jewish marriage do not identify with Judaism.[2] But they have at least recognized the problem. Jain community appears to be completely oblivious of the future it faces. There are no debates or discussions.

Many Jains today discount the census count (44,51,753 Jains in 2011) and claim that the actual number of Jains is much higher, although without any supporting data. The only reason given is that during the census, many Jains either do not identify themselves as Jains or the census takers on their own put them in the Hindu category.

Even if we assume that there is a significant undercount of the Jains, trends show that actual number of Jains is going down as a percentage of total India's population, and this decline will accelerate. For a number of sociological reasons, the survival of Jainism overseas is also threatened. Let us examine the current status and the trends.

Jains in India

Before independence, the Jain population of India dropped from 0.49 per cent in 1881 to 0.37 per cent in 1941.[3] For three decades after the partition, the Jain had a healthy growth about equal to the rest of India. The Jains were 0.47 per cent in 1981. But the proportion dropped sharply in 1991 to 0.40 per cent and stayed about the same in 2001. As we feared earlier, there was significant drop during 2001–2011, the fraction dropping to 0.37 per cent (Table 9.1).

Table 9.1

Population of India by Major Religious Communities, 2011

Religious Community	*Total Population*	*% of Total*	*Decadal Growth Rate, 2001–2011*
Total	1,21,08,54,977	100	–
Hindu	96,62,57,353	79.80	24.6%
Muslim	17,22,45,158	14.23	16.8%
Christian	2,78,19,588	2.30	15.5%
Sikh	2,08,33,116	1.72	8.4%
Buddhist	84,42,972	0.70	6.1%
Jain	44,51,753	0.37	5.4%
Parsi	–	–	–17.7%[4]

Jainism has historically been present all over India. There are native Punjabi Jains and Tamil Jains. States with largest Jain populations are Maharashtra (1.25% Jains), Rajasthan (0.91%) Madhya Pradesh (0.78%), Gujarat (0.96%) and Karnataka (0.72%).[5] There is not a single state where Jains are 2 per cent or more. There are only three districts with Jain population exceeding 4 per cent (Mumbai 4.10%, Kolhapur 4.00% and Belgaum 3.73%). The cities such as Delhi, Bombay, Ahmedabad, Indore, Udaipur, Jaipur, Baroda and Pune have a significant population of Jains, but all of them with less than 10 per cent Jains.

The 2011 census has confirmed what was feared earlier. For the decade 2001–2011, the Jain growth rate is one-third of the rate for Hindus and one-fifth the rate for the Muslims.

Jains Overseas

Outside India, significant presence of Jains has risen only during the second half of the last century. The first major emigration of Jains took place to Kenya and Uganda and later to United States, Canada and United Kingdom. In 1997, it was estimated that the Jain population in United States and Canada was 85,000.[6] Since then the number[7] may have gone up to about 1,60,000. There are about 20,000 in the United Kingdom,[8] 14,000 in Kenya area[9] and some in Belgium, Dubai, Abu Dhabi, Nepal, Singapore, Malaysia, Indonesia, Japan and Australia.[10]

The earlier emigrants who initially moved to East African countries had modest educational levels. They have prospered through their enterprise and many have moved to United Kingdom. The recent migration to the West since 1970s includes highly educated professionals such as engineers, doctors, IT professionals, financial experts and businessmen.

The Jains in Eastern Africa, Singapore, Malaysia, Middle East and Japan have nearly remained very Indian as if they never left India. The Jains in United States and Canada being professionals interact and socialize with non-Jains. They have started changing their habits to suit the conditions they are in. This includes language, customs, religious practices and even marriages.

Trends Affecting Jains in North America

The number of Jains in North America has been going up because of the continuous arrivals of Jains from India. However, the number of practicing Jains in the second generation is going down. If this trend continues, then we will see its dramatic result in the next one to two generations. The following can be considered as the major factors behind this trend:

1. About half of Jain youths in United States are marrying non-Indians, and another 30 per cent marry non-Jain Indians.[11] Thus, only about 20 per cent are marrying fellow Jains. When this happens, the bonds to Jainism in the new family get diluted or lost, depending on the upbringing of the Jain partner, who generally tends to be less aggressive. The Jain identity is then likely to be lost over a period of time.
2. Most of the Jain organizations have not recognized the needs of the Jain youths and as a result they feel alienated, sometimes even allergic towards the Jain tradition. The Jain centres often cater to the older generation. Sometimes they become highly ritualistic and dominated by regional or sectarian affiliations. Jain youths and young Jain professionals are losing bonding with the Jain SANGH.
3. Many of our religious speakers who mostly come from India are unaware of the needs of the young Jains, having never been exposed to the Western society and their discourses consist of other-worldliness, and academic intellectualism.
4. There is no appreciation of activism in Jain Community unlike the American groups. The Jain youths who are highly motivated feel no connectivity with the Jain organizations.
5. Often there is a lack of pride of being a Jain and the practice of *ahimsa* and vegetarianism. What used to distinguish Jains from rest of the pack is very quickly getting lost.
6. Many Jain families are regularly visiting non-Jain institutions such as Chinmaya Mission, Swami Narayan and even Christian organizations. This causes them to gradually drift away.

In North America, there are institutions that are making positive contributions, but they need support and encouragement. The two major Jain youth organizations YJA (Young Jains of America) and YJP (Young Jain Professionals) are well organized and dynamic but represent only a tiny fraction of Jain youths. The Federation of Jain Associations in North America (JAINA) is a significant institution in North America, however its main energies are devoted to organizing a convention every two years. Many of the issues affecting the Jain community in North America need careful attention.

In several Jain centres, there are Sunday Jain Pathshalas for youths aged 5–17. Beyond that, there is nothing to sustain this teaching. Many teachers emphasize rote learning of *mantras* and *stutis*. One more contributing factor is the lack of quality teaching material in English language.

Concerns about the Jains in India

In India, the Jain population has declined greatly in many regions. In some regions such as coastal Karnataka and Tamil Nadu, several communities used to be mainly Jain but now only traces remain. In Rajasthan and Gujarat, a large fraction of Vaishnavas are descendants of former Jains. The history of Agrawals in North India is entirely Jain until the Mughal rule. Only a couple of centuries ago, texts suggest that even half of the Agrawals used to be Jain.[12] Today only about 8 per cent Agrawals remain Jain.[13]

Here are some of the factors contributing to the continual decline of Jain population in India.

1. Gender selection and female foeticide/abortion is a new trend. The recent Indian census data show that in Jain community there are only 89.5 girls for 100 boys between the ages of 1 and 4 years. This will cause a disintegration of the Jain society. A few Jain monks have now started speaking out against this.[14]

2. Most Jain couples today have two or fewer children. This is below the number needed for maintaining the same population.[15] The population of the prosperous KDO (Kutchi Dasa Oswal) community in Mumbai has already started declining.[16]
3. Demands of dowry by young men and their parents. Because of this, either many a girls remain unmarried, have bad marriage or end up in messy divorce. Some girls become a victim of extortion.
4. Euphoria on building more and bigger temples but not preservation of Jain knowledge and traditions. We need classes, workshops, seminars and academic organizations to provide teaching and training in Jainism.
5. We tend to identify with a region or a specific sect rather than as Jains who follow Lord Mahavira. Identifying us as Jains, for example, using Jai Jinendra as a salutation unites us all with a common heritage.
6. Hinduization of Jain society in India as well as overseas. While respecting other religions is proper, many Jains are unable to overcome pressure to assimilate. The distinct lines of difference between Jainism and Hinduism are becoming increasingly blurred. In some Jain homes, worship of Hindu gods is becoming common. Many Jains visit Hindu places of worship, gurus and faqirs seeking miracles.

What Can Be Done?

Following are some steps that can be taken:

- We need visionary leadership and organizations who can understand the societal issues. We get lost in awards and other recognitions. We have to find solutions to today's issues using today's tools.
- We need involvement of leading professionals in the Jain community. The Jains are the most educated community in India with a large number of Supreme Court and High

Court Justices, Vice Chancellors, officers, educationists and others. They have skills to contribute to the urgent issues and debates affecting the society. While many of these are aloof, we see some awareness now and some of them are coming forward to contribute.

- *Youth Movements*. The youth bring life into a moribund society. For a long time, a strong Jain youth movement had been missing. In India, fortunately there are now organizations such as Young Jains of India and Jain Medical Doctors Association. We should all support and encourage this trend.
- *Visionary Media*. Media plays a very important role in debating the issues and shaping the society. We have hundreds of Jain newspapers and magazines but their quality and readership need much to be desired.

The change is inevitable. As an affluent and highly educated Jain community, we need to have healthy debates, action plans and road maps. These issues are not easy and similarly their answers and solutions are not easy. Collectively, we need to take that first step now in the right direction.

Learning from Jewish and Parsi Communities

As already mentioned, there exist two communities that are remarkably similar to the Jains. The Parsis, concentrated in Mumbai, and the Jews, who have a significant presence in United States, are both elite minorities that tend to be urbanized wealthy merchants with much higher levels of education compared with others, just like the Jains.

The Parsi population, after having flourished in India for centuries, has been declining for the past seven decades since 1941. Even with the special attention given by the Parsi institutions and the government, their population declined by another 18 per cent during 2001–2011.[17] Many of the Parsis appear to have resigned to the fate leading to eventual disappearance and have lost the will to fight.[18] The key factor is well known, they marry late and some never get married. Intermarriage (39%) with others is a threat, but some researchers believe it to be of secondary importance.[19] Their fertility rate (average number of children per woman) is about 1 which is less than half of the rate of 2.1 required to maintain a constant population.[20]

On the other hand, the Jewish population in the United States has stabilized, even though majority of the Jews (72 per cent among non-orthodox) marry outside, and most tend to have a low fertility rate of about 1.7.[21] There are two factors that are helping. The minority Orthodox Jews, who significantly lag in education, have a fertility rate which is much higher (3.4–6.7). Secondly, Judaism has the reputation of being a superior religion (which is in fact a part of the Jewish dogma), and thus many children of the intermarried families tend to identify as being Jewish.

It should be noted that a large percentage of the Jewish population are Jewish by identity rather than by religious practice.[22] Some of the notable Jewish schemes (such as the Taglit-Birthright Israel) rely on strengthening the Jewish identity.[23]

The Jain fertility rate has recently been about 1.5,[24] which is better than the current Parsi rate, but much lower than the rate needed to sustain the current Jain population.

What can the Jains draw from the two examples? Possibly this two-pronged approach:

1. *Address the Jain Fertility Rate.* To a considerable extent, the fertility rate is a function of education level (lower level often correlates with a higher fertility rate) and marriage age. The highest fertility rate for a woman occurs during the age 20–24 and then starts dropping. The rate drops sharply after age 29. The Jewish and Parsi communities have fertility programmes that attempt to help low fertility couples. The Mormons have managed to combine early marriages with high educational levels.

2. Bring dynamism in the Jain society that will bring a sense of identity and pride among Jains. That would involve having active Jain organizations that promote the awareness of the Jain traditions among not only Jains but also among those with a mixed Jain and non-Jain heritage. It should be noted that the Jains tend to be non-aggressive and often the non-Jain spouse dominates.

Unfortunately overwhelming majority of Jains is oblivious to the threat to Jain survival, although occasionally informed Jains have been warning about it for more than a century.[25] The Jains should follow the lead of the Jewish community to ensure that Jainism continues to flourish. The Jewish community is not only an elite and successful community, but it also has successfully addressed the challenges to its existence for many centuries. The Jain scholars and leaders should carefully study the approaches used by the Jewish leaders. While the Parsis too have been financially successful, they have continued to make the mistakes that are threatening their existence. The Jains should identify and avoid these mistakes.

Notes and References

1. Samanth Subramanian, 'India's Zoroastrians Dying Out for Lack of Parsi Clergy', *The National, Australia*, 28 January 2011.
2. A. Gordon and R. Horowitz, 'Will Your Grandchildren Be Jews', http://www.aish.com/jw/s/48910307.html.
3. V.A. Sangave, *Jaina Community: A Social Survey*, 1959.
4. Nergish Sunavala, 'Alarming 18% Decline in Parsi Population since 2001 Census Has Community Worried', *Time News Network*, 25 July 2016,
5. Based on 2011 census data.
6. Y.K. Malaiya, 'Jainism in America', *Lansing Jain Society Pratishtha Souvenir*, 2000, pp. 26–29.
7. Since then the number of listed telephone numbers with last name 'Jain' has gone up by a factor of 2.8. If annual rate of increase is taken as 7.6 per cent based on census data for Indians, the estimate would be 1,62,000.

8. *Religion in England and Wales 2011*, Office for National Statistics 11 December 2012, http://www.open.ac.uk/blogs/boh/wp-content/uploads/2013/01/dcp171776_2905101.pdf (accessed on 23 October 2016).
9. http://cesa.imb.org/peoplegroups/jains.html (accessed on 23 October 2016).
10. See Prakash C. Jain, 'Exploring the Global Jain Diaspora', in Jayaram (Ed) *Diversities in the Indian Diaspora* (Delhi: Oxford University Press, 2011), pp. 155–172; Also Prakash C. Jain, *Jains in India and Abroad: A Sociological Introduction* (Delhi: International School for Jain Studies, 2011), Chapter 3.
11. Based on Amazon.com wedding registry, accessed 23 October 2016.
12. For example, Navalsah Chandeia, *Vardhamana Puran* 1768 AD.
13. Based on the 1911 census count of Agrawals (10,19,698) and *1914 Bharatvarshiya Digambar Jain Directory* (67,121 Agrawal Jains), and the observation that about 20 per cent of the Agrawal Jains are Shvetambar, mainly Sthanakvasi (from the matrimonial data bases).
14. Muni Tarun Sagar, 'Fight Female Infanticide as Women Play Crucial Role in Society', *Ahimsa Times*, January 2006.
15. J. Craig, 'Replacement Level Fertility and Future Population Growth', *Population Trends*, 1994, Winter, Vol. 78, pp. 20–22.
16. 'KDO Jains Attempt Tracing Causes of Fast Decline', *Times of India*, 25 April 2004.
17. 'Alarming 18% Decline in Parsi Population since 2001 Census Has Community Worried', *Times News Network*, 25 July 2016.
18. Dinyar Patel, 'Understanding Parsi Population Decline in India: A Historical Perspective', Jawaharlal Nehru Centre, Mumbai, 7 May 2011.
19. Zubin C. Shroff and Marcia C. Castro, 'The Potential Impact of Intermarriage on the Population Decline of the Parsis of Mumbai, India', *Demographic Research*, Vol. 25, 26 August 2011, pp. 545–564.
20. Roshan Rivetna, 'The Zarathushti World: A Demographic Picture', Presented at the XVI North American Zarathushti Congress, 2–5 August 2012 in Rye, New York.
21. Steven M. Cohen, 'What Is to Be Done? Policy Responses to the Shrinking Jewish Middle', *Berman Jewish Policy Archive*, Stanford, 22 May 2014.

22. 'A Portrait of Jewish Americans', Pew Research Center, 1 October 2013.
23. Leonard Saxe, 'Take-Aways' from the Pew Research Center's 'A Portrait of Jewish Americans'.
24. Fertility Tables F-9, F-9 SC, F-9 ST AND F-10, Census of India, 2011.
25. See, Ganesh Prasad Varni, *Meri Jeevan Gatha*, Pt. I (in Hindi). Varanasi: Bhargav Bhushan Press, 1949, p. 248. The book refers to the decline in Jain population from 14 lakh in 1891 to 12 lakh in 1911. See also, Sulekh C. Jain and Yashwan K. Malaiya, 'Can Jainism Survive in 21st Century?', *JAINA Digest*, 2011, pp. 125–128.

10

Under-Enumeration of Jain Population

Evidence from Two Delhi Surveys

Shugan C. Jain and Prakash C. Jain

This chapter confirms the long-held contention of a number of knowledgeable Jains that Jain population in India has been under-enumerated in the census taking exercise. The issue came into sharp focus with the 2011 census data suggesting only 5.4 per cent decadal growth rate of the total Jain population in India during 2001 and 2011.[1] Under-enumeration of Jain population in Indian census has been a major issue in the minds of Jain leaders and opinion makers for over a century now. In 1881, the total Jain population as per census records was only 12 lakh which after 130 years has now increased to about 45 lakh (Table 10.1). Many Jains believe that their population presently is not less than 1 crore. Some even claim it to be 2 crore.[2] They believe that a considerable number of Jains are enumerated as Hindus in each census, resulting in consistently low population enumeration of the Jains.

Table 10.1

Jain Population in India Since 1881

Census	*Number of Jains (in 000s)*	*Percentage of Total Population*	*Decadal Per cent Change in the Number of Jains*	*Urbanization*	*Sex Ratio*
1881	1,222	0.49	–	–	–
1891	1,417	0.51	15.94	–	–
1901	1,334	0.47	-5.83	30.0	929
1911	1,248	0.41	-6.47	29.6	940
1921	1,177	0.39	-5.26	33.9	931
1931	1,251	0.37	6.28	34.6	940
1941	1,440	0.37	15.81	41.4	930
1951	1,618	0.45	11.67	–	927
1961	2,027	0.46	25.17	53.9	924
1971	2,605	0.47	28.48	59.8	940
1981	3,193	0.48	23.17	64.0	941
1991	3,352	0.40	4.42	71.0	946
2001	4,225	0.40	26.0	75.0	940
2011	4,451	0.37	5.41	80.0	954

Sources: 1. Kingsley Davis, *Population of India and Pakistan* (New York: Russell and Russell, 1951), pp. 178–179.

2. Census of India, 1961, Paper No. 1 of 1963, Religion (New Delhi: RGO, 1963), pp. ii–viii.
3. Census of Indian, 1971, Paper No. 2 of 1972, Religion (New Delhi: RGO, 1972), pp. 2–5.
4. Census of India, 1981, Paper No. 4 of 1984, Household Population by Religion of Head of Household (New Delhi: RGO, 1984), p. 26 (figures amended as per Errata issued subsequently by this office).
5. Census of India, 1991, Paper No. 1 of 1995, Religion (New Delhi: RGO, 1995).
6. Census of India, 2001, First Report of Religion Data (New Delhi: RGO, 2004).
7. Most 2011 census data in this chapter are taken from Dheeraj Jain (2017).

It is against this background that the Jain population study in India projects were conceived by International School for Jain Studies, New Delhi. The foremost idea was to check the veracity of census data, to begin with, in specific administrative areas of Delhi NCR, namely Hauz Khas tehsil of South Delhi and New Delhi district.

Map

Location Map of Hauz Khas Tehsil and New Delhi District, 2011. With Two More Districts, Shahdara and South East Delhi now has 11 Districts Since September 2012

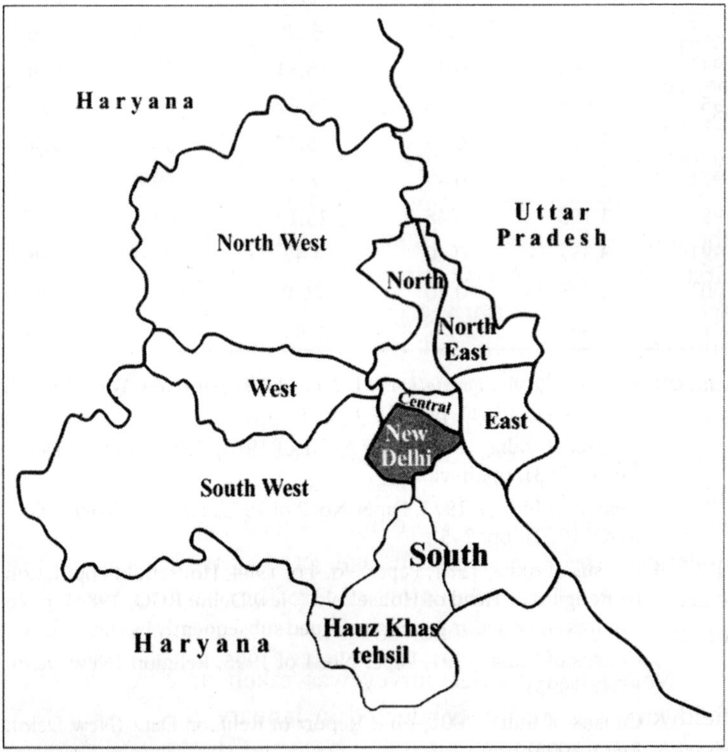

Two Delhi Surveys[3]

Hauz Khas is one of the three subdistricts of South Delhi district which is widely spread and whose population is heterogeneous in terms of occupational structure, income groups and religious affiliation. Centrally located New Delhi district consisting of Connaught Place, Parliament Street and Chanakyapuri is dominated by central government employees' residential quarters, parliamentarian and ministerial bungalows and private houses of Delhi business and commercial elites. The total Jain population of South Delhi district in 2011 was 11,020 and that of Hauz Khas tehsil was 5,448. The Jain population of New Delhi district was comparatively miniscule at 960 in 2001 and 679 in 2011. Besides, the population size of the two districts also widely differ in terms of Jain population growth rate. During the 2001–2011, the growth rate of Delhi Jain population was 7.16 per cent and that of the South Delhi district was 3.32 per cent. On the contrary, the New Delhi district registered the decadal growth rate during the same period at –25.06 per cent.

The idea of conducting these surveys was mooted during the middle of 2017. The Hauz Khas tehsil survey was taken up first. With the help of an steering committee consisting of scholars and community leaders a questionnaire was finalized and about two dozen volunteers, mostly Jains, were given an instant training for conducting field work during the *Paryushan Parva* (18 August–5 September 2017). This resulted in about 60 per cent of the data collection. Subsequently, a market survey agency was hired for the collection of the remaining data. A total of 1,123 Jain families were interviewed with the help of a questionnaire. The data thus collected until November 2017 were subjected to tabulation and further analysis. The final report was out in December 2017.

New Delhi district survey was taken up next for which fieldwork was mostly conducted in January 2018 by the same market survey agency which had collected the Hauz Khas tehsil data. In all, 253 Jain families in the area were contacted. Of these, 138 heads of the household were interviewed using a slightly modified questionnaire used in Hauz Khas survey.

The field work in both areas was not without pitfalls. A considerable number of people who took the questionnaire to fill in at home did not return them. Some others were reluctant to give mobile number, or at times information about income, or about family members. A few respondents even refused to provide any information whatsoever about them or their families. Of course, these are the usual problems associated with the questionnaire as a technique of data collection. The other problem in field work was to identify the potential respondents belonging to the Jain community, particularly in Hauz Khas tehsil, due to the following reasons:

1. A large number of Jains, particularly those who have migrated from Rajasthan do not write Jain as their surname. To counter this problem, we had collected lists of members of Chhoti Dadabari; Green Park, Lodhi Road, Vasant Kunj and R.K. Puram temples and Acharya Sushil Muni Ashram, all in Hauz Khas tehsil. We also made a list of approximately 250 surnames, which we came across as being used by Jains, though this list was not comprehensive. However, searching for these surnames in Voters list was very cumbersome as most of the people we talked to with such names turned out to be non-Jains.
2. Because of the issue indicated above, it was not possible to exactly determine the total number and details of addresses of Jains for complete field survey. Therefore, we restricted the field survey to a large extent to those Jains who used Jain as surname. Exceptions to this were Jains who met us during *Paryushan Parva* as well as some from Directory for Chhoti Dadabari available with us.
3. The spatial spread of Hauz Khas tehsil is very large. Most of the far flung areas have scanty Jain population as most of the Jains are concentrated in few colonies. Therefore, 100 per cent survey, though aimed at in the beginning, became a difficult exercise. We, however, tried to cover at least 50–60 per cent of Jain households to determine their actual numbers with a confidence level of 95 per cent or above along with the socio-demographic data associated with Jains.

4. A small number of Jains were hesitant to respond to our survey out of fear of being seen as drifting from Jainism or loss of privacy of family information in spite of our assurance for strict adherence to confidentiality and non-disclosure of personal information even in writing.

Hauz Khas Tehsil Survey

Methodology Adopted

A two-pronged strategy was used to collect data for analysis and estimation as follows:

Collection of Secondary Data

1. *Voters List*: Comprehensive and almost complete up to date data of adult Jains could be extracted from the Voters list for all India available with Government of India by district, tehsil and ward. Even before starting this work, it was ensured that the list of wards used in census 2011 for Hauz Khas tehsil was retained in our field survey as well as Voters list analysis.
2. Census of India data for 2011.
3. Directories of Jain temples/sthanaks and Jain residents welfare associations where large Jain population is concentrated.
4. Reports of surveys of Jains conducted earlier.

Field Survey/Primary Data

In order to collect field survey data, we used the following multi-pronged strategy:

1. *Data Collected from Jain Temples in Hauz Khas Tehsil (by ISJS staff)*: Normally Jains do visit temples during *Paryushan Parva*. So this trait was used by us to collect data from select temples in Hauz Khas tehsil (Chhoti Dadabari SE-II, Green Park, Sarojini Nagar, Acharya Sushil Muni Ashram, Defence Colony, Chirag Delhi, Ahimsa Sthal, Badi Dadabari, Mehrauli, Sangam Vihar, R.K. Puram, Vasant

Kunj, New Friends Colony Sthanak, Bhogal, Kalkaji, Govindpuri and Tughlakabad). The ISJS teams mentioned above were spread to different temples to collect information from Jains visiting the temples for 18 days (Paryushan and Das-Lakshan).

2. Personal meetings and telephone calls by ISJS staff with Jains known to them as well.
3. Field survey by outsourced agency by home visits and telephone interviews.

Approximately 50 per cent complete data (Jain households listed in Voters list) was collected by the above methods to cover as many families as possible.

Data Collected for Hauz Khas Tehsil

1. Jains (with Jain surnames) in Voters list by wards:
   Number of Jain Household addresses: 2,218
   Number of Jains: 6,629
2. Number of Jains as per Census 2011: 5,448 Jains (2,735 males, 2,713 females)

   Ratio of non-adult Jains to adult Jains: 0.37: 1.00 (as per census 2011)
3. Actual field survey by ISJS and external survey agency

Survey Agency	*Jain Addresses*	*No. of Jains*
ISJS	706	3,180
Contractor	417	1,702
Total HK	1,123	4,882 (2,464 males, 2,418 females)

Number of households, as per Voters list, visited by the survey agency but did not get data due to the following reasons:

Premises locked	3
Refused to give data	57
Shifted	72
Deaths	110
Incomplete data	26

Similarly we gave survey forms to Jains who were in a hurry to fill the form on the spot but did not return the filled forms for a total of 227 as 'no response'. Thus, the total households visited/contacted for data collection is 1,123 + 3 + 57 + 110 + 26 + 227 = 1,546 or 69 per cent of total Jain house-holds as per Voters list.

Data Analysis

Secondary Data Collected

1. *Census Data 2011*

   All India factors like

   Urban to rural Jain population : 76.11 per cent

   Decadal growth of Jain population : 5.37 per cent

   Jain population in Hauz Khas Tehsil : 5,448 Jains (2,735 males and 2,713 females)

2. *Voters List*: The list contains data of adult Jains (over the age of 18) who are eligible to vote (updated data published by government was used for elections for Delhi assembly in 2015).

   Jain population in Hauz Khas tehsil: 6,629 Jains

   Jain households in Hauz Khas tehsil : 2,218

   Average number of adult Jains per household : 6,629/2,218 = 2.99

   Average number of Jains including non-adults per household: 2.99 × 1.37 = 4.09

   (Census 2011 gives 21 per cent below 15 and our survey gives 6 per cent between 15 and 19 age group for a total of 27 per cent giving a factor of 100/73 or 1.37 to come up with total population).

3. *Directories*: These sources were used to contact potential Jains for survey as their telephone numbers were available. Also these directories were used to establish a factor for adjusting the number of Jains in Voters list to include Jains

who do not use Jain as their surname as Delhi has a sizeable population of Jains from Rajasthan. Generally they belong to Shvetambar Jain subsects, Murtipujak and Terapanth. They use non-Jain as surnames, such as Nahata and Singhvi, more often. It becomes difficult to identify such Jains as surnames such as Shah and Mehta are used more by non-Jains than Jains. Our analysis of these directories indicated result for Hauz Khas tehsil as tabulated in Table 10.2.

Table 10.2

Persons/Families Using Jain and Other Surnames as per Jain Temple/Sthanak Directories

Temple	*Number of Jain Households Using Jain as Surname*	*Number of Jain Households Not Using Jain as Surname*	*Total*
Green Park	296	4	300
Lodhi Road	145	22	167
Chhoti Dadabari	160	154	314
Grand Total	601	180	781

Based on the above, the ratio of total number of Jains to Jains using Jain as their surname comes to 781/601 or 1.3.

Field Survey

Analysis of survey data collected reveal:

Jains who participated in the survey and provided data

Total Jains Households: 1,123
Total Jains: 4,882 (2,464 males, 2,418 females)

Jains who were contacted but did not participate in the survey

Premises locked	3
Refused to give data	32
Shifted	64
Number of households given survey forms but did not respond	227

Total households visited for data collection: 1,123 + 3 + 32 + 64 + 227 = 1,449 out of a total of 2,218 as per Voters list (55%)

Analysis of data shows that:

1. As many as 506 Jains used non-Jain surnames while 3,489 used Jain as their surname. This gives us a ratio of total Jains to those using Jain as their surname as 3,595/3,489 or 1.145
2. Sixty four households out of a total 167 surveyed did not appear in Voters list for Green Park, Safdarjung Enclave and Arjun Nagar (all adjoining areas in Ward 163).
3. Sixty four households who shifted from the Hauz Khas tehsil as per survey
4. Average household size as 4,884/1,123 = 4.35 as against 4.09 as per Voters list.

Estimation of Jain Population in Hauz Khas Tehsil

Three different methods were used to estimate the likely total number of Jains in Hauz Khas tehsil. These are discussed as follows:

1. As per Census 2011: Census figure of 5,448 × 1.0537 (decadal growth in Hauz Khas for 2001 to 2015) = 5,740
2. As per Voters List: Total number of Jains as per Voters list 6,629 × 1.15 factor for non-Jain surnames (1.145 as per survey and 1.3 as per directories) × 1.37 (to include non-adult Jains) = 10,444
3. As per Survey
   (a) Mean or average family size/household = AVG = 4,884/1,123 = 4.35 with standard deviation of 1.843.
   (b) The mean/average size limits for a confidence level of 95 per cent = 4.35± 0.108 or 4.24 to 4.46.
   (c) Estimated likely Jain population AVG × 2,218 × 1.15 = 11,095

(d) Estimated number of Jains for 95 per cent confidence interval
   (i) Lower limit = Number of households as per Voters list × AVGL × factor for including non-Jain surnames = 4.24 × 2,218 × 1.15 = 10,815
   (ii) Upper limit = Number of households as per Voters list × AVGH × factor for including non-Jain surnames = 4.46 × 2,218 × 1.15 = 11,376

Table 10.3

Actual and Estimated Population of Jains in Hauz Khas Tehsil

Basis	*Actual*	*Estimated (2017)*	*Estimate Limits @ 95% Confidence*
Census 2011	5,448	5,740	–
Voters List	6,629	10,444	–
Field Survey	–	11,095	10,815–11,376

To sum up, the total number of Jain estimated as per survey is 96 per cent more than the census 2011 number. Even total number of Jains as per the Voters list is 82 per cent more than census 2011 number and is only 8.2 per cent less than the estimate based on our field survey. So census 2011 data of Jains appears to be under-estimation.

Comments

1. It can easily be observed from Table 10.3 that there is a very large difference in Jain population data even from the two government sources, namely census 2011 (5,740 adjusted for decadal growth) and Voters list (10,444 adjusted for non-adult population and Jains with non-Jain surnames). The estimates based on our field survey and Voters list data are almost similar. The difference can be assigned to the use of average household size and assumption for non-adult Jain population.
2. The above estimates of Jain population is in contrast to South Delhi of which Hauz Khas tehsil is part, which shows only 3.32 per cent decadal growth only.

3. It came to our notice that in 2001, the census field staff was asked to get the forms signed by the respondents to ensure that proper recording is made along with ethical revival amongst Jains. That year saw a spurt of 27 per cent Jain population growth from 1991 figures that is almost in line with the average decadal growth for the period 1941–2001 as per census figures.
4. Delhi has a sizeable population of Jains from Rajasthan. Generally they belong to Shvetambar Jain subsects Murtipujak and Terapanth. They generally use non-Jain as surnames, such as Nahata and Singhvi. It becomes difficult to identify them as surnames such as Shah and Mehta are used more by non-Jains than Jains. However, the Jains of the same sects from Punjab, Haryana and Uttar Pradesh use Jain as their surname. This seems to be the trend. As an example, directory of members of Green Park Jain Mandir belonging to Digambar Jain sect shows just 4 out of a total of 300 members (households) use non-Jain surnames.
5. *Immigration:* Our survey shows a large number of Jains from areas such as Bundelkhand and South India are migrating to Delhi. Most of such immigrants live in low cost city villages, such as Jia Sarai, Gautam Nagar, Arjun Nagar, Sangam Vihar and Tughlakabad. On the other hand, we also found a number of new comers (professionals) living in guest houses/paying guest accommodation in Green Park, that is, where temples and large Jain population exist. We also feel that more Jain migrants are coming to Hauz Khas tehsil per the trend in recent two decades (urban Jains 76.11 per cent in 2001 vs 79.08 in 2011)
6. *Emigration:* The emerging trend in Jain community is the large number of Jain youth opting for profession than family business. This results in large number of Jains migrating to other cities and even overseas. This becomes difficult to estimate in our survey except the discussions we had during the survey when we have some respondents (when specifically asked for such reasons) who identified

education and jobs and in some cases shortage of space and deaths.

7. Voter list data were selected only for those voters who use Jain as their surname. This factor will become more significant in Maharashtra, Karnataka, Rajasthan, Gujarat and Tamil Nadu more than 80 per cent Jain population do not normally use Jain as their surname. Chances of such people not being reported in census as Jains are significant
8. Due to economic trend and opportunities, it is likely that more and more Jains are migrating from rural or semi-urban areas to metros. This fact becomes evident from large number of Jains living in Sangam Vihar, Tughlakabad and city villages. This is substantiated by census data for 2001 and 2011 (76.11 per cent Jains in urban areas growing to 79.08 per cent).
9. Jains using Jain as surname and not reporting religion as Jain during census survey.
10. Jains using non-Jain surnames and not reporting religion as Jain during census survey.
11. Census surveyors not visiting Jains and hence not reporting. (It is highly likely). Census surveyors visiting Jains and reporting Hindu as religion (likely for those using non-Jain surnames).

New Delhi District Survey

As in the case of Hauz Khas tehsil, in the New Delhi district case too, primary and secondary sources of data were used. The primary sources mainly included the field survey of Jain population in the district, whereas the secondary sources used included Voters list as well as census 2011 data. A questionnaire consisting of 25 items/questions was used for data collection. The data were collected by a survey agency by home visits. About 50 per cent of the Jain household heads were contacted for interviews. The extrapolation of Jain population was done on the basis of this source.

Data Collected

1. Number of Jains as per Voters list.
2. Number of Jain Household addresses: 253
3. Number of Jains: 805
4. Actual field survey by ISJS and external agency

   Jain addresses: 138

   Number of Jains: 514

   Other details of data that could not be procured or not applicable in Jain population estimation are given below:

Reason	*No. of Addresses*	*No. of Jains*
Premises locked	3	–
Refused to give data	15	–
Shifted (no one was there)	83	–
Shift reported	7	22
Deaths	–	16
Migrated	–	9
Not traceable	4	–

Total households visited/contacted for data collection is 138 + 3 + 15 + 83 + 4 = 243.

Data Analysis

1. *Census Data 2011*

   Jain population in New Delhi district: 679 Jains (318 males and 361 females)

2. *Voters List:* The list contains data of adult Jains (over the age of 18) who are eligible to vote (updated data published by government was used for elections for Delhi assembly in 2015).

   Jain population in New Delhi district: 805 Jains

   Jain households in New Delhi district: 253

Average number of adult Jains per household: 805/ 253 = 3.18

Average number of Jains including non-adults per household: 3.18 × 1.37 = 4.35

(Census 2011 gives 27 per cent below18 years of age giving a factor 1.37 to come up with total population)

3. *Directories:* Only the Lodhi Road Jain temple directory was available which listed 167 Jain families as its members. Of these 145 members were using Jain as their surnames.

   Based on the above, the ratio of total number of Jains to Jains using Jain as their surname comes to 167/145 or 1.15.

4. *Field Survey*

   Analysis of data collected reveal:

   Jains who participated in the survey and provided data

   Total Jain households: 138

   Total Jains: 514 (258 males, 256 females)

   Data Not Collected

Reason	*No. of Addresses*	*No. of Jains*
Premises locked	3	–
Refused to give data	15	–
Shifted (no one was there)	83	–
Shift reported	7	22
Deaths	–	16
Migrated	–	9
Not traceable	4	–

Total households visited for data collection: 138 + 3 + 15 + 83 + 7 + 4 = 250.

Actual data collected per cent of total 138/253 = 54 per cent as per Voters list

(a) All Jains surveyed use Jain surnames except two heads. This is so as we surveyed on the basis of Voters list having Jain surnames. We shall use the same ratio as used in Hauz Khas (a ratio of total Jains to those using Jain as their surname as 1.145).

(b) 72 Jains were not listed in Voters list, so these are new immigrants in New Delhi district.

(c) Jain population in New Delhi estimated for surveyed households = 514

(d) Average Household size: 514/138 = 3.72 as against 4.33 as per Voters list

Estimation of Jain Population

Three different methods were used to estimate the likely total number of Jains in New Delhi district. These are discussed as follows:

1. *As per Census 2011:* Census figure of 679 × 1.0 (even though in New Delhi there is decrease of 25 per cent for 2001 to 2017) = 679
2. *As per Voters List:* Total number of Jains as per Voters list 805 × 1.15 factor for non-Jain surnames (same as in Hauz Khas) × 100/82 (to include non-adult Jains) = 1,129.

3 *As per Survey*

(a) Mean or average family/household size = AVG = 3.72 with standard deviation of 1.64

(b) The mean/average size limits for a confidence level of 95 per cent = 3.72 ± 0.14 or 3.86 to 3.54.

(c) Estimated likely Jain population AVG ×1.15 × 253 = 1,082

(d) Estimated number of Jains for 95 per cent confidence interval

(i) Lower limit = Number of households as per Voters list × AVGL × factor for including non-Jain surnames = 3.54 × 253 ×1.15 = 1,041

(ii) Upper limit = Number of households as per Voters list × AVGH × factor for including non-Jain surnames = 3.86 × 253 × 1.15 = 1,123

Table 10.4

Actual and Estimated Population of Jains in New Delhi District

Basis	*Actual*	*Estimate (2017)*	*Estimate limits @ 95% Confidence*
Census 2011	679	679	–
Voters list	–	1,129	–
Field survey	–	1,082	1,041–1,123

To sum up, the total number of Jain estimated as per our survey is 60 per cent more than the census 2011 number adjusted for 2017 with no decadal growth even though a decline of 25 per cent was reported during 2001–2011. Even total number of Jains as per the Voters list is 54 per cent more than census 2011 number and is 17 per cent less than estimate based on our field survey. So census 2011 estimate of Jains appears to be too low (Table 10.4).

As in the case of Hauz Khas tehsil, in New Delhi district too there is a large difference in Jain population data between the census 2011 figure (730 adjusted for decadal growth) and Voters list figure (1,129 adjusted for non-adult Jains and Jains with non-Jain surname). The estimates based on our field survey and Voters list data are almost similar. The above estimate of Jain population also contradicts the 2001–2011 decadal growth rate of –25.7 per cent for New Delhi district. Comments made on the estimation of Jain population in Hauz Khas tehsil also generally apply on the New Delhi district.

Sociological Issues

Both the surveys also attempted to seek opinions on a number of socio-religious issues such as inter-faith marriage, remarriages of widows/divorcees, young generation of Jains moving away from the religious values and the way of life, daily routine of life and the nature of Jain identity. It was important for us to raise such issues as they have serious repercussions on the Jain population dynamics. It was hypothesized that the lower rate of growth of Jain population and consequently the unavailability of suitable life partners within the community not only increases the possibility of inter-religion marriage and drift, but also dilutes the key elements of the typical orthodox Jain identity primarily based on *ahimsa*.

In both the surveys, it was found that the Jain population was very well educated, with about 58.4 per cent to 82.10 per cent of them having graduate or post-graduate educational qualifications. The Jain women too happened to be almost equally qualified. About 22 per cent of the total Jain population in New Delhi district engaged in their own businesses, and another 14 per cent in numerous professions and service. About 38 per cent of the Jain population is that of students. Unfortunately, a significant number of Jains (6%) were also found to be illiterate, which should be a matter of great concern for the community (See Table 10.5).

Coeducation and coworking have been suggested by the majority of respondents (51.4%) to be the main cause of inter-religion marriage. In Hauz Khas study, about one-third of our respondents further admit the non-availability of suitable match within the community as the second important cause of inter-marriage. These two causes underline the acceptability of 'love marriage' or marriage by choice as the preferred mode of marriage which leads us to conclude that the majority of Jains are not very rigid about their Jain values and the way of life. Similarly, the great majority of respondents (99.2%) are supportive of widow/divorcee remarriage. Again, a good majority of respondents are flexible about temple/sthanak visit, eating before sunset and occasionally having a drink (Table 10.5).

Table 10.5

Two Delhi Surveys: Summary of Major Findings

Indicators	*Hauz Khas Tehsil*	*New Delhi District*
Estimated Population (2017)	11,095	1,082
	Education	
Graduate +	58.4%	82.10%
Illiterate	8.4%	5.64%
	Occupation	
Own Business	25.4%	21.98%
Professionals	5.0%	0.39%
Services	6.4%	13.89%
Students	23.5%	37.94%
	Income	
₹ 50,000+	20.6%	23.15%
Major Cause of Interfaith Marriage		
Coeducation and Coworking	50.4%	51.45%
Support for Widow and Divorcee Remarriage	80.8%	99.28%
	Temple Visit	
Visit occasionally	61.8%	50.72%
	Eating before Sunset	
Not relevant in present times	15.5%	35.51%

Concluding Remarks

Delhi population surveys are truly the path-breaking studies. Their major objective was to check the veracity of census data regarding the total population of Jains and their characteristics in small census areas, that is, a tehsil and a district. While our surveys positively validate some major population characteristics of the Jain community such as age and gender structure, family size, sex and child sex ratios, literacy and educational levels, occupational structure and others, they raise serious doubts about the correct head count of the members of the community. For a number of reasons, some Jains, particularly those who write other than 'Jain' surnames, are often registered as Hindus by census enumerators resulting in under-enumeration of the Jain community in census figures. In our studies, this under-enumeration is in the range of 60 per cent to 100 per cent. In view of this, such studies need to be replicated at a number of places in India with a sizeable Jain population. The studies also require a wider publicity through media as well as extension lectures.

Notes and References

1. For 2011 census data on Jain population, see Dheeraj Jain, *Population of Jains in India (A Perspective from the Census 2011)* (New Delhi: International School for Jain Studies, 2017).
2. A brief discussion on the subject is also there in the introductory chapter of this book.
3. For full details of the two surveys, see (a) *Jain Population Study in India: Hauz Khas Tehsil, Delhi* (New Delhi: International School for Jain Studies, 2017); (b) *Jain Population Study in India: New Delhi District, Delhi* (New Delhi: International School for Jain Studies, 2018). In fact, much of this chapter is extracted from the two reports which were written by the authors.

Appendices

APPENDIX I

Demography: Concepts and Definitions

(Based on Census of India, 2011)

Age-Dependency Ratio: The ratio of persons in the ages defined as dependent (under 15 years and over 64 years) to persons in the ages defined as economically productive (15–64 years) in a population.

Age Sex Structure: The composition of a population as determined by the number or proportion of males and females in each age category. The age sex structure of a population is the cumulative result of past trends in fertility, mortality and migration.

Ageing of Population: A process in which the proportions of adults and elderly increase in a population, while the proportions of children and adolescents decrease. This process results in a rise in the median age of population. Aging occurs when fertility rates decline while life expectancy remains constant or improves at the older ages.

Birth Rate (or Crude Birth Rate): The number of live births per 1,000 people in a given year.

Census: Data collection of all individuals living in an area, resulting in an enumeration of the entire population and often the compilation of other demographic, social and economic information pertaining to that population at a specific time.

Census Towns: All administrative units satisfying the following three criteria simultaneously are treated as census towns:

1. A minimum population of 5,000
2. At least 75 per cent male main working population engaged in non-agricultural pursuits
3. A density of population of at least 400 per sq km

An administrative area that is not classified as urban (statutory/census town) is treated as rural area.

Death Rate (or Crude Death Rate): The number of deaths per 1,000 people in a given year.

Demographic Transition: The historical shift of birth and death rates from high to low levels in a population. The decline of mortality usually precedes the decline in fertility, resulting in rapid population growth during the transition period.

Demography: The scientific study of human population, including their sizes, compositions, distributions, densities, growth and other characteristics, as well as the causes and consequences of changes in these factors.

Fertility

Age-Specific Fertility Rate (ASFR): It is defined as the number of births per year per 1,000 women of a specified age. It may be computed either for single years of age or for age intervals for 5 year age group

$$\text{ASFR} = \frac{\text{No. of live births to mothers of a specified age group}}{\text{Mid-year female population of the specified age group}}$$

Replacement Level Fertility: It is the total fertility rate – the average number of children born per woman – at which a population exactly replaces itself from one generation to the next, without migration. This rate is roughly 2.1 children per woman.

Total Fertility Rate (TFR): Total fertility rate is defined as the number of children which a woman of hypothetical cohort would bear during her lifetime if she were to bear children throughout her life at the rates specified by the ASFR for the particular year if none of them dies before crossing the age of reproduction.

$$\text{TFR} = (\sum \text{ASFR}) \times 5$$

(This index gives the expected number of children born per woman as she passes through the reproductive ages under the given fertility schedule.)

Gross Reproduction Rate: The average number of daughters that would be born alive to a woman (or group of women) during her lifetime if she passed through her childbearing years conforming to the age-specific fertility rates of a given year.

Growth Rate: The increase or decrease in population in a year expressed as a percentage of the population at the beginning of the time period.

Household: A 'household' is usually a group of persons who normally live together and take their meals from a common kitchen unless the exigencies of work prevent any of them from doing so. Persons in a household may be related, unrelated or a mix of both.

Life Expectancy: The average number of years a person could expect to live if current mortality trends were to continue for the rest of that person's life.

Literate: A person aged 7 years and above who can both read and write with understanding in any language is taken as literate. It is not necessary for a person to have received any formal education or passed any minimum educational standard for being treated as literate.

A person, who can neither read nor write or can only read but cannot write in any language, is treated as illiterate. All children of age 6 years or less, even if going to school and have picked up reading and writing, are treated as illiterate.

Literacy Rate: Literacy rate of population is defined as the percentage of literates to the total population aged 7 years and above.

$$\text{Literacy rate} = \frac{\text{Number of Literateas}}{\text{Population aged 7+}} \times 100$$

Natural Increase (or Decrease): The surplus (or deficit) of births over deaths in a population in a given time period.

Net Reproduction Rate: The average number of daughters that would be born to a woman (or a group of women) if she passed through her lifetime confirming to the age-specific fertility and mortality rates of a given year. This rate is similar to the gross reproduction rate but takes into account that some women will die before completing their childbearing years.

Population: Population refers to the total number of persons who were found to be residing in India at the Census Moment of 0.00 hours of 1 March 2011.

Population Projection: Computation of future changes in population numbers, given certain assumptions about future trends in the rates of fertility, mortality and migration. Demographers often issue low, medium and high projections of the same population, based on different assumptions of how these rates will change in the future.

Sex Ratio: Sex ratio has been defined as the number of females per 1,000 males in the population. It is expressed as 'number of females per 1,000 males'.

$$\text{Sex ratio} = \frac{\text{Number of females}}{\text{Number of males}} \times 1{,}000$$

Child Sex Ratio (0–6 Years): Child sex ratio (0–6 years) has been defined as the number of females in the age group 0–6 years per 1,000 males in the same age group in the population. It is expressed as 'number of female children age (0–6) years per 1,000 male children age (0–6) years'.

Child sex ratio (0–6 years) =

$$\frac{\text{Number of females children } (0-6)}{\text{Number of males children } (0-6)} \times 1{,}000$$

Statutory Towns: All administrative units that have been defined by statute as urban such as municipal corporation, municipality, cantonment board, notified town area committee, town panchayat and nagar palika are known as statutory towns. Further, statutory towns with population of 1,00,000 and above are categorized as cities.

Stable Population: A population with an unchanging rate of growth and unchanging age composition as a result of age-specific birth and death rates that have remained constant over a sufficient period of time.

Survival Ratio:

$$\text{Survival ratio} = \frac{\text{Mean no. of children surviving}}{\text{Mean no. of children born}}$$

Mean number of children ever born (MNB) to women in a particular age group is the mean number of children born alive to women in that age group.

Urban Areas: Urban areas comprises two types of administrative units: (a) statutory towns and (b) census towns.

Work Participation

Work and Workers: Work is defined as participation in any economically productive activity with or without compensation, wages or profit. Such participation may be physical and/or mental in nature. All persons engaged in work as defined above are workers.

Non-workers: A person who did not at all work during the reference period was treated as non-worker. The non-workers broadly constitute students who did not participate in any economic activity paid or unpaid, household duties who were attending to daily household chores such as cooking, cleaning utensils, looking after children, fetching water and other such activities and are not even helping in the unpaid work in the family farm or cultivation or mulching, dependant such as infants or very elderly people not included in the category of worker, pensioners those who are drawing pension after retirement and are not engaged in any economic activity. Beggars, vagrants, prostitutes and persons having unidentified source of income and with unspecified sources of subsistence and not engaged in any economically productive work during the reference period. Others, this category includes all non-workers who may not come under the above categories such as rentiers, persons living on remittances, agricultural or non-agricultural royalty, convicts in jails or inmates of penal, mental or charitable institutions doing no paid or unpaid work and persons who are seeking/available for work.

Main Worker: Any person who had participated in any economic productive activity for six months or more during the last one year preceding of enumeration is defined as main worker.

Marginal Worker: If a person has participated in any economic productive activity for less than six months during the last one year preceding of enumeration is defined as marginal worker.

Work Participation Rate: Work participation rate is defined as the percentage of total workers (main and marginal) to total population and is computed as:

$$\text{Work participation rate} = \frac{\text{Total workers (main + marginal)}}{\text{Total Population}} \times 100$$

Work Categories/Occupations: The Indian census operations identify the following four broad work participation categories, namely cultivators, agricultural labourers, household industry workers and other workers.

1. *Agricultural Labourers:* A person who works on another person's land for wages in money or kind or share is

regarded as an agricultural labourer. She or he has no risk in the cultivation, but merely works on another person's land for wages. Agricultural labourer has no right of lease or contract on land on which she/he works.

2. *Cultivator:* A person is classified as cultivator if he or she is engaged in cultivation of land owned or held from government or held from private persons or institutions for payment in money, kind or share. Cultivation includes effective supervision or direction in cultivation. A person who has given out her/his land to another person or persons or institution(s) for cultivation for money, kind or share of crop and who does not even supervise or direct cultivate on land, is not treated as cultivator. Similarly, a person working on another person's land for wages in cash or kind or a combination of both (agricultural labourer) is not treated as cultivator.
3. *Household Industry Workers:* Household industry is defined as an industry conducted by one or more members of the household at home or within the village in rural areas and only within the precincts of the house where the household lives in urban areas. The larger proportion of workers in the household industry consists of members of the household. The industry is not run on the scale of a registered factory where more than 10 persons with power or 20 persons without power is in use as it would qualify or has to be registered under the Indian Factories Act.
4. *Other Workers:* Workers other than cultivators or agricultural labourers or workers in household industry, as defined above are termed as 'Other Workers (OW)'. Examples of such type of workers are government servants, municipal employees, teachers, factory workers, plantation workers, those engaged in trade, commerce, business, transport, banking, mining, construction, political or social work, priests and entertainment artists.

APPENDIX II

Number of Jain Ascetics in India

The ascetics, whether male or female, are those fully dedicated souls who have renounced worldly life and pleasures, adopted a life of renunciation and asceticism, and devote themselves to the 'pursuit of moksa or liberation, by attending primarily to their own spiritual well-being and secondarily to the moral welfare of the society in general' (Jain, 1983: 81–82). Thus, the ascetics are not only the spiritual self-seekers but also the 'community builders' (Folkert, 1993). They are in regular interaction with the laity – the interaction being especially intense during the four-month rainy season (*chaturmas*). As in other religions, in Jainism too the ascetics constitute a tiny minority, perhaps numbering about 5,000, including women ascetics. However, their authority and influence over the laity is extraordinary. Apart from the personality factor, much of their institutionalized legitimacy and authority is derived from their spiritual attainment along the path of salvation.

The four-fold Jain Sangh consists of male ascetics, female ascetics, laymen and laywomen. Traditionally, Jainism allows women to join monastic order as per their desire and capacity. In this context, it is often maintained by Jain scholars that women ascetics far outnumber their male counterparts. Thus, for example, in the Sangh of Lord Mahavira there were only 14,000 male ascetics, whereas the number of female ascetics was 36,000. Contemporary data on Jain ascetics also support this trend, especially in the case of Shvetambars (Appendix Table II.1). However, the situation has been different in Contemporary Digambar Jainism, where, except until very recently, the monks always outnumbered the nuns (Appendix tables II.1 and II.2).

Table II.1

Jain Mendicants by Sect/Subsect and Gender, Mid-1990s

Sect/Subsect	*Monks*	*Nuns*	*Total*
Shvetambar	2,157	2,596	10,853
1. Murtipujak	1,474	5,420	6,894
2. Sthanakvasi	536	2,638	3,174
3. Terapanthi	147	538	685
Digambars	415	350	765
Total	2,572	8,946	11,518

Source: Manisha Sethi (2012), p. 4.

Table II.2

Number of Digambar Jain Ascetics by Gender and Spiritual Status

Ascetics	*2000*	*2005*	*2010*	*2015*	*2017*
		Monks			
Acharya	51	62	71	97	95
Acharyakalp	4	1	2	0	0
Balacharya/Yuvacharya	1	1	4	4	5
Ailacharya	3	4	6	9	7
Upadhaya	16	13	18	11	8
Muni	269	338	385	466	437
Ailak	26	34	50	30	28
Chhullak	80	108	142	183	142
Sub Total	450	561	678	800	722
		Nuns			
Ganini Aryika	10	11	21	27	37
Aryika	312	356	458	512	527
Chhullika	46	80	109	180	174
Sub Total	368	447	588	719	738
Total	818	1008	1266	1519	1460

Source: Adapted from www.sanskarsagar.org, monthly magazine, August 2017, p. 62.

Census enumerations in India do not have a count of ascetics belonging to any religion, including Jainism. However, some religious, sectarian organizations do attempt to enumerate their respective ascetic orders – both male and female.

Presently the total population of Jain ascetics is estimated around 17,000. This proportionately rather a large ascetic order (17,000 ascetics for estimated 4.7 million Jains, i.e. one ascetic for 276 members of the community) must be having significant demographic impact on the Jain population dynamics which needs to be assessed.

Select Bibliography

Banks, Marcus (1986) 'Defining Division: An Historical Overview of Jain Social Organisation', *Modern Asian Studies*, 20(3): 447–460.

Banks, Marcus (1992) *Organising Jainism in India and England*. Oxford: Clarendon Press.

Banthia, J.K. (2004) 'Introduction', *The First Report of Religion Data*. New Delhi, R.G. Office.

Carrithers, M. (1989) 'Naked Ascetics in Southern Digambar Jainism', *Man* (NS), 24: 210–235.

Census of India 1961 (1963) Paper No. 1 of 1963, Religion. New Delhi: R.G. Office.

Census of India 1971 (1972) Paper No. 2 of 1972, Religion. New Delhi: R.G. Office.

Census of India 1981 (1984) Paper No. 4 of 1984, Household Population by Religion of Head of Household. New Delhi: R.G. Office.

Census of India 1991 (1995) Paper No. 1 of 1995, Religion. New Delhi: R.G. Office.

Census of India 2001 (2004) First Report of Religion Data. New Delhi: R.G. Office.

Colebrooke, H.T. (1872) *Miscellaneous Essays*. Madras.

Cort, John E. (1991) 'The Shvetambar Murtipujak Jain Mendicant', *Man*, 26(4): 651–671.

Cort, John E. (2001) *Jains in the World: Religious Values and Ideology in India*. New York/Delhi: Oxford University Press.

Davis, Kingsley (1951) *Population of India and Pakistan*. New York: Russell and Russell.

Desai, P.B. (1957) *Jainism in South India and Some Jaina Epigraphs*. Sholapur.

Dundas, Paul (1992) *The Jains*. London/New York: Routledge.

Flugel, Peter (2006) 'Jainism and Society', *Bulletin of SOAS*, 68: 91–112.

Flugel, Peter (ed.) (2006) *Studies in Jain History and Culture: Disputes and Dialogues*. London: Routledge.

Flugel, Peter (2011) 'Jain Monastic Life: A Quantitative Study of the Terapanth Swetambara Mendicant Order', *Tulsi Prajana*, 38(150): 66–80.

Folkert, Kendal W. (1993) *Scripture and Community: Collected Essays on the Jains*. Atlanta: Scholars Press.

Gopal, Surendra (1984) 'Jain Merchants in Eastern India under the Great Mughals', pp. 69–81, in Dwijendra Tripathi (ed.) *Business Communities of India: A Historical Perspective*. Delhi: Manohar Publishers and Distributors.

High Level Committee (2001) *High Level Committee Report on Indian Diaspora*. Delhi: Indian Council of World Affairs.

ISJS (2017) *Jain Population Study in India: Hauz Khas Tehsil*. New Delhi: International School for Jain Studies.

ISJS (2018) *Jain Population Study in India: New Delhi District*. New Delhi: International School for Jain Studies.

Jain, Dheeraj (2017) *Jain Population in India: A Perspective from Census 2011*. New Delhi: International School for Jain Studies.

Jain, Hiralal (1962) *Bharatiya Sanskriti Mein Jain Dharam Ka Yogadan* (in Hindi). Jabalpur: Shidhi Printing Press.

Jain, Jyoti Prasad (1983) *Religion and Culture of the Jains*. Third Edition. Delhi: Bharatiya Jnanpith.

Jain, M.K. (1975) 'Jains in India: How Many and Where?' *Tirthankar*, 1(2): 8–23.

Jain, M.K. (1986) 'A Demographic Analysis on the Jains', *Jain Journal*, 21(2): 33–50.

Jain, Muni Uttam Kamal (1975) *Jain Sects and Schools*. Delhi: Concept Publishing Company.

Jain Prakash C. (2010) 'For a Sociology of the Jain Community', *Tulsi Prajna*, 37(146): 63–76.

Jain, Prakash C. (2010) 'Status of the Contemporary Jain Community', *Arhat Vachan*, 22 (1 and 2): 71–83.

Jain, Prakash C. (2011) 'Exploring the Global Jain Diaspora', pp. 155–172, in N. Jayaram (ed.) *Diversities in the Indian Diaspora*. Delhi: Oxford University Press.

Jain, Prakash C. (2011) *Jains in India and Abroad: A Sociological Introduction*. New Delhi: International School for Jain Studies.

Jain, Prakash C. (2014) 'Contemporary Jain Demography', in Jain, Shugan C. and Prakash C. Jain (eds.) *Social Consciousness in Jainism*. New Delhi: International School for Jain Studies and New Bhartiya Book Corporation.

Jain, Prakash C. (2015) *Socio-Economic Change among the Jains of Bundhelkhand: A Sociological Study*. New Delhi: Indian Council of Social Science Research (Mimeographed).

Jain, Ravindra K. (1999) *The Universe as Audience: Metaphor and Community among the Jains of North India*. Shimla: Indian Institute of Advanced Study.

Jain, Shugan C. and Prakash C. Jain (eds.) (2014) *Social Consciousness in Jainism*. New Delhi: International School for Jain Studies and New Bhartiya Book Corporation.

Jain, Surendra Kumar (1996) *Golapurav Jain Samaj: Itihas Evam Survekshan* (in Hindi). Sagar: Paras Shodh Sansthan.

Jain, Yogendra (2007) *Jain Way of Life*. Getzville, New York: Federation of Jain Associations in North America.

Jaini, Padmanabh S. (1979) *The Jain Path of Purification*. Delhi: Motilal Banarsidass.

Jaini, Padmanabh, S. (2000) *Collected Papers on Jaina Studies*. Delhi: Motilal Banarsidass.

Joshi A.P., et al. (2005) *Religious Demography of India*, Chennai, Center for Policy Studies.

Kapadia, K.M. (1966) *Marriage and Family in India*. Bombay.

Karve, Irawati (1965) *Kinship Organization in India*. Second Edition. Bombay: Asia Publishing House.

Kavyateerth, Pt. Mohanlal Jain (ed.) (1941) *Shree Akhil Bharatvarsheeya Digambar Jain Golapurav Directory*. Barayatha, Sagar: The Author.

Kavyateerth, Pt. Tulsiram (ed.) (1924) *Digambar Jain Parwar Directory*. Amravati: Singhai Bansilal Pannalal Parwar.

Kumar, Bhuvanendra (1996) *Jainism in North America*. Mississagua, Ontario: Humanities Press.

Laidlaw, James (1995) *Riches and Renunciation: Religion, Economy and Society among the Jains*. Oxford: Clarendon Press.

Long, Jeffery D. (2009) *Jainism: An Introduction*. London/New York: I.B. Tauris.

Mahmood, Tahir (1993) 'Hindus, Buddhists, Jains and Sikhs: Religious Identity, Beliefs and Practices under the Indian Legal System', *Religion and Law Review*, 2(2): 5–28.

Mehta, D. (n.d.) *Shrimad Rajchandra: A Life*. Ahmedabad: Shrimad Rajchandra Janma Shatabdi Mandal.

Mehta, M. and D. Tripathi (1991) *Business Houses in Western India*. New Delhi: Manohar Books.

Nevaskar, Balwant (1971) *Capitalists without Capitalism: The Jains of India and the Quakers of the West*. Westport, CT: Greenwood Publishing Corporation.

Premi, M.K. (2004) 'Religion in India: A Demographic Perspective', *Economic and Political weekly*, XXIX(39): 4297–4302.

Reynell, Josephine (1985) 'Renunciation and Ostentation: A Jain Paradox', *Cambridge Anthropology*, 9(3): 20–33.

Reynell, Josephine (1991) 'Women and the Reproduction of the Jain Community', pp. 41–68, in M. Carrithers and C. Humphrey (eds.) *The Assembly of Listeners*. Cambridge: Cambridge University Press.

Risley, Herbert. (1915) *People of India*. Calcutta.

Sangave, Vilas A. (1980) (1959) *Jain Community: A Social Survey*. Bombay: Popular Prakashan.

Sangave, Vilas A. (2001) *Facets of Jainology: Selected Papers on Jain Society, Religion and Culture*. Mumbai: Popular Prakashan.

Sangave, Vilas A. (2006) (1990) *Aspects of Jaina Religion*. Fifth Edition. New Delhi: Bharatiya Jnanpith.

Sethi, Manisha (2012) *Escaping the World: Women Renouncers among Jains*. New Delhi: Routledge.

Shah, C.J. (1932) *Jainism in North India*. London: Green and Co.

Shah, Natubhai (1998) *Jainism: The World of Conquerors*. 2 Vols. Brighton: Sussex Academic Press.

Shah, Sneh (1977) 'Who Are the Jains?' *New Community*, 7: 369–375.

Sharma, Jagdish P. (1976) 'The Jains as a Minority in History and Society', *Jain Journal* 5(April): 137–148.

Singh, K.S. (1998) 'Jain', pp. 1327–1338, *India's Communities, H–M* (People of India National Series, Vol. V). Delhi: Anthropological Survey of India and Oxford University Press.

Singh, Yogendra (1973) *Modernization of Indian Tradition*. Delhi: Thomson Press.

Singhi, N.K. (1987) *Studies in Jainism: Ideal, Ideology, and Practice*. Jaipur: Printwell Publishers.

Singhvi, L.M. (1990) *The Jain Declaration on Nature*. London: Office of the High Commissioner of India.

Spratt, P. (1966) 'Jainism', pp. 300–314, in *Hindu Culture and Personality: A Psycho-Analytic Study*. Bombay: Manaktalas and Sons.

Stevenson, Sinclair (1995) (1915) *The Heart of Jainism*. Third Edition. Delhi: Munshiram Manoharlal Publishers.

Syamlal (1992) 'The Jain Movement and Socio-Religious Transformation of the "Bhangis" of Jodhpur, Rajasthan', *The Indian Journal of Social Work*, LIII(1): 59–67.

Roy, B.K. (1989). 'Census Based Trends in Religions of India', pp. 276–288, in S.N. Singh, et al. (eds.) *Population Transition in India*, Vol. 2. New Delhi: B.R. Publishing Corporation.

Thornton (2003) (1898) *Parsi, Jaina, and Sikh: Or Some Minor Religious Sects in India*. New Delhi: Mittal Publications.

Timberg, T.A. (1978) *The Marwaris: From Traders to Industrialists*. Delhi: Vikas Publishing House.

Tripathi, Dwijendra (1981) *The Dynamics of Tradition: Kasturbhai Lalbhai and His Entrepreneurship*. New Delhi: Manohar Books.

Tripathi, Dwijendra (ed.) (1984) *Business Communities of India: A Historical Perspective*. Delhi: Manohar Publishers and Distributors.

Upadhye, A.N. (1946) 'Studies in Jaina Gotras', *Jain Antiquary*, II(3): 61–69.

Vallely, Anne (2002) 'Ethical Discourses among Orthodox and Diaspora Jains', in Michael Lambek (ed.) *A Reader in the Anthropology of Religion*. London: Blackwell Publishing.

Varni, Ganesh Prasad (1949) *Meri Jeevan Gatha* (in Hindi). Kashi: Bhargava Bhushan Press.

Varma, Subodh. (2016) 'Now Majority of Families Have 2 or Less Kids', *The Times of India*, New Delhi.

Varma, Subodh (2016) 'Triple Talaq Effect? 5 in 1,000 Women Divorced', *Times of India*, New Delhi.

Wagle, Nagendra K. (1966) *Society at the Time of Buddha*. Bombay: Popular Prakashan.

Weber, Max (1958) 'The Heterodox Soteriologies of the Cultured Professional Monks', pp. 192–204, in *The Religion of India*. New York: Free Press of Glencoe.

Weber, Max (1958) (1920) *The Religion of India: The Sociology of Hinduism and Buddhism*. New York: The Free Press of Glencoe. German Original in 1916.

Williams, R. (1963) *Jaina Yoga: A Study of the Medieval Sravakacharas*. London: Oxford University Press.

Williams, Raymond Body (1988) *Religions of Immigrants from India and Pakistan*. Cambridge: Cambridge University Press.

Index